W9-CDE-543

The New Kids

Kids

Big Dreams and Brave Journeys
at a High School for Immigrant Teens

BROOKE HAUSER

Free Press
New York London Toronto Sydney New Delhi

*f*P

Free Press
A Division of Simon & Schuster, Inc.
1230 Avenue of the Americas
New York, NY 10020

First Free Press hardcover edition September 2011

FREE PRESS and colophon are trademarks of Simon & Schuster, Inc.

For information about special discounts for bulk purchases, please contact Simon
& Schuster Special Sales at 1-866-506-1949 or business@simonandschuster.com.

The Simon & Schuster Speakers Bureau can bring authors to your live event. For
more information or to book an event contact the Simon & Schuster Speakers
Bureau at 1-866-248-3049 or visit our website at www.simonspeakers.com.

Designed by Jill Putorti

Manufactured in the United States of America

10 9 8 7 6 5 4 3 2 1

Library of Congress Cataloging-in-Publication Data

Hauser, Brooke.
   The new kids : Big dreams and brave journeys at a high school for immigrant
teens / Brooke Hauser.
      p. cm.
   1. Children of immigrants—Education (Secondary)—New York (State)—New
York—Case studies.   2. High school seniors—New York (State)—New York—
Case studies.   3. International High School (New York, N.Y.)—Students—Case
studies.   I. Title.
   LC3746.5.N7H38 2011
      373.18—dc22   2010051302

ISBN 978-1-4391-6328-3
ISBN 978-1-4516-2080-1 (ebook)

For my family and
In loving memory of Saul Shapiro

They asked us questions. "How much is two and one? How much is two and two?" But the next young girl also from our city, went and they asked her, "How do you wash stairs, from the top or from the bottom?" She says, "I don't go to America to wash stairs."

—PAULINE NOTKOFF, A POLISH-JEWISH IMMIGRANT WHO PASSED
THROUGH ELLIS ISLAND IN 1917. INTERVIEWED IN 1985.

Contents

Part I

PASSAGES

Chit Su's First Day

Everybody has The Outfit—the outfit they bought for America. The students who have lived in the country for longer have learned how to blend in better, disappearing in brand-name sneakers and low-riding jeans. But each September on the first day of school, the new kids are easy to spot.

Some arrive in their native dress, like the Bangladeshi girls in colorful *shalwar kameez,* or the African boy who walked the halls in goatskin sandals lined with bristly hair. Others try to fit in and fail, like the boy who came from a country that no one had heard of. He wanted American blue jeans but settled for a pair hand-sewn by his uncle instead. Then there are the kids who dress the part of model student, a few in starched shirts and slacks still wrinkled from the plane, as if they were headed to an immigration interview instead of first period. One Yemeni boy showed up in a business suit, and a Haitian freshman carried a backpack filled with books that weren't on any syllabus, his notebook thin from all the used pages torn out. Still, he was better off than the refugees who seem to arrive with nothing at all. Everyone remembers the Burmese sisters who wore flip-flops through the first winter snow.

Sitting behind a cluttered desk in her office on the fourth day of school, Dariana Castro examines the new girl from behind cat's-eye glasses. Somehow, Student No. 219870508 got it almost right. Today is her first day at the International High School at Prospect Heights, a Brooklyn public school that teaches English to new immigrants, but at least by appearances she could be any girl entering the ninth grade at any high school in any city or small town across America. She has silky brown hair, which is half up, and small eyes, which are cast down at the floor. Her lips are glossed and her nails polished, but that doesn't stop her from nibbling on them. She wears brand-new blue jeans (factory made), a black-and-red Mead backpack, and a T-shirt the fluorescent-green color of Nickelodeon slime. Her clothes fit too well to be hand-me-downs, and they leave no trace of a foreign country. It's as if someone undressed a mannequin in the back-to-school display in the tween department of Target, and re-created the ensemble on her.

"What's your name?" Dariana asks.

"Chit Su," the girl says, twisting a flower-shaped ruby ring on her finger.

"*Cheet Sue*," Dariana repeats carefully.

Cradling a phone receiver to her ear, she motions for the girl to take a seat. Especially during the first week of school, it's rare that an extra chair is available. Throughout the day, a steady tide of visitors flows into this air-conditioned room, located in the back of the student-government office on the fourth floor, keeping Dariana in a perpetual state of distraction.

Officially she is known as the Coordinator of Special Programs, but a better job title would be The Fixer. Every immigrant community has one, and the International High School at Prospect Heights has Dariana, a twenty-five-year-old Dominican with pale skin, curly red-tinted hair that will change colors and styles many times in the coming months, and a solution for everything. Teachers go to her for glue sticks, information about scholarships, or a squirt of hand sanitizer from the giant container on her desk.

To students, Dariana is like Craigslist and a big sister rolled into one, offering everything from job opportunities and relationship advice to home remedies for any number of ailments. For instance, how to get rid of a hickey. Step 1: Address the problem, as she had to do with a Parisian junior who came to school with a blotchy purple stain above his collarbone. *What's on your neck? That's disgusting!* Step 2: Rub the inflicted area with a penny to disperse the blood. *It works with black and blues, too.* Step 3: Cover what's left of the love bite with concealer, dismissing any protests that the student in question, in this case a boy, might make about not wanting to wear make-up. *Well, why'd you let her do that?* Step 4: Send the student back to class.

As soon as the new girl walked into her office to pick up her class schedule, it was obvious to Dariana that Chit Su was suffering from a bad case of nerves. But that's just about the only thing about Chit Su that *is* obvious. Other than the ID number assigned to her by the New York City Department of Education, very little is known about Student No. 219870508. No one is exactly sure where she came from, or how she got here this morning, up three flights of stairs and past security. To Dariana, she looks like an ordinary American girl. But she is from Burma. Or Thailand. Her answer changes depending on who asks. Either way, she is the only person in the entire school who speaks her language, now that the flip-flop-wearing Burmese sisters have relocated to Texas. She is seventeen years old, and her English is very limited. That much is clear.

"Are you happy to be here?" Dariana asks, leaning forward. "Are you nervous?"

Silence. Shifting her weight in the chair, the girl smiles, her teeth crowded on top of each other like subway riders at rush hour.

"You're not nervous?" Dariana asks again, this time speaking more slowly. More silence.

Dariana stands up and walks over to the corner of the room, where a large plastic bag is filled with snacks and small cartons of juice.

"Here," she says, handing Chit Su a package of peanut-butter crackers, along with her class schedule. "Eat these every time you feel nervous. It will make you feel better." Rubbing her stomach, Dariana pretends to chew. "Mmmm. That's what I do."

*   *   *

The International High School is located in north-central Brooklyn on the third and fourth floors of a massive, sandy brick building, formerly known as Prospect Heights High School. In the mid-1980s and early 1990s, amid gang warfare, it was considered among the most violent schools in the city. But since then, the Prospect Heights High School closed, and in its place are four small schools: the Brooklyn Academy for Science and the Environment, the Brooklyn School for Music & Theatre, the High School for Global Citizenship, and the International High School at Prospect Heights.

Every morning on the way to first period, students have to pass through a metal detector. Located on the southern side of the school building, the security area is better known as "scanning," and was set up as part of a citywide effort to reduce violence and weapon possession in schools. The rules are pretty simple: In addition to guns, knives, and glass bottles, no headgear, belts, or electronics are allowed. Nevertheless, day after day, a battle of wills plays out on the patch of sidewalk where boys and girls form double lines under the watch of various administrators and blue-uniformed school-safety officers who guard the entrance to the cafeteria. Despite countless PA announcements throughout the year about dress code, students show up in bandannas and bandies (bandannas tied around the chest like a bra), do-rags and chains, country flags festooning from their pockets, and dingy boxers ballooning from their low-riding jeans like puffs of smog.

For the most part, the upperclassmen are wise to the campuswide restrictions from 8:40 AM to 3:10 PM A few bury their cell phones in Prospect Park until school is out, while others grudgingly deposit their Sidekicks and iPods into numbered brown paper bags, which, for a small fee, cashiers at any number of nearby delis will stow behind the counter, along with the scratch-off cards, Wet N' Wild condoms, and E-Z Wider rolling papers. The Yemeni clerk on Franklin Avenue is known to have the best deal on the block, one reason why his store is always packed with International students in the minutes before class. Occasionally kids manage to stash their phones in their shoes and get through the metal detector without incident, but it is hard to sneak much past the flat stares of the guards.

One person who always manages to slip by is Alex Harty, a twelfth-grade math teacher. Tall, lanky, pierced, and tattooed—a multicolored portrait of "the gunslinger" from Stephen King's series The Dark Tower covers his right arm—Alex lopes through the halls of the International like a walking DO NOT DISTURB sign, when he isn't rolling through on his skateboard. On most days, he comes to work wearing a Toronto Blue Jays cap and baggy cargo shorts, publicly flouting the schoolwide ban of hats and disregarding the administration's distaste for low-riding pants. He did wear a suit on his job interview: his prom suit. Despite the no-iPod rule, Alex is rarely seen without his headphones. Not just any headphones. These are Shure SCL2 sound-isolating earbuds in black, which, according to the product description, are "great for use in noisy environments such as bus stations, airports, or live stages."

Or high schools. In the past, everything from the metal band Tool to the bluegrass fusion of Bela Fleck has helped Alex keep his sanity, but not this year, not during the first week of school. Over the summer he lost his iPod, and when he walks into the halls of the fourth floor, there is no buffer, no noise rock or soothing Flecktones to drown out the sound of his students crying out, "Mr. Haaaaaarrrrrttttttyyyyyyyyyy!"—and more than four hundred other voices shrieking simultaneously in foreign tongues.

"*Aiiiiiiiii, Te ves muy morena!*"

"*Salaam Aleikum!*"

"What's crackin', yo? What's poppin'?"

"*Kire ki obostha!*"

"*Jarama!*"

"Hey, Plátano," a French junior calls out to a curly-haired Dominican girl, her brown skin oozing like fresh taffy out of too-tight jeans.

"Hey, Frenchie," she says, smiling over her shoulder before folding herself into the arms of her boyfriend.

Three years ago, when Alex first began teaching at International, it all sounded the same to his ears: "'*JABBA-JABBA-JABBA*.' When the hallway would come into the room, it was insanity," he says. "It felt like the Tower of Babel."

In some ways, Babel is an apt metaphor for the International High

School at Prospect Heights, which is part of the Internationals Network for Public Schools, a nonprofit organization formed in 2004 that serves recent immigrants and new English-language learners from around the world. (In addition to twelve schools in New York City, the Network has opened schools in Oakland and San Francisco.) At the school in Prospect Heights, students come from more than forty-five different countries and speak more than twenty-eight different languages. At any given moment hundreds of tongues are flapping in Arabic, Bengali, Creole, French, Fula, Hindi, Krio, Mandarin, Mina, Nepali, Punjabi, Russian, Spanish, Tajik, Tibetan, Urdu, and Uzbek.

Despite his efforts to tune out the cacophony, Alex has picked up a few things over the years. At first, he was boggled by the fact that some of the Tibetan and Bangladeshi students seemed to understand one another; then he learned that they share the common language of Hindi, which the Tibetans learned in Dharamsala, India, home to the largest Tibetan exile community as well as their spiritual leader, the Dalai Lama. Their native "*Tashi delek*" means "hello" or "good luck." The Haitians speak Creole, not to be confused with Krio, the broken English dialect of the Sierra Leoneans, who greet each other with the somatic salutation, "Ow di bodi?" (How's the body?) Typically, the answer is, "Di bodi fine!"

Everyone who walks through the halls of International on a daily basis has a different way of dealing with the noise. (Aspirin helps.) The effect can be overwhelming, like audio spam. Imagine being trapped in a small, windowless room and tuning into dozens of AM radio stations at once. Some frequencies are low, such as the soft chatter of the Pakistani girls who gather in black *hijabs*, moving like shadows against the rows of rusting blue lockers; or the Bangladeshi girls, who giggle behind their palms and form a colorful garden with their streaming silk scarves in marigold, bluebell, rose, and lime.

Others are head-splittingly strong, like the Dominican girls who do running jumps into each other's arms, or the Haitian fashionistas who clog the halls, screaming at the top of their lungs, their hugs more like body slams in a cage match.

Chaos and confusion always reign during the first week, but the administrators and school-safety officers who police the third and fourth floors still try to impose order. For the rest of the year the classrooms will never be as clean as they are in September. By June every year, barnacles of dried gum encrust the undersides of tables and chairs, and every August they are scraped away. The restrooms are stocked to the hilt with toilet paper, the bowls pristinely awaiting an answer to a communal plea that has been laminated and taped to the girls' bathroom door: FLUSH, it says, IF YOU LOVE YOUR SCHOOL. At least for a little while, the hallways smell of disinfectant and not body odor—or, worse, stink bombs. The mottled blue floors are practically spit-shined, like linoleum lagoons, dimly reflecting Nikes and Pumas on their surfaces, as students pounce on each other, their shrieks rocketing off the walls.

Leaning against a row of lockers and sporting a pair of Nike Airs in red, white, and blue, a sinewy African boy named Freeman Degboe lives up to his reputation as the class flirt, stroking his goatee and chatting up girls in various tongues.

"Did you miss me?"

"Where are you from?"

"*Hola, flaca!*"

"*Bonjour!*"

"Hey, it's my wife!" he greets a cute Chinese junior with short-cropped hair and broad shoulders. "*Ni hao!*"

Over the summer, Freeman traded in his round John Lennon specs and the acoustic guitar he always carried around in the halls—both more for effect than actual use—for those white Nikes, a gold Jesus head pendant, and the nickname Pollo Frito, which his Dominican rapper friends call him in honor of his appetite for Spanish-style chicken and rice. Wind Liu, a whippet-thin Chinese girl with a penchant for patent-leather stilettos, rechristened herself Dinice, even though she still heads her homework with her birth name, Dong Er. Owen Zhu, a geeky senior with a few sparse chin hairs and a flash drive on a cord around his neck, came back with fresh skills, which he hopes will impress Wind/Dinice/Dong Er.

"I got really into Rubik's Cube over the summer," he tells her. "I like it to make my fingers smoother and my thinking smarter." Oblivious to the cloud of boredom misting over Dinice's milky-blue contact lenses, he fishes out the puzzle cube from his backpack and works it with thick, sweaty hands. "I learned how to do this on YouTube," he explains, when each side is a single wall of color. "My best time is one fifty-seven."

Most of the faces that pass through the halls are familiar. But every year approximately 110 freshmen are accepted into the school, many arriving in the country just months, weeks, or even hours before the first day. Tiny and burdened by huge backpacks, the new kids grip their class schedules and wander the halls lost and confused, watching as teachers pull over other kids like traffic cops stop speeding, swerving cars for Breathalyzer tests. *Do you know where you're going? Who's your advisor? Who, who, who? She's waiting for you!*

On the first day of school, every student is directed to an "advisory," a group of about a dozen kids who meet with each other and their advisor, usually a teacher in their grade, for sixty-five minutes twice a week. A few advisors have already led their freshmen charges through the halls, pointing out important landmarks, like the cafeteria in the basement and various classrooms, including 444, which is the room number for Chit Su's first-period class, global studies.

Because Chit Su came late, she is on her own until she meets her advisor, who also happens to be her first-period teacher. Outside Dariana's office, Chit Su passes through a harsh, seemingly lawless world on the way to Room 444. Gripping her class schedule in one hand and half-eaten peanut-butter crackers in the other, she walks with her head down through the halls, her backpack molded to her like a turtle shell, her sneakers squeaking against the bluish-gray linoleum. On her right is a mural left by the Class of 2008. The entire wall is covered with a colorful patchwork of squares painted in different shades, representing the skin tones of the inaugural class: peach, parchment, ebony, cocoa, and umber. On her left, locker doors open to reveal stick-on mirrors and photos of teen idols like Zac Efron and Selena Gomez, before banging closed.

Room 440, 441. Chit Su squeezes by a knot of Dominican boys

wearing sunglasses and long chains of colored rubber bands—their rap group's very own discount bling. "718! All day!" someone screams in honor of the posse's name and Brooklyn's area code. Nearby, a Haitian girl wearing a single, black lace Michael Jackson glove teases her hair with a purple pick.

Room 442, 443. More classroom doors swing open, and students spill out, shrieking, laughing, hugging, high-fiving, and talking—so much talking. Even their T-shirts talk, getting louder and bolder over the year: "Sexy Baby," "Sexy Bitch," "Mean Girls Finish First," "I'm Looking for a Rich Man." A stringy African girl in a T-shirt emblazoned with the words "Hi, Hater" sprints down the hall, leaving Chit Su to stare blankly at the blocky lettering on her back: "Bye, Hater."

At Room 444, Chit Su comes to a squeaking halt and peers through a rectangular glass window in the door. The room is bright and filled with students, their faces turned toward a thin woman standing in front of a huge map. Her name is Suzannah Taylor, and she teaches global studies. Two days ago she made the students step up to the map, point out their countries, and then say one thing they liked about where they were from and one thing they liked about New York City. Everyone agreed that the best thing about America was TV. A boy from Mauritania said he liked his country because it's large. One girl couldn't find Haiti on the map and was surprised to see how small it looked when Suzannah pointed out a speck of green amid so much blue. When Suzannah asked a Puerto Rican girl what she missed most about her country, her eyes welled up with tears. *"Todo,"* she said. *Everything*.

Suzannah told the class that she missed her home, too, but it was hard to tell where she was from. Fair-skinned with fine brown hair, glasses, and a tiny silver nose stud, she looked like she got dressed in an African market that day. She wore a grass-green skirt in a bold flowered print, big black hoop earrings made of wood, and ivory bangle bracelets that clanged together when she pointed to a gigantic mass of land on the map. "Texas," she said. "The capital of Texas is Austin. It's not the biggest city, but it's where the government is. My country's capital is Washington, D.C. That's where the president lives. One thing I like about my country is that there are so many different kinds of people. My second country is Mali because I lived in Africa for a year."

"Where are you from?" Suzannah asks Chit Su, when she walks into her classroom on the fourth day of school.

"Thailand," Chit Su says, looking around the room. The peach walls are covered with posters of laminated world currencies and flags. If she had been in class on the second day of school, she would have drawn her country's flag in crayon on a four-by-six-inch index card along with the other students. But because Chit Su is late, Suzannah gives her a worksheet to fill out. It is divided into three columns: "Words I don't know," "Words I kind of know," "Words I know."

From her backpack, Chit Su pulls out a pencil bag and selects a sparkly silver-and-blue pen, poising it over the page but never touching the nib to the paper. From the corner of her eye, she watches Suzannah show the class pictures of maps on a projector.

"Who can tell me what a continent is?" Suzannah asks.

Several hands shoot up.

"It's like an island, but bigger!"

"A group of countries!"

"Something you find on a map!"

Biting the tip of her pen, Chit Su stares at the assignment. As the other students get to work, she stares at the walls, and at her classmates. Like in the mural in the hall, their faces range from ivory white to cake-batter brown to dusky black. Only, up close, they are in high definition. There are a surprising number of mustaches and lots of acne, some of it covered up with patchy foundation or hidden behind heavy bangs. A couple of the girls wear dark veils wrapped around their heads and shoulders.

"We're going to talk about maps today. Pretend I'm from a different planet," Suzannah says, cocking her head to the side. "What's a 'map'?" More hands shoot up, and she shows the class a map of Central Park. "Is that Costa Rica?" a Haitian girl asks.

At moments, the outside world seeps in, breaking up the chorus of voices. Through the open window comes the whoosh of braking trucks and distant cries of ambulance sirens. In a nearby classroom, the English teacher Minerva Moya claps her hands for attention, her voice ringing down the hall. "Students! STUDENTS!"

When the clock hands hit 9:45 at the end of the period, the effect is already Pavlovian. Students zip their backpacks closed and shove out of their seats, grinding metal chair legs against the floor. Chit Su is still clutching her sparkly silver-and-blue pen, but her page is blank.

Frequently Asked Questions

The little things are the most daunting. Like not knowing when the teacher is talking to you, and then suddenly feeling the heat of so many stares on your back as she asks again, "Can you introduce yourself to the class?" Like having to pee but finding all of the stalls in the girls' bathroom have been locked from the inside. Do you climb under? But then your pants would get dirty from crawling on your hands and knees on the tile floor. So you hold it—or at least that's what Chit Su does, after rattling the door doesn't work. Chit Su hadn't gone to the three-day summer orientation for new students, which is held every year at the International High School at Prospect Heights, so she missed the full tour. That's when the staff passed out a list of frequently asked questions compiled by the school's first-ever graduating class: *Where is the bathroom? When is lunch? Where is the office for different things? Who speaks my language? What teachers speak what? How big is the school? How safe is the school? Do you have a swimming pool?*

Many of those questions are answered again when students show up on the first day of school and meet their principal, Alexandra Anormaliza. Each September, Alexandra stands by the scanning line and personally welcomes each new student who walks through the wide double doors of the cafeteria. Petite, with long licorice-black hair, a broad face, and a closet full of cute outfits that offset her businesslike demeanor, Alexandra knows what it's like to feel lost. She attended English as a Second Language, or ESL, classes as a child, after her family immigrated to Brooklyn from Ecuador, and the experience of navigating her way through a large high school where she often felt anonymous and over-looked has defined her to this day. Alexandra became the founding prin-cipal of the International High School at Prospect Heights in 2004. A former classroom teacher, she was in her early thirties at the time and represented a new kind of leader being cultivated by New York City's small-schools initiative.

In 2002, Mayor Michael Bloomberg and Schools Chancellor Joel Klein launched an effort to overhaul the city's public-school system by shutting down large, failing schools and creating nearly two hundred small schools in their place. One of Klein's pet projects was the NYC Leadership Academy. Based in Long Island City, Queens, the academy offered an intensive, privately financed fourteen-month program to train principals. Alexandra was a member of the academy's first class, which graduated in 2004. Around the same time, the Internationals Network for Public Schools—an external nonprofit organization that works with New York City's Department of Education (DOE), but re-mains apart from it—had received funding from the Bill & Melinda Gates Foundation and was looking to open a new International High School in Brooklyn.

After scouring the borough for possible locations, the Network landed on the Prospect Heights campus. Not only was it close to several sub-way lines, it was the nearest viable location that the Network could find to an area in southwest Brooklyn that, according to the DOE's analyses of eighth- and ninth-grade students at the time, had one of the city's highest-density populations of recent immigrants who also were new English-language learners. "We really have simple criteria," says Claire Sylvan, the Network's founding executive director, who helped Alexandra start the school. "We're looking for the basic minimum requirements. We're not looking for the Waldorf Astoria."

In the beginning, the International High School at Prospect

Heights was very much a grassroots operation. Alexandra herself recruited students from middle schools in the surrounding community. For the first few months before school started, she didn't have an office or a work phone and gave prospective students and their parents her personal cell-phone number, which they continued to call for years. Her teachers held part of freshman orientation in the public park across the street.

Even without an office, Alexandra had a vision of what the school could be. She imagined filling the spacious classrooms with students of every color and painting the putty-gray walls a warm peach. "I used to say, 'We're going to turn around people's perceptions of what a school for immigrants should look like,'" Alexandra recalls one afternoon in her office, which is decorated with black-and-white photos of students from the founding class. "It's going to be the prettiest school, it's going to have the best teachers. It's going to be a happy place."

Since the school opened in 2004, Alexandra has filled it with a staff that is almost as diverse as the students. The majority of the teachers are in their twenties and thirties. They are from Puerto Rico and the suburbs of Philadelphia, the Deep South and Nairobi. They are straight, gay, single, married, black, white, Jewish, Muslim, atheist, Taoist, conservative, radical Democratic Socialist, pierced, parents, tattooed, graying, blue-eyed and blue-haired.

With the exception of the bathrooms and the stairwells, the school is pretty, just as Alexandra had imagined. In the student lounge outside Dariana's office, neon-colored throw pillows line a seating area by a wall painted with a mural of past and present world leaders, including the Dalai Lama. Classrooms and hallways are wallpapered with student artwork and projects; for one, underclassmen re-created the native dress of ancient Aztec, Sumerian, and Greek civilizations. Despite the utopian feel inside the school, however, the building crouches on the edge of a neighborhood, Crown Heights, that was home to one of the ugliest race riots that this country has ever seen.

In August of 1991, the vicious fighting between the neighborhood's black and Jewish communities made headlines around the world. Since then tensions have cooled, and the surrounding area reflects an eclectic mix of young professionals, new immigrants, and old settlers. Bodega owners eke out their livings in the shadows of rising luxury condos. Muslim women in burkas stroll down the same stretch of Eastern Parkway where West Indians in sequined costumes gyrate on feathered floats every Labor Day weekend during the annual Caribbean Parade. In the spring, cotton candy vendors sell cumuli of pink fluff on wooden sticks, like artificial effigies of the cherry blossom trees that burst within the perimeters of the Brooklyn Botanic Garden. Near the Brooklyn Museum, the Prospect Heights campus occupies most of a block on Clausson Avenue.

Getting to school is the first test. Some students had never left their villages before coming to the United States. Suddenly they face the challenge of navigating mass transit in a foreign country where they don't speak the language. Every year freshmen get lost on the way. One African girl ended up at the wrong school, and when she and her father finally made it to International, she begged him to stay with her throughout her first day. In addition to giving tours inside the building during summer orientation, teachers have tried everything from mapping exercises to leading kids on scavenger hunts through the surrounding blocks to familiarize them with the area. Still, students get turned around and often don't communicate their confusion until it's too late. One teacher belatedly realized that many of her students were not only unable to point out where they lived on a map, some couldn't read a map. Last year a popular Chinese senior surprised everyone when he wrote his college essay about how he didn't eat lunch for the first month of his freshman year because he couldn't find the cafeteria.

Fortunately, that won't be a problem for Chit Su. After global studies, Suzannah calls her over and introduces her to a Nepali sophomore named Chhoki Sherpa who will be Chit Su's guide for the rest of the day. Tall and slim with a long sable ponytail, Chhoki wears a light pink T-shirt that says "Cocktails First Question Later." She is the one who leads Chit Su down four flights of stairs to the lunchroom, where a line of International students is already snaking down the wall.

Located in the bowels of the school building, the cafeteria is a close, dank room where every sound is trapped and magnified, including the feedback of the walkie-talkies that the school-safety officers carry on their hips. On a low ceiling, fluorescent panels cast a dull glow on whatever happens to be the gruel of the day. The only other light comes from the windows near the double doors at the side exit. Despite the brightly painted blue-and-yellow walls, the space has an institutional feel. Students sit at long oval tables and short round ones, with attached stools and benches, which, unlike chairs, can't be thrown in a brawl. As an extra precaution against fights, Nedda de Castro, one of the school's assistant principals, regularly patrols the lunch line looking for line cutters. The crafty kids wait for some distraction to capture her attention before making their move. Nedda is scouring the floor for ketchup packets when Chhoki skips the line, taking Chit Su with her.

Inching forward, Chit Su looks at the pictures of different foods on the bulletin board. To many new students, lunchroom staples like chicken nuggets and meat loaf are unfamiliar. So are the utensils that come wrapped in plastic on their trays. Some of the African girls, who grew up eating a cassava porridge called *fufu* with their hands and never learned how to use a fork, have been asking for etiquette lessons. Unglamorous as it is, the cafeteria is the first step to dining in public, one reason why the girls sit in the back of the room, near the wall of Snapple vending machines.

"Next!" the lunch lady barks.

Somewhere, the pop of a plastic sandwich bag shatters the air like a gunshot, and Chit Su jumps. Clutching the straps of her backpack, she keeps her eyes trained on Chhoki's pink shirt. At the head of the line, Chhoki says something to the lunch lady, who hands Chit Su a white Styrofoam tray with pizza and a carton of milk. Inside a clear wrapper is a folded napkin and a white plastic spork that Chit Su examines with interest. When she looks up, the pink shirt is gone.

Standing at the front of the cafeteria, Chit Su grips her tray. It is only the fourth day of school, but already cliques have formed. Near the entrance is one of the Haitian tables. Several of the guys belong to a rap group called the Get Money Flyboys, or GMFB for short. Despite the no-hat rule, they wear black do-rags and Yankees caps with the price tags in plain sight: $31.99. Most days they slam their palms on the Formica tabletop and improvise on big themes like "pain" and "humanity," trying to drown out the beats of International's other rap group, 718 La Familia.

Sitting on the opposite side of the lunchroom, the boys in 718 hail from the Dominican Republic and Peru. They take their cues from Keith Longa, a sixteen-year-old with soft cheeks and a Caesar haircut who goes by various nicknames: King Capo, The Leader, The Boss, and Number One. The shortest member of the group, King Capo is the one responsible for their discount bling. Over the summer he bought a ton of colored rubberbands, which he assembled into long chains bearing the group's name in marker on silver medallions that are actually Memorex CDs. King Capo may be the image maker, but everyone knows that the best rhymes come from a skinny sophomore named Alan Caceres, who calls himself Crazy Flow The Professional and keeps a Daddy Yankee notebook filled with raps in Spanish and English. "We're number one in Brooklyn. We run this school. I'm not kidding—we don't play," Caceres boasts, adding thoughtfully, "We only play with music."

With few exceptions, the lunchroom's gray-and-blue tables are as clearly demarcated as the city's ethnic neighborhoods. Not far from the rappers are the Dominican jocks, with their gelled curls and manicured nails and names like Odanis (in honor of the godly, handsome youth Adonis, but misspelled). In between playing dominoes and eyeing cute girls, they talk about baseball, always *béisbol*. It's almost impossible to pass their table without hearing Major League names like Cano, Cabrera, or Martinez.

Geographically close, but galaxies apart in every other respect, are the Uzbek freshmen. A throng of boys who went to the same middle school together have re-formed their alliance in the lunchroom, where they sit next to each other in decreasing sizes like Russian stacking dolls. With their peach fuzz, nascent pimples, and pungent boy smell, they repel girls with as much force as the Dominicans attract them and use their sporks to launch chicken-nugget missiles across the room.

Should one of those missiles hit the next table, all hell will break loose. The eleventh-grade Haitian girls are among the fiercest fighters in the school. Despite the short fuses of an infamous few, they are almost always willing to forgive a fellow Haitian, and they reserve a special tender spot for Wave Pascal Saint Fleur Michelot, a tiny squeak of a sophomore whose ceremonious name came to his father in a dream. As the story goes, a voice told his father: "You gonna make a son, he gonna be your only son, and you gonna call him Wave Pascal." Scrawny and dark-skinned with a smile like a thousand glow sticks snapped at once, Pascal, as he is more commonly known, has a reputation for getting out of trouble almost as easily as he gets into it. On mashed-potato day, he is the first to smack his hand into the gluey mound of starch and gravy and start a food fight. The girls for the most part give Pascal a free pass and look for trouble elsewhere. The social workers have yet to figure out why their biggest rivals are the Yemeni boys, aka The Arabic Family, but one wrong look can ignite jihad. Not to be confused with "Jehad," who is a student.

Sporting XXL T-shirts and copious amounts of facial hair, the Yemeni boys sit at one of the tables closest to the exit doors and stare longingly at the Dominican *chicas* in stretch jeans and halter tops, while they still can. Their bachelorhood is fleeting, and arranged marriages await several of the boys in the near future. Until then, they court the Latin girls with the passion of Saudi princes. Every Valentine's Day boys with names like Kassim and Musheer send girls with names like Geraldine and Juliana two-dollar roses delivered in class and love notes that are more carefully composed than any homework assignment. Once in a while the group has one fewer member. Boys drop out to marry girls back home or work full-time. Among those who stay, several are grocers by night and wannabe gangstas by day. Kassim Almalahi, a mustached sophomore who goes by the name Sammy, raps about the deli where he toils behind the counter. "Sammy Sammy's my name / I don't play no new game / Sammy Sammy eat pastrami / Stay behind the deli / Make eggs and cheese and salami." Today he's not eating anything. From sunrise to sunset, he and the other Muslim students are fasting for Ramadan throughout the month of September.

Chit Su tucks a loose piece of hair behind her ear and heads toward the Chinese tables. If she wanted to, she could rest her tray there. The

Chinese kids occupy several outposts throughout the cafeteria, which subdivide according to age and attitude. For the most part, the Chinese students stick together. But occasionally someone breaks away from the mold of geek, gamer, or popular girl. Dinice Liu can't stand the Abercrombie girls who gossip behind her back. "All of those Chinese girls, they don't even talk to me, and they say mad shit about me, like I fuck with every single boy I know, and I'm so ghetto," she says, fuming. "They don't even know me." Instead, she sits with two friends who are widely considered to be the hottest girls at school: Kalsang Choekyi, a Tibetan girl who resembles Megan Fox, and Elaine Vasquez, a Dominican who likes to wear black bras under white tank tops and has curly hair that always looks wet.

As in any high school, there are also the nomads: lost freshmen who wander from table to table looking for a place to settle, as well as upperclassmen who don't fit into any one group. Now a senior, Freeman speaks four languages fluently and uses all of them to hit on hotties from every corner of the world. Since the second semester of his freshman year, when Freeman arrived fresh off the plane from Togo, he has racked up countless nicknames, which vary from group to group. The Dominicans know Freeman as Pollo Frito; the Tibetans know him as the lone black guy who joined Students For a Free Tibet and then rechristened himself The Freedom God; and the teachers know him as Mr. International, on account of all of the above. In Freeman's unfinished autobiography, entitled *Freeman's Book*, he insists that in his hometown in Africa he was known as *Le Beau Gars de la Ville*, which he translates as "the Cute Guy of the Town." He also responds to Fatoosh, The Pimp, Frenchy, Sexy Lips, The Sexy Nerd, and The Popular Guy. (He came up with the last two monikers himself.)

Still, in trying to fit in everywhere, Freeman belongs nowhere— certainly not at the table of younger West African boys who scoff at his shameless pickup attempts, nor with the girls from Guinea who simply pretend that he doesn't exist. None of those girls seems to have much interest in boys her own age, but one senior is more mature than some of her teachers. Her name is Bilguissa Diallo, and at nineteen, she is a wife to a Fula taxi driver and mother to their baby, born last year. Every morning before school Bilguissa wakes at 7:30 to pack her daughter's pink knapsack with Huggies diapers and two plastic bottles filled with milk, which she hands over to the child-care specialists who work at a campus nursery on the first floor. Soft-spoken, with a round face and a gap-toothed smile, Bilguissa emits a sense of graceful calm in nearly everything she does, and despite her responsibilities at home, she has managed to become one of the top students in her grade.

Also at the top of the class is Harold Montilla. Unlike the Dominican jocks, Harold can't play baseball to save his life, and dancing *bachata*—forget it—too much hip shaking and leg grinding. With his close-cropped hair and a silky black trace of a mustache, Harold doesn't look like a typical dork, but underneath the Aéropostale shirt is a gentle soul who is obsessed with Star Wars and comic books and who seems to love two things above all: studying and spending time with his girlfriend Jessica Tan, who just arrived from China last year. If they aren't comparing their SAT scores or finishing up their articles for the school newspaper, chances are good that Harold and Jessica are deep in conversation, sitting across from each other at a round table at the edge of their own little world.

Finally, there are the actual nomads: Tibetan kids who grew up tending yaks and foraging for food and never knowing their birthdays. Several had been farmers in their native country. They are sisters and brothers, cousins and long-lost neighbors, and many of them, male and female, are named Tenzin. Some of the Tibetan students were raised in the same section of eastern Tibet. Others met later in Dharamsala, India. A few were introduced by friends or relatives in New York. But however they ended up here, almost all of the Tibetan students have crazy pilgrimage stories about how they fled: crossing the Himalayas by foot in the middle of winter, getting thrown in jail, and being held at gunpoint by Chinese police.

The leader of the Tibetan Club is Ngawang Thokmey, a senior known around school as Mr. Free Tibet. Small-boned and muscular with a perfect swell of black hair, Ngawang is usually the first person to volunteer to help out a new student, and in the coming weeks and even months, there will be many among the Tibetans—always arriving with vascular cheeks as rosy as a Red Delicious. Sitting with his older brother Lobsang and their friend Tenzin, a boy who wears a diamond stud in his ear and a cannabis leaf on his T-shirt, they form a base camp for just about anyone who comes from a country bordered by the Himalayas.

Despite their open-door policy with most students, the Tibetans sit a few tables away from the Chinese kids, partly to avoid fights. Even thousands of miles away from home, age-old animosities between the two cultures play out in the cafeteria. Ngawang makes an effort to be friends with Chinese students, but one day when he distributed flyers advertising an upcoming meeting of the Tibetan Club, which is affiliated with Students for a Free Tibet, a group of boys defaced it by writing, "Bullshit! Tibet is inside of China first go to Chinese Club." The flyer eventually made its way back into Ngawang's trembling hands. Every once in a while, a comment like that threatens to disturb the peace, but for the most part the Tibetans are nonviolent, hospitable, and welcoming to outsiders. A few seats down, Chhoki is already tucking into her lunch when Chit Su spots her pink shirt and heads over to join her and another Nepali girl, a senior with teased reddish hair and chipped purple nail polish.

Though her real name is Yangi, the girl with the teased hair introduces herself as Angie Sherpa, "You know, like Angelina Jolie," she says.

"Where are you from?" she asks Chit Su.

Unaware that she is being spoken to, Chit Su stabs at her rubbery pizza with a spork.

"Where are you FROM?" Angie asks again.

Startled, Chit Su looks up. "Thailand," she mutters.

"Oh, I was the only girl from Nepal. How old are you?"

"Seventeen." Despite Chit Su's attempts, the pizza is unyielding to the spork's flimsy plastic tines. After sniffing a bit of cheese that has collected on the spoon's edge, she tries a scooping motion instead. It's a no-go.

"You're seventeen?" Angie says with a snort. "You look twelve or thirteen! What grade are you in?"

No answer.

Angie tries again. "GRADE?"

"Ninth grade," Chit Su says, pushing her tray aside.

Angie takes another bite of her cheeseburger and examines the new girl more closely. As she chews, her thoughts practically telegraph themselves. Compared to other kids her age, Chit Su looks too young to be in high school, but if she is actually seventeen, she is too old to be a freshman.

"Ninth grade," Angie says finally, in between gulps. "Why?"

Over the Counter
and Under the Radar

Every year, new kids who are afraid to speak arrive at the school. At least for the first week, many freshmen sit in monklike silence, and classrooms are so quiet that teachers have to laugh. That's because they know something the students do not: in just a few days, most of them will be screaming and bouncing off the walls like at any other high school.

While the majority of the students eventually warm up, some choose not to talk for weeks, sometimes months. Most of the kids know at least a few words of English, but they use them in strange ways. There was the Bangladeshi boy who wished his classmates a good evening every morning, and the well-meaning Tibetan girl who innocently greeted her social-studies teacher in the halls by saying, "Hey, sexy!" Words could come out all wrong—like tones made by a deaf person who has no way of knowing what those noises sound like to the outside world.

Although Chit Su didn't say much on her first day of school, every once in a while a word in English escaped her when she thought no one was in earshot. Before lunch, she was on the fourth floor standing in front of a bulletin board covered with student art when her finger alighted on a drawing of an insect with bright, colorful wings. "Butter!" she cried in a low and guttural voice. "Fly!" Then she started pointing to different colors and naming them, playing a private game of I Spy.

Throughout the day, some questions were easier to answer than others. Did she know her ABCs? How about her 123s? The answer, as her English teacher determined from a quick battery of assessment tests, was yes and yes. But by far the hardest questions were the ones that began with "Why." Why was she seventeen and only going into the ninth grade? Why did she leave Burma? Why did she sometimes say that she was from Thailand? Why had she come to America?

Each year the school admits students who leave their countries for a variety of reasons. Some immigrate to the United States to join family members who are already here, some to simply get a better education. Other students are fleeing wars or political persecution, their very lives vivid testimonies to the headlines of the world. In every grade, there are witnesses to hunger in Haiti, horror in Sierra Leone, police brutality in Tibet, and religious extremism and poverty in the Middle East. Students have trekked mountains, crossed deserts, and survived imprisonment to make it to International, which has as its motto: "Opening Doors to the American Dream."

No matter where they started off or where they are headed, at a certain point everyone meets Miguel Antunes, the school's resident parent coordinator. An amiable twenty-nine-year-old guy from Elizabeth, New Jersey, with a shaved head and a penchant for Ben Sherman jackets and cool sneakers, Miguel oversees the intake process of almost every new referral who walks into the pod of offices that he shares with the school's social workers on the fourth floor.

Using a translator when necessary—the DOE provides translation in nine languages as well as interpretation services in more than one hundred languages—Miguel first goes over the basic qualifications that a prospective pupil needs to meet in order to be accepted at International. According to the criteria set by the Internationals Network and the DOE, at the time of intake, a student must have lived in the United States for fewer than four years and must be a new English-language learner, or ELL. All International students take an English language assessment test—the catch is, they have to fail to get in.

Miguel's office is luridly lit by fluorescent panels and sparsely decorated with a subway map on one wall and a whiteboard with an endless "TO DO" list on another. Not exactly a welcoming space, but for many families, especially those who have come to America for their children's education, it is memorable: a place where hopes and dreams are buoyed or dashed. An Ellis Island to the school's bustling metropolis, Miguel's office is a gateway to the New World and he is the processing agent.

Students come to the school in a few different ways. Some are sent by their middle schools. Others find out about International from the DOE or from a friend. Every year Miguel sees plenty of "over-the-counter kids," as they are known, students who more or less have wandered into the school off the street or from a local borough enrollment office. Generally, parents and guardians of newcomers to the country are supposed to go to one of the DOE's fourteen main enrollment offices, where they begin the process of finding a school. For many families, that process feels more like an endless odyssey through an enormous bureaucracy that is unable to address all of their needs.

Despite the nearly two hundred new schools that have been created as part of Mayor Bloomberg and Chancellor Klein's small-schools initiative, ELLs still get lost in the shuffle. Even when they have a referral form from one of the enrollment offices in hand, newcomers often get turned away because a particular school can't accommodate them. Families may be told that there is no room when, in fact, there are limited or no resources available to ELLs at many schools, even though these students are legally entitled to receive additional services, including instruction to learn English.

The International schools help fill the gap in the system. Funded by the DOE as well as by grants from Internationals Network partners, these small public schools are set up exclusively to serve newcomers who are also English-language learners—two separate qualifications. "You can be an English-language learner and not be a recent immigrant, or you could be a recent immigrant and not an English-language learner, because you came from England or Jamaica," explains Claire Sylvan, the Network's executive director.

At the International High School at Prospect Heights, cultural acclimation goes hand in hand with English instruction. Students from various ethnic and educational backgrounds are mixed together in all subject area classes, where they speak and write in English as well as in their native languages, often working in small groups so that they can help each other. Sylvan compares this style of learning to riding a bicycle: "People learn to ride a bicycle by getting on it—not by watching."

Though the Network is relatively new, the model that it adheres to can be traced back to 1985, when Eric Nadelstern, who later became the DOE's chief schools officer, founded the original International High School at LaGuardia Community College in Queens. A joint venture by the Board of Education and the Board of Higher Education of the City of New York, the school was set up to deal with the influx of immigrant students. In the years since Nadelstern served as principal at LaGuardia, his vision for a public high school that would prepare ELLs for college has spawned almost a dozen more International schools around the city, and two in California. Every year, however, more newcomers arrive and there is less space for them at the International schools, which are increasingly in high demand for a population that has been treated as a low priority.

"So many times, I've said to enrollment counselors, 'Look, we really don't have the space,' and asked if they could find another placement," Miguel says. "But the counselors push me because they know that, at another school, a student might not get any support. Maybe there's no ELL program at all. The student ends up sitting in the back of the class for the whole year, or dropping out."

For many students who already have been rejected by other public schools, the International High School at Prospect Heights is a last resort. Miguel can tell which families have spent days trudging from school to school looking for an empty seat: their papers stick together from so much handling. Those who have lived in America for a couple of years and become more established might organize their records in a three-ring binder or a plastic briefcase, but newer arrivals sometimes stuff their children's identities into brown paper bags—dumping onto the conference table outside Miguel's office birth certificates, passports, yellow vaccine forms, and utility bills as proof of address, often not their own.

Almost all of the families who come to International look lost. The school-safety officers who guard the building get used to the sight of nervous mothers and slack-jawed kids, dressed to impress, as if the right outfit could guarantee a seat, as if a seat could guarantee a future. Nga-wang Thokmey thinks it can. "Once you get into this school, your life is fine. Even if you never become famous or successful, you don't have to do dangerous work," he assures a thirty-something Tibetan father who has come to the school to enroll his daughter, a former yak herder. Although she has never been to school in her life, clearly the girl has done some studying in the hope of passing her first test: the interview. She wears rhinestone-encrusted jeans and a purple scrunchie in her long black hair. Her father, a family friend who has asked Ngawang to serve as their translator, carries her documents in a white plastic bag emblazoned with the message, "I Love America."

The new kids start coming in as early as July and continue to show up at the school as late as the following June. They arrive in trickles and tidal waves, with parents and siblings, friends and distant relatives, and occasionally a representative from the International Rescue Committee, an organization that aids refugees. Many prospective students hear about International via word of mouth within their own communities, or from in-house recruiters who visit middle schools in the area. Once, Dariana Castro attempted to recruit a student at a Laundromat.

Technically, Miguel is supposed to take every child who is referred by one of the DOE's enrollment offices and meets the criteria set forth by the Internationals Network and the DOE. Because every year there are more referrals and fewer seats, however, Miguel is forced to turn kids away. "Our hands are tied. If the principal tells me I have no space, I have no space. As far as the DOE is concerned, we should take all of those students," Miguel says. "But then, it becomes much more difficult for individual students to get the attention they need. It really does destroy the whole idea behind the small-schools initiative."

August and September are the busiest months, and the cruelest.

Miguel adds: "I call myself the Grim Reaper. In some cases, you're turning a whole family away."

The job takes an emotional toll on Miguel. He sees the Uzbek mother playing with the hem of her gray pencil skirt as she implores the bodiless voice of a Russian translator whom he has summoned on the speakerphone to implore Miguel to allow her son into the ninth grade. He listens as the Haitian stepmother speaks on behalf of her silent stepdaughter, who arrived in the United States only two months before. "She don't know train or bus yet," the woman pleads in a thick Creole accent. "She's gonna lost."

Certain words are universal: "Please," "Thank you," "I'm sorry." In the best-case scenario, Miguel is able to help a family find a spot at another International school. Depending on the level of education in a student's native country, he might recommend repeating the ninth grade if there is no space in tenth. If nothing else works, he has to send another family back onto the street.

If there is space, the actual intake lasts thirty minutes to an hour. For many of the Tibetan students who were nomads or farmers back home, there are no easy answers.

How old are you? Take Ngawang, for example. He is seventeen, but his birth date is unknown. His grandmother calculated that it was sometime in June 1991, based on the height of the weeds on the day he was born, during the Year of the Sheep on the Chinese zodiac calendar.

What is your name? That seems pretty straightforward, but not if you are asked to fill in two names when you only have one. Take Sonam Sonam—or Lucky Lucky—a freshman whose given name also became her surname when she entered the United States.

Where are you from? Though a few Tibetan students were born in Dharamsala, India, most are from eastern Tibet, but their birth certificates are officially Chinese, reflecting decades of government control. "I hate that," Ngawang seethes.

When did you arrive in this country? That's easy. Almost everyone remembers the exact day.

What was the last grade you completed in your country? The rare female student from Yemen and the West Africans from war-torn villages take pause before answering. Every year kids who are classified as SIFE—

Students with Interrupted Formal Education—are given extra academic attention in a special program at the school. But there is no such label for the students whose formal education never even began before they entered the United States.

How do you like New York? Where are you living? Who are you living with? In his two years on the job, Miguel has processed kids who were sleeping in homeless shelters or squatting with friends. "I try not to pry too much into their living situation," he says. "If a student registers with their aunt and uncle, for instance, I won't necessarily ask where their mother or father are, since that could be a tough emotional question."

Any medical problems? Do you have health insurance? Often, the answer to the second question is no.

Legal status is "a don't-ask-don't-tell thing," Miguel explains. All students, whether documented or not, are legally entitled to attend public school from kindergarten through the twelfth grade as a result of the 1982 United States Supreme Court ruling, *Plyler v. Doe*, which came about after a group of undocumented Mexican children living in Tyler, Texas, were effectively denied free public education at local schools. The ruling has been called into question several times over the past three decades, with each new anti-immigrant wave. However, the alternative—not educating the hundreds of thousands of undocumented children who currently live in this country—could help grow an impoverished underclass.

"Children will become adults, and could become productive members of society—or they could become members of society that cost a huge amount of money. Prisons are infinitely more expensive than schools," says Sylvan. "We look at it as lowering the cost to society in the long term by enabling a large group of people, many of whom will eventually become legal for a variety of reasons: the jobs they choose, the people they marry, the changes in laws. Any number of things can happen. Better to have those people functioning as productive members of democratic society than not."

Despite the current open-door policy at American public schools, there are still conspicuous absences among certain populations of immigrant students at International. It is a crisp fall afternoon, and one problem in particular has been dogging Nedda de Castro, the Dominican assistant principal, as she sits in her office near a picture of her daughter playing the violin. "Where are the Uzbek girls?" she wonders aloud. "We have a whole crew: ten kids from Uzbekistan, not a single girl. Do they have sisters? What's up?"

"School is different, culturally—how things are taught, that school is taught at all," Nedda continues. She credits books such as Khaled Hosseini's *A Thousand Splendid Suns* for helping her grasp just how far some students have traveled, not just physically, but in psychological miles. "It helps to understand where they are coming from, so we know how far we have to reach."

Of course, the less that is known about a particular country—the less visible it is on the world stage—the more difficult it can be to bridge that gap.

In September of 2007, a hundred thousand people in Myanmar (still known as Burma to its refugees and to many countries who don't recognize the junta's renaming of the nation) took to the streets to protest more than forty years of being held hostage by the military junta in power that has left the country poor and isolated, with almost no access to the outside world. Those who have attempted to oppose the dictatorship have been killed or punished. Most notably, Daw Aung San Suu Kyi, the prodemocracy opposition leader in Myanmar, was jailed in her own home for most of two decades, until November 2010. Her decaying house on a compound overrun with weeds became a symbol of an entire nation imprisoned on its own soil, cut off and unknowable.

One year after the uprising, Chit Su had walked into Miguel's office with a white referral slip and a family friend, a man who spoke Burmese and limited English. Their meeting was brief, but far briefer were Miguel's notes, a combination of handwritten observations in a burgundy spiral notebook, and a slightly more detailed assessment in a Microsoft Word document:

Chit Su
- 17-year-old female originally from Myanmar/Burma
- U.S. arrival date was July 2008

- Completed 9th grade in Burma. This year she'll begin in 9th grade.
- SIFE—Education interrupted for the last three years while living in a refugee camp in Thailand
- Understands and speaks very limited English

Miguel wasn't surprised when the family friend explained that Chit Su had lived at a refugee camp in Thailand for the past three years, during which time she didn't go to school. However, he was concerned, just as he always is whenever he hears the words "refugee camp."

"Alarms go off in my head. Red flags. Depending on where they lived, anything could have happened to them in that time: Was there neglect? Was this a poor girl who was sitting in a corner by herself for a year?" Miguel says one September morning in his office.

"All the students are a total mystery, for the most part. We always ask them for some sort of transcript, but depending on what country they're coming from, they might not have one. Like the students who come from Tibet—there's no infrastructure. They have no records. They get asylum in the U.S., and they're basically a blank slate, and they have to start over with us.

"I don't ask the families what happened in between," he adds. "I just focus on making the transition into the school as easy as possible. Three years from now, maybe Chit Su will write an essay about her experience at the refugee camp. It's amazing, some of the trials and tribulations that our kids have gone through just to get a foot into our school."

From Journey to Journal

"Where *are* they?" Ann Parry wonders aloud. She glances at the plastic digital clock leaning against the whiteboard. The period officially started five minutes ago, but her classroom is still empty, except for the lone gray mouse scaling the leg of a wooden bookshelf and Nora Mendez, a tiny Guatemalan girl sitting at one of the light blue trapezoidal tables by the window. Twisting her long, dark-brown hair into a thin funnel down her back, Nora wears liquid black eyeliner and a disheartened expression, as if she were the first guest to arrive at a really lame birthday party.

There was a time when Ann would fill her classroom with visual distractions: photos of the kids, plants, and a worm bin when she taught science. But this year, other than throwing some books on the shelves and arranging the tables into their familiar horseshoe-shaped groupings, she hasn't done much else in the way of decorating. It seems unnecessary now that her students are seniors and no longer need her to hang a subway map on the wall and label the sprawling beige mass that is Brooklyn, "You are here." She knows that, when her kids walk through the cafeteria, up the stairwell grouted with ancient wads of gum and fresh spit, to the third floor, and finally into Room 340, it will feel like coming home.

"How was your summer?" Ann asks Nora, walking over to the window to sit in the navy-blue metal chair beside her.

"Good, Mees Ann," Nora squeaks. "Working working working."

"Where were you working?"

"Sweater factory," Nora says.

What is a sweater factory? Ann thinks. *Does she mean a sweatshop?*

"That sounds like an awful job in the summer," Ann says, eyeing the door.

There is still no sign of her other advisees, but if she put her mind to it, Ann could probably guess why they are late. She knows who is having trouble getting up in the morning because of a late shift, and who's just playing grab-ass in the hall. She also knows who is going to have a hard time when the entire senior class starts applying for federal financial aid, because of an undocumented status. She doesn't need a crystal ball to predict that, sometime in the next few minutes, Genesis Carolina Matamoros Pozo is going to walk through the door wearing the tightest, lowest-cut shirt she could find, her breasts like shrink-wrapped billiard balls, despite multiple requests from Ann over time to "put the girls away."

Smoothing her khakis, Ann stands up and paces like an expectant host, pushing in chairs and checking her attendance sheet as if it were a VIP list. For the rest of the year, she will shuttle between two classrooms, teaching English and social studies, but she is never late. Twenty-nine years old, she has sunny blond hair, cut to her shoulders, and a light spray of freckles across her nose. Her eyes are pale blue, specked with bits of green and yellow and rimmed with puffy half-moons, which will get puffier over the next few weeks as she readjusts to the BEEP-BEEP-BEEP of her 5:30 AM alarm, and the steady soundtrack of voices yelling, "*Miiiiissssss!*" At the end of the year, one student will give her wrinkle cream as a parting gift.

In the next two hours alone, she has to distribute class schedules, forms for free lunch and field trips, and the four-by-six-inch index cards where her advisees update their contact information. She will also talk about graduation requirements, college essays, résumés, internships, and registering for the SAT. It's a lot, but she feels ready. Her laptop bag is packed with a peanut-butter-and-jelly sandwich and her daily planner filled with good intentions: the first month of her social studies curriculum, prompts for English class, and Important Things To Do highlighted in attention-grabbing hues. "Announcements: Register for the SAT," "Think about clubs to participate in," "What do you enjoy reading? Describe a favorite book."

This year is going to be different, Ann told herself when she woke up, giddy with nerves and slightly amnesiac with optimism.

That was three hours ago.

It always takes a few minutes, but eventually the stragglers come in, the CoverGirl compacts are put away, and the composition books come out. By the second week of school, the seniors in Ann's first-period English class know the drill. Most days when they walk into Room 337, there is a journal assignment written on the whiteboard. *How do you feel about the senior year so far?* Ngawang, from Tibet: "I feel good and weird." *If you could have one superpower, what would it be?* Harold, from the Dominican Republic: " 'Supersonic Speed.' I want to be able to do things fast and move at an incredible speed to make the most of my time." *Why do we read?* Hasanatu Sowe, from Sierra Leone: "We read to survive in the world, because when we know how to read, we can have gob."

Ann is usually at the front of the room, her palm smudged with blue ink as she writes the topic of the day, but this morning her co-teacher, a Russian immigrant named Vadim Feyder, came up with the prompt: *Write everything you can about your hair.* Within seconds pens start scribbling and Ann begins her daily loop through the maze of light-blue tables, once in a while stopping to share tidbits about her own hair, like how it turns darker in the winter and white blond in the summer.

Ann is used to being the only blonde in the room. Like her blue eyes, her flaxen hair has made her a bit of a celebrity in the halls of the International High. There was that time when the Bangladeshi girls swarmed her, running their fingers through her ponytail as if she were some life-size Barbie right out of the box. "So pretty!" they cooed, until she had to physically remove herself from their grip and use her teacher voice: "Okay, we're done now—please stop doing that!"

For the most part, Ann tries not to call attention to her appearance, but she has to admit that Vadim's idea is inspired. Every student has something to say. Peering over hunched shoulders, Ann catches glimpses of journal entries that are surprisingly revealing. Wearing a gold Buddha charm around his neck, his jet-black hair in a bristly faux-hawk, Ngawang writes about his Chinese barber. Despite whatever political differences they may have, Ngawang trusts the barber to make him look cool. "Since we have similer face, they know which hair cut will look good on me," he scribbles. Sitting at the next table, Harold looks deep in thought as he describes his regimen, getting his hair trimmed every three weeks and brushing it regularly to avoid looking sloppy, and his impeccable handwriting quickly fills up the page. A few feet away, Hasanatu picks at a nubby braid with one hand as she scratches out letters with the other, holding her pencil in a curved, clawlike grip.

> *My hair is hort, most of the time my hair is hard it use to be brown color, I change it to redcolor and I have wash it every two weeks or go to the salom to make it more soft and beautiful. I also braid my hair.*

In fact, a couple of the African girls are professional hair braiders and work at salons after school when they're not beautifying themselves. A startling number of the Chinese boys want to be "hair designers," and several talk about opening a salon together. They would have discovered the cure for cancer by now if they had spent as much time studying as they do teasing, tin-foiling, perming, and perfecting the art of the emo haircut: long, ratted-out bangs and a pinwheel of feathery spikes in the back. Every day is a hair show, an array of Edward Scissorhands styles. "You just became interested in hair designing because everybody else is interested in being hair designers!" Ann tells one of her advisees, a girl who suddenly changed her career focus from "I don't know" to "hair designing," after getting a cool new haircut. "Half of my students want to be hair designers!"

The rest of the kids are obsessed with their hair simply because they are teenagers. Walking around Room 337 one morning in late September, Ann sees hair that's been crimped, curled, straightened and spiked, braided, plaited, picked, and ponytailed—but all in shades of black or brown. The ethnic makeup of her first-period class couldn't be more different from her own experience of high school in Chester County, Pennsylvania, known for its rolling hills and horse farms. And yet, Ann's memories of Unionville High School, Home of the Indians, are fresh enough that she can relate to her students at the most basic level. When she looks at Genesis twirling her ponytail, she remembers what it felt like to want to be wanted. When she looks at Marco, slinking into class with his long inky black hair askew from sleeping late again, she remembers what it felt like to hate authority and being told what to do. "I remember all those feelings of resentment. I see that in my students, and I think, 'Ooh.' They're just a ball of hormones. They're going through growing pains; they're finding themselves. Underneath all of these cultures and ethnicities, there's this sameness which is startling," Ann says. "A teenager is a teenager."

In many ways, Ann's students seem like typical American teenagers. They spend way too much time on Facebook and way too little time on homework. In other ways, they are anything but typical American teenagers. For one, they were not born in the United States. They come from Tibet, Sierra Leone, Ecuador, China, Mexico, Togo, Yemen, Haiti, the Dominican Republic, Honduras, Nepal, Bangladesh, Guinea, Uzbekistan, Poland, and Colombia, among other countries. Of the eighty-four students in the Class of 2009, approximately 15 percent are undocumented. Many are the first in their families to go to high school, and many more are hoping to be the first in their families to go to college. More than half of the seniors work, some six or seven days a week. Their job descriptions include convenience-store cashier, factory worker, manicurist, waiter and waitress, food runner, cook, and maid. Three girls are already mothers, and before the end of the school year, at least two more will be pregnant.

But those are just a few nameless statistics that don't even begin to capture the complexity of the students' lives outside the classroom. Just this morning, Ann helped her first-period student Hasanatu begin a rough draft for a college essay about how her African girlfriends are pressuring her to find a husband. It was either that or spruce up a story she wrote last year about the day she caught on fire in Sierra Leone when a car she was traveling in was bombed. She titled it, "I Grew Up in a War."

It's said that there are eight million stories in New York City. At International High, there are more than four hundred walking memoirs waiting to be translated. By fall of their senior year, Ann has heard many of her students' stories before, but getting them on paper is another matter entirely, and the stakes couldn't be higher. One essay can make or break a student's chance of getting into college, which is why Ann and Vadim have been using journal warm-ups to prepare the seniors for the challenge that lies ahead: writing college essays. Their American-born peers have the advantage of speaking English as a native language and may score higher on their SAT's, but a great story can blow away the competition. Last year a Tibetan girl who had grown up as a nomadic yak herder won a Gates Millennium scholarship to Middlebury College, in part because of her essay about escaping to India on foot through the Himalayas. "I am only seventeen years old," her first line began, "and I have already had three lives."

Ann checks the clock, and as the students put down some last thoughts about their hair, she winds her way past the windows and wooden bookshelves. Most of the picture books came with the classroom. *Runny Babbit: A Billy Sook* by Shel Silverstein—not exactly college reading material. The rest are way over most of the kids' heads, like *For Whom the Bell Tolls* or *Jurassic Park*—a total waste of space when those shelves could be filled with books that her students might actually read, like *The Joy Luck Club* or *The Color Purple*. Other than the rows of foreign-language and visual dictionaries, there's no rhyme or reason to the way the titles are organized. *The Catcher in the Rye* is next to *Ramona Quimby, Age 8*, and maybe that's somehow appropriate, considering that her students' reading levels range from third grade to college.

On the fourth day of school, Ann plopped a bunch of books on a table and asked the kids to read the synopses on the back of each cover, the front flap, and one page, before filling out a response sheet. "Can you understand it?" "Do you want to read it?" "Will this reading challenge you?" One of Ann's most important tasks this year will be matching the right books to the right kids for silent reading. For Hasanatu, who entered the ninth grade barely knowing how to read or write, that means finding a copy of *Superfudge* by Judy Blume. For Harold, who brings in a copy of *The Elements of Style* by Strunk & White, that means finding something a bit more fun. Ann gives him *The Brief Wondrous Life of Oscar Wao* by Junot Díaz.

"Okay, guys, put your journals away," Ann says, poking a few book spines back into place. She cracks a window, letting in a cool breeze, and passes out sheets of marigold paper photocopied with the writing prompt that students will develop into their college essays over the next few weeks.

"Assignment," she reads aloud. "Write a true story from your life that demonstrates your strengths as a person."

In a far corner of the room a skinny Haitian boy with a huge Afro who didn't close his journal continues to draw a portrait of Homer Simpson eating a bag of M&M's. Sitting an elbow's length away, Kalsang, the modelesque Tibetan girl, examines a pimple in her compact mirror through smoky eyes. "This zit hurts like crap!" she hisses.

"Pop it!" Freeman shouts, catching her scowl.

"Guys, guys!" Vadim waits for their attention and then writes some key words on the board: "HOOK," "SETTING," "PLOT," "CHARACTER."

"Use a 'hook' at the beginning to grab the reader's attention," Ann continues. "You need to clearly establish a 'setting.' Have a 'plot' that moves a story along. Fully develop at least one 'character.' Your story must show your audience your personal power. What is your personal power?"

In preparation for today's lesson on setting and sensory details, Ann had taken a stab at writing her own story. As usual, she procrastinated until the last possible second, dashing off a first draft at 11 PM the night before in her room, a glass of merlot in hand. She tried to put herself in her students' shoes as she sat at her old wooden desk under a shelf of her books: *Encyclopedia of Herb Gardening, Automotive Excellence, Smart Women Finish Rich, Teacher with a Heart*. She saw herself as seventeen again, applying to college. What would she write about? She hadn't yet traveled to Ecuador or India or hiked the Appalachian Trail. Unlike her students, she never had walked barefoot over a desert or crossed the Himalayas in a snowstorm. But she had spent years waitressing at a nursing home—where her mother was head nurse and her grandmother was a patient—that was something to explore. Everyone has a grandmother. Everyone could relate to having a relative who is sick.

The result of her effort is a two-page essay entitled, "Creamed Corn and Pureed Hamburger." Wearing a white tank top and khakis, Ann rotates slowly so that everybody can get a good look at the Xeroxed copy that she holds in her hands. Times New Roman. One-inch margins. Double-spaced lines. "As you can see, it's twelve-point font. Not something that looks like you wrote it with a paintbrush," she says drolly, to scattered laughs. "It's not a comic book."

Despite multiple warnings throughout the year, there will be one student who turns in a social-studies essay, in thirty-six-point font, that ends with the simple conclusion, "DONE." But that hasn't happened yet. Ann is still hopeful. She's also nervous, a pink flush creeping down her neck and to the tips of her ears. Standing at the front of the room, she grips both sides of her paper, takes a shallow breath, and begins to read in a loud, clear voice.

"'Creamed Corn and Pureed Hamburger.' Her eye sits on the nightstand. It's hazel green, sometimes blue, sometimes gray; the same color as my eyes. My mother picks it up and grasps my grandmother's head and wiggles the eye into the empty socket."

"What's a socket?" asks Kalsang.

"It's the hole where your eye goes," Ann says.

"Aww, Miss! That's nasty."

Ann reads on, occasionally interrupting herself to explain what "glaucoma" is, and how her grandmother needed a glass eye to replace the one that she had lost to disease; the other was stitched shut. In the end, the essay is less about Ann and more about her grandmother, a tough widow who raised six children by herself before going blind. But Ann inherited her mother's pragmatism (*Teaching is a lot like nursing*, Ann thinks. She spends half her day checking for vital signs) and she has her grandmother's sometimes green, sometimes blue, sometimes gray eyes.

Once she's done reading, Ann walks over to the whiteboard and marks in three-inch letters: "SETTING." Underneath, she scrawls: "Sight," "Taste," "Smell," "Touch," "Hearing."

"So," she says, "what's the 'setting' of the story?"

"Sort of like a hospital?" Ngawang ventures.

"Does everyone know what a nursing home is?" Ann asks.

"It's for old people," says Hasanatu, twisting a nub of her reddish-brown hair. "People who are so old they have their own room."

"Okay . . ." Ann says, suppressing a smile. "Now, did you guys get a picture of what the nursing home looked like?"

A few heads shake no.

"Not really. So, we're going to brainstorm 'sensory details,' because that's what stands out for me. A lot of old ladies wore perfume with a lavender scent."

"What's lavender?" asks Ngawang.

"Lavender is a purple flower." Her hand smudged with blue ink, Ann writes "Lavender" on the board, under "Smell."

Ngawang writes "lavender" in the bottom margin of his composition book. "Did you have to wash dishes?" he asks.

"Yeah, there was always old food on the plate—peas, peanut butter and jelly. And I had to vacuum the carpet. Sometimes I would reach down and pick food off the carpet."

Once again, Ann points to the board. " 'Hearing.' You hear people mumbling and the nurses talking to themselves. But it's also extremely quiet. 'Taste?' " She scrunches up her face in disgust. "Maybe when I was on my break, I would go back into the storage room and grab a piece of fruit or a peanut-butter-and-jelly sandwich. You really didn't want to have the meal that you were serving that day."

"Did you get paid?" Freeman asks.

"What was the fun part?" Ngawang cuts in. "It sounds sad."

"Do you get the sense that I thought it was a terrible place?" Ann asks in reply. "It really wasn't. I had all these friends in the kitchen. When my grandmother became a resident, that was kind of sad. But maybe I do need to include some fun things about the place." Ann lowers her voice into a conspiratorial whisper. "This is actually my second draft, not my shitty first draft."

From the corner of the room comes Jovita Victoriano's Tickle-Me-Elmo giggle. *Hee hee hee.*

"I had to cut out lots of things, and you guys will probably have to do that, too, because your memories are so *vast*," Ann says, spreading her arms. "I had to focus, focus, focus—on her eyes, on the things that I did for her."

As Ann ties up, Vadim passes out another photocopied assignment and explains the activity for the second half of the period. The worksheet features five bubbles, each labeled for the different senses. In the middle of the page is a question: "Where is the story taking place?" Once they figure out the story they want to tell, the students are supposed to brainstorm sensory details to create a setting. "For now, just write whatever comes to mind," Vadim says.

In the remaining minutes, Ann sits down with Jovita, who wears a loose sienna-colored top with blue jeans and big silver hoops. Three years since she started at International, Jovita hides behind a hank of jet-black bangs, and wears her eyeliner as heavy as she likes her Spanish rock. Short and stocky with broad brown shoulders and shapely legs, she is one of International's best soccer players, but joining the team was its own challenge. When she first came to the United States from Mexico, Jovita was afraid to leave her apartment, and she didn't talk for the first six months of her freshman year. Every time she was called on in class, her jaw quivered. "How long did it take for you to start speaking in English?" Ann prodded Jovita one afternoon, on the way to an informal parent-teacher conference at the local taqueria where Jovita's mother worked behind the counter. "Two years," Jovita said. "Two years!" Ann cried. "Finally, I had to say, 'You have to speak in English, or else!' I wouldn't respond to you if you spoke in Spanish."

In class, they have a deal. As long as Jovita speaks in English, Ann will accommodate her in other ways. "I'll be your secretary," she often tells the kids who struggle.

Ann scoots her chair closer to Jovita and leans in close. "Where is the story taking place?" she asks, already knowing the answer.

"Sonoran Desert," Jovita says, her blouse sliding down her shoulders as she bends over the paper. "Arizona–Mexico border."

Borrowing Jovita's pen, Ann writes "Sonoran Desert" on her paper.

"What did the desert smell like?" Ann asks, probing. "What did it look like?"

Jovita plays with her big hoop earring, translating her thoughts into English. "Cactus? *Espina?*"

"Okay, there were cactus spines. Maybe that goes under 'Touch,'" Ann says. "What about your feet? How did your feet feel while you were walking?"

Jovita smiles. The right word in English is lodged in a place where she can't reach it. "Blood," she says.

"Do you mean *blisters?*" Ann asks. "That would be under 'Touch,' too—you felt pain." Ann shows her the corresponding bubble and writes "Blisters." "So, you walked all day and night with the coyote?"

"No, because at night I couldn't see anything." Jovita cups an invisible orb in the palm of her hand. "Only when the moon was out."

"How long?"

"One week."

Ann points to the bubble labeled "Taste." "What did the water that you were drinking taste like?"

"Sometimes we drank water from the lake."

"What kind of animals did you see?"

Jovita laughs, *hee hee hee*. "Cows, only cows."

"So, you were drinking the same water the cows were drinking?"

"Yes," Jovita says, in a thick accent. *Jess.*

Across the room, Kalsang has begun putting on her rings again. At the beginning of every period before she starts writing, she removes all of her rings, leaving a small pile of silver and semiprecious stones on her desk, and at the end of every period she reverses the ritual, whittling away a total of ten minutes of class time—fifteen to twenty if she can get her hands on the laminated yellow bathroom pass. She is on the last one, a silver band featuring a slab of turquoise, twisting it as slowly as possible.

Ann taps Jovita's pen on the table. She only has a few minutes left to extract as much information as possible from her, and they work with the intense concentration of two girls playing Ouija, trying to summon a past life into the classroom, before the door between the two dimensions slams shut.

"So," Ann says, "you got tall cactus, short cactus . . . maybe we should look up the different species of cactus."

"And also, mmm, *una fruta de color rojo y verde*," Jovita says, taking a minute to translate. "We ate the fruit of the cactus."

"What did it taste like?" Ann asks.

"Sweet, but too many spines, so we take it out."

"This is good. You're starting to think of more things you were eating," Ann says. "What did you hear? What sounds does the desert make at night? You must have heard something, because when you're outside at night, there's always noise. Did you hear dogs barking?"

Jovita nods, digging her chin into the meat of her palm, a fleshy hammock. From outside comes a bang on the door, rattling its rectangular windowpane. "*Maricón!*" a boy yells, followed by the sound of sneakers squeaking up and down the hall. Ann is still trying to peer into Jovita's past when the clock blinks to 9:45, and her student packs up to leave.

The smiley, blue-jeaned girl Ann knows bears little resemblance to the one who scavenged for cactus fruit in the desert and drank the same water as cows. Remembering the past is not a useless exercise. A good essay could help secure a private scholarship for someone like Jovita, who is undocumented and ineligible for federal financial aid. Still, sometimes Ann wonders if it would be better for the students to forget and move on. Ann watches Jovita link arms with another Mexican girl and disappear into the halls. Then she clears an empty milk carton off the table as the next class shuffles in for second period.

Twenty-Four Hours in a Suitcase

"Get in," the man said to Ngawang, motioning at a small suitcase on the ground. It was the fall of 2003, about two years before Ngawang would arrive at International, and they were standing on a quiet side street in Lhasa. Ngawang looked at the man, and back at the suitcase. The man was his father's friend, a farmer with a wide, tanned face sowed with worry in the encroaching dawn. The suitcase looked very fancy—black nylon with a plastic handlebar, rubber wheels, and metallic zippers. Ngawang had never touched a suitcase before, and he inspected it closely. There was some Chinese lettering on it that he could not read. The main compartment was only about two by three feet, the size of a baby's coffin. Ngawang was small for eleven, but he wasn't that small. He thought the farmer must be joking.

The black suitcase would soon be one of many bags stacked in the backseat of a beat-up silver Toyota that was supposed to deliver Ngawang to the border of Nepal, the first leg of a journey that would end in Dharamsala, India. In the tea-colored light, Ngawang could make out a few tired faces, older Tibetans who had paid to drive out of Lhasa before the capital city stretched out of its slumber. He was about to join the others when the farmer motioned again toward the suitcase.

"Get in," he said, unzipping the top.

Ngawang stared blankly at the man and the suitcase.

"Hurry!" the farmer said. "Before the police come and take us to jail!"

"How long?" Ngawang whispered.

"One night and one day."

That was how long it would take to travel from the capital to the border, assuming they didn't get caught. The actual distance was much shorter, but the driver would be circumventing several Chinese police checkpoints along the way. They didn't have much time. Except for the glowing apparition of the Potala Palace rising from the valley, Lhasa was still dark. But soon the sun would rise, shining a spotlight on anyone who dared to flee.

Ngawang got in. He imagined himself back in his grandma's wide bed, where he had slept with his older brother Lobsang and their little cousins only a few weeks before, their bodies crisscrossed in every direction like a network of roads, all leading to home. Inside the suitcase, he crunched his knees to his chest and rocked to the side. For a brief moment he saw the farmer's face, its broad planes darkened in shadows like a field under a passing cloud. Then there was a zipping sound, and everything went black.

Nine hours into the journey Ngawang vomited, the bitter remnants of a black tea and barley breakfast singeing his throat and clinging to the fibers of his camouflage pants. Thirteen hours in, he urinated, a gush of warm liquid rushing down his leg, cooling in his sneakers. In the upside-down dark, his tears flowed in uncharted directions, tracing saline paths from the corners of his eyes to the hollows of his ear, where they pooled like hot springs.

When the suitcase first closed, Ngawang felt scared but strong. He still wore the white silk scarf that his grandmother had placed around his neck as a parting gift. Clasping his hands between tucked knees, he whispered a Buddhist prayer: "*Om mani padme hum.*" Those were the last words he spoke. He was afraid to make a sound. In the village he had heard tales about Tibetans who were caught midpassage by

Chinese police. Friends told Ngawang about prisoners who had been beaten with clubs, shot at, and subjected to strange torture techniques like one called Digging in Bamboo Sticks, and he imagined police hammering the sharpened rods under their victims' fingernails.

Even if Ngawang wanted to scream, no one would hear him. He couldn't hear anyone, either. Within seconds of the zipper zipping, he lost control of his senses. He couldn't see, but he smelled the gasoline leaking from the car engine. Half of his body went cold—the half that was closest to the icy ground. He tried moving his arm and leg on his other side, but found that he was trapped. *Thumpphh!* Something had fallen on him, but he wasn't sure what. It sounded like a dead body being thrown into a grave, but then Ngawang realized: It was the sound of suitcases stacking. *THUMPPHH! THUMPHH!*

In, out, in, out. Breathing had become such an impossible task that it was hard to believe it had ever been automatic. The more he thought about it, the more he panicked, gasping for air and swallowing dust. His right arm ached from pushing up against the weight of the other suitcases that were piled on top of his own. His left arm was frozen against the cold car floor. He felt every bump and every rock on the road. He heard the engine sputter to a halt at what must have been the police checkpoints and clenched his fists until it started again, thundering in his ear. He summoned a world beyond his own eyelids. The saffron-robed monks and Chinese soldiers who crowded the streets of Lhasa would be far behind now. He imagined lakes and rivers and animals roaming in big, empty spaces.

Sometimes his thoughts drifted to his grandmother, Mashi. His own mother had died three days after he was born. Mashi was the one who suckled Ngawang with a glass bottle filled with milk from a female yak—known as a *dri*—when the village women weren't able to breastfeed. The day he and Lobsang left Golok, their village in eastern Tibet, Mashi cooked a meal of *momo* dumplings and yak-butter tea, one last taste of home before Ngawang and his brother Lobsang mounted their horses and headed west. In the blackness of the suitcase, Ngawang could see her still standing in the tall green grass, waving good-bye.

Since the Dalai Lama fled in 1959, tens of thousands of Tibetans have followed his path to Dharamsala, India. Ngawang knew their stories. He had heard about the men and women who crossed the Himalayas, many dying of starvation or getting trapped in the ice during the long trek. For years his father had planned his own escape, and he was the first of Ngawang's family to flee, arriving in America in 2003. A few months later he sent for his two sons. Ngawang caught bits and pieces of the plan from neighbors whenever they came back from Nyakchu, the nearest district with a phone. From Golok, Ngawang, Lobsang, and their father's friend would ride on horse to Nyakchu, where they would board a bus to the county of Markham and get on a truck headed for the capital. After getting their bearings in Lhasa, they were supposed to join up with a paid guide to make the trek across the mountains to the border of Nepal. If they made it that far, a Nepali man would meet them. For 2,500 yen per boy, he would pose as their grandfather and he would be waiting with a piece of coal and a car. The car was supposed to transport the brothers to a Tibetan refugee center in Kathmandu. The coal was for Ngawang and Lobsang to paint their faces a shade darker, so that they would look more like Nepali children. Tibetan children are known for their unusually ruddy red cheeks, the extra blood flow resulting from the high altitude and low oxygen of the plateau—Plateau Red, the Chinese sometimes called it. The first part of their journey had gone as planned. But in Lhasa, a crucial part of the plan changed. One evening the farmer told Ngawang that he had gone to see an oracle earlier that day. Ngawang had never met one, but he knew that oracles were wise men who traveled between the physical and divine worlds and could see into the future. The farmer passed on the oracle's message. Lobsang, who was two years older and much bigger, should walk through the mountains with a paid guide, a trek that could span thousands of miles and several weeks. Ngawang was too small. He simply wouldn't survive the trip. "The oracle said it's better to come with me in the car," the farmer explained.

Ngawang's father used to talk about how tiny he was when he was born—he fit into two outstretched palms, not much larger than one of the potatoes plucked from their fields. Despite his small size, the lama in their village had given him a big name: Ngawang Thokmey. Loosely translated, it meant Voice of Power, Never Stuck.

Several thousand miles west of where Ngawang Thokmey was born, Ann Parry sits at a glass-topped table in the shade of her backyard in Bedford-Stuyvesant and rereads the paragraph before her.

> *The suet case closed and I went blind. My body was squeezing under many suet cases and I can Barely breath. After hours and hours squeezing under suet cases, I felt depress and hot. I just wanted to escape, but many suet cases were stacked on me. I was sweating, I wanted to scream, but I knew that it would be worst. They could go after my sweet grand ma and hurt her because she was sending me to freedom. I could get beat up or killed. I knew I would never get to see my single dad. I would never achieve what my mom's hope and my grandma's hope. So I made my hands fist and breath strongly.*

It is 7 AM, and the October sun blinks in the clouds like a cursor on a blank page. Ann's cereal is getting soggy, and her coffee is already lukewarm. In between sips from her favorite glazed brown mug, she stares at the purple morning glories creeping up her chain-link fence and back at Ngawang's college essay. A suitcase? He is lucky to have survived. Grading pen in hand, she tries to imagine an eleven-year-old Ngawang balled up in the darkness, his fists clenched. Surely, he understands things that she doesn't about life. Or does he? His ending is brief. He is in the suitcase, and then he is in India. Ann never learns what really happened next: as planned, Ngawang met the Nepali man at the border, disguised himself with the coal, switched cars, and headed to Kathmandu. His brother wasn't so fortunate on his first attempt to make it to the border. While trekking through the Himalayas, Lobsang was arrested and jailed by Chinese police. The boys later reunited in Dharamsala, and in 2005 they joined their father in the United States, where they were granted political asylum.

Clearly, Ngawang's story is too complex to squeeze it all into a three-page college essay, but there is no final message, no deeper sense of understanding. In the minutes before she heads to school, Ann wonders about the father who also fled, the mother who died, and the grandmother whom Ngawang might never see again. She wonders about his daily life in eastern Tibet, where he had worked on his family's farm. Was he still the same boy when he emerged from the suitcase, twenty-four hours later? He never says. The editor in Ann sees a story with a great hook but an emotionally limited narrator who hasn't even begun to unpack the events of the past few years. Then she remembers that Ngawang is only seventeen.

It's easy to forget sometimes that by the time they walk into Room 337 on the first day of senior year, many students had already survived more trauma and hardship than she could imagine. But that hasn't necessarily made them wiser, and she doesn't see her kids as victims. When Ann looks at Ngawang, she doesn't see the Boy in the Suitcase but a punky kid wearing Converse and a black T-shirt inscribed with a yellow smiley face and the message "I Hate You." She sees a teenager who has started turning in his assignments late, and who would rather read the *New York Post* and comment on how Miley Cyrus looks fat than pay attention in class. He could seriously fall behind in college if he doesn't make an attitude adjustment, quick. She sees a boy who is much more than a myth, and much less.

Ann refuses to feel sorry for her students. As she views it, she has a couple of options: either she can know more about a student's life outside school, and expect less, or she can know less and expect more. "If a student can't write a sentence or is having trouble filling out an application, it's much easier to deal with that problem than 'This kid's life is a crazy jumble of disasters right now,'" Ann explains. "Then you start making all these excuses for them, and you don't want to do that. You want them to pull themselves up and get done. 'You have to type your paper, you don't have any excuses.' I can maintain that attitude if I don't know too much."

There was a time when Ann thought she'd be able to close the door to Room 337 and focus on each student in the moment, at least for the one hour and five minutes when they were hers, safe within the confines of the classroom's four peach walls. But that hope vanished as soon as she left school to read forty life stories in various stages from first drafts to finals that she had stuffed into her gray laptop bag.

For the past few days she has been averaging forty-five minutes per essay, grading up to three in a sitting, usually before school. She never grades the roughest draft. The first step is to determine where each student is academically. Can he write a sentence? Can she express a thought clearly and tell a story? A few years ago Ann would have written comments on every essay, but now she delivers most of her feedback verbally. She adds her grammar and spelling edits on the second draft because there are just too many in the beginning: missing articles, run-on sentences, capitalization errors, and plurals and singulars that don't agree, even a few that don't actually exist. Despite the twelfth-grade teachers' constant chiding, students will continue to use the misnomers "childs" and "childrens" throughout the year.

For now, Ann tries to read without being judgmental. There is always the danger of turning off a student with too much slashing and red ink and bricking up a secret passageway that may never open again. "How do you correct a sentence about someone's family dying in a car crash?" she asks after reading one Ecuadorian girl's account of waking up in a hospital to find out that she and her aunt were the only survivors of a fatal accident.

She reads the account of a heavyset Dominican girl named Milagros who works as a cashier in a supermarket, where she has become a de facto translator for Spanish-speaking customers. "In the supermarket that I work in the first thing you smell when you go in, is fresh vegetables like celery, Cole, letters and papers. You also smell the deli, when the person is making sandwiches, it smell hot and like cheese." Ann underlines "Cole," draws a question mark, and reads on.

> *Sometimes alot of wird people go in there like this guy who goes there from tow blocks way you know is him because he screms so loud and talks to you like if you are three blooks away. A lot of the timens Im in my register and I see people having trouble getting what they need because they don't know English. And a lot of this time I help them because of tow*

reazon, one reazon is that Im one of the workers who know Spanish, and
secand reazon is because I know how those persons fell when they cant get
what they want because they dont know how to speak English.

"There are many spelling errors here that could have been easily fixed
by getting a teacher/advisor/friend to correct the paper," Ann writes on
the grading sheet that she will return to Milagros, along with her first
draft, which she had turned in two weeks late. "Your description of the
supermarket is great. This would have been a C if it were on time." Ann
gives her a D.

When she's on a roll, Ann is reading minds as much as she is reading
papers. What is this kid trying to say? Would the same sentence make
sense if it were translated word by word into Spanish or Creole or Urdu?
Even if the words are jumbled, is there a coherent thought behind them,
so that if they were arranged in the right order, meaning would emerge?

Fulani people say, "A women is nothing without a husband." In Fulani
tradition, they don't care how old a girl. Is once they see there first period
it means you have to get married. They don't care about feelings or love.

There must be more to this, Ann thinks, as she reads Hasanatu's essay
about attending the West African wedding of her friend who became a
bride at fourteen years old.

The day of her wedding many people were there. Women were cooking all
different kinds of African foods. They killed a cow and a goat, children's
were running all over the place, and playing all different kind of games,
other people were bring water from the well too. Also they was playing all
kind of African songs, people were dancing all over the place they was so
happy. Family, friends, and neighbor brought lot of money and gift. But
[she] was so sad because she was too young to get married; she doesn't even
know her husband.

She wrote about her girlfriend, but what about Hasanatu? Ann wonders.
Hasanatu rarely mentions her previous life—those memories seem to be

locked away in another place, sealed off like a dusty room that is too painful to enter. And even if she chose to enter, what would she salvage? Which story would she tell? Her essay, "I Grew Up in a War," is just one chapter. Ann has heard enough about the widespread practice of female circumcision in Sierra Leone and Guinea to understand that Hasanatu must have survived much more than war. Better not to dwell on the past, but to keep moving forward. "I am glad that I came to America," Hasanatu concludes her essay. "When the right time comes I will get married to the man of my dream."

In the shade of her garden, Ann travels across continents and time zones, the issues of the world made manifest in the lives of her students. She reads about the one-child policy through the gray-lensed eyes of Dinice Liu, who reveals herself to be a budding feminist. "What is so great about boys? Huh? Just because they've got a penis and balls?" Dinice rages, recalling the day she heard her mother say that if her younger brother had been born first, she wouldn't exist. "I have known I was extra since I was a little girl. But nobody ever said it out loud in front of my face. I felt embarrassed. No! More like humiliated. Shame wrapped its red, hot claws around me and squeezed."

Dinice is a living contradiction: a girl who has as many different identities as she has names. There is Dong Er, the jilted extra daughter; Wind, the girl in between; and Dinice, who is obsessed with her appearance and will write her spring-term research paper on vitiligo because part of her eyebrow turned blond. As with all of her students, Ann's job is to comb through the unfinished layers and extract the student's best self, the one that most effectively declares, in less than five hundred words, "This is who I am."

More often than not, the students write about who they are expected to be. When Odanis Rosario turns in an essay about baseball, Ann's eyes roll. *The Dominican kid writing about baseball*, she thinks, *Oh, come on.* Yes, the game is his passion; he plays center field. But she wants to know what drives the real Odanis, a fiercely intelligent boy who was so determined to learn English when he arrived in the United States that fear wasn't an option—day after day, he would raise his hand in class and pour out completely incomprehensible sentences. Ann is wrenched out of her thoughts and back into the reality of his paper by one such sentence, which shows that she must make further efforts as his English teacher and as his former biology teacher: "I grew up with diversity since I was in the stomach of my mother." She makes a mental note to talk to Odanis about uteruses.

Ann worries about Odanis, but at least he isn't afraid to talk. She reads the newest draft of Jovita's essay, about crossing the Sonoran Desert.

> *The first night in Nogales Mexico was bad. The dark night not let saw anything, but the coyote tell us "we walking all the night to make best time and cross the border in few days," nobody think that was be imposible. After the coyote said "be careful with the cactus," was too late because the spine were into my feet and leg "is only a spine not problem with me" I said. But a few minutes late I felt like if someone put on me a vacune liquid make me numb all my feet and didn't let me walk anymore that night.*

Ann knows that crossing the border is just the first of many difficult trials that Jovita will have encountered in America by the end of this year. Without her papers, she has little possibility of going to college. Ann can talk to Jovita and her mom about options, but she is competing against more than apathy. In the direst cases, Ann is competing with necessity, with mothers who need help babysitting, fathers who need help paying the rent, and students who need sleep or even shelter, and who gave up on the idea of going to college a long time ago . . . or just recently.

The deeper she gets into the pile, the more Ann notices a theme. There are so many sad stories, it's overwhelming. Somehow, the assignment asking, "What is your personal power?" got processed as, "What is the worst thing that ever happened to you?" She and Vadim have to laugh about it; it's laugh or cry. "Every kid poured their hearts out onto the paper, but none of them made it into a college essay," Ann bemoans.

Don't make any decisions when you are mad or tired of what life is putting you through, people say.

This paper belongs to Yasmeen Salahi, a normally studious Yemeni girl who has been in and out of school for weeks, dealing with the death of her father and her ailing mother. Ann reads her emotional account of learning about her father's cancer diagnosis around the same time that her mother, who had long suffered from kidney problems, had a heart attack that left her in a coma.

This is therapy, Ann thinks, after she finishes the last paragraph. *She is cracking open.* She imagines Yasmeen sitting by her father's bedside in the hospital and what that must have been like for her. Her next thought is, *This is not a college essay. She doesn't talk enough about herself.* An admissions officer might feel sorry for Yasmeen, but that doesn't guarantee that he would accept her. They don't know the student that Ann knows: an outspoken Muslim girl who was the president of the Arabic Club last year, despite being its only female member. They only know the tragic figure in the essay. The fact that it is full of grammatical mistakes is almost a relief to Ann, as if each error were a buffer between her and the raw emotion coming off the page in hot waves. She can correct a run-on sentence, if not a life run off course.

Of course, some kids float by on good grades and high test scores and never seem to need help at all. "Get out of here! You do not belong to this family!" No title precedes this opening sentence, no date, just the name at the top of the page: Yuan Tan. Ann knows her better as Jessica Tan, one of the strongest students in her fourth-period English class, despite having arrived in America only last year.

That was the first sentence I heard when I first saw my stepmother. "How can you say this to my daughter?" My father said gently and put his left hand around my shoulder. After a 14 hours'-flight from China to America, what I faced was making me more exhausted and sad. My stepmother went insane when she saw me. Her piercing voice penetrates my ears and my mind. "She is not my child! Why I need to take care of her? If she doesn't go, then I will!" She closed the door loudly and my step

brothers began to cry. "Daughter. I'm sorry. After all, she is not your real
mother." "I know, dad." "Your step mother won't be nice to you and your
step brothers are too young." "Don't worry. I'll go." I said calmly but my
heart was broken. My father came to America when I was 10 and we
have not seen each other for 7 years. After all these years of waiting, now
I could finally be with my father. But he "abandoned" me again for his
new family. I did not say anything; the choice was made.

Ann is stunned by the revelation. So many of her students bring their
problems at home into the classroom, if they bother showing up at all.
But Jessica always seems so cheerful and well-adjusted, and unlike some
of the other Chinese kids, she has an air of privilege about her. She is
light-skinned and has wispy, shoulder-length hair, liquid black eyes, and a
round chin that dimples when she is deep in thought, which she often is.
Her contemplativeness is at odds with her personal style, which appears
to have been culled from bargain bins across Chinatown and inspired by
old episodes of *Punky Brewster.* She favors stripes and sequins and clothes
in My Little Pony colors, which she pairs with little punk touches like
an Arabic *keffiyah* scarf in robin's egg blue or a single silver star dangling
from her ear.

In a few hours, Ann will look at Jessica in class and think back to her
essay, back to one line in particular that will stay with her for the rest of
the day:

Today is my 18th birthday. "I'm very busy today so I cannot come." I
couldn't tell you how many times my father had told me that he was busy.
I sat on the bed and sang the Happy Birthday song to myself.

Ann pictures Jessica sitting on her bed, singing to herself, and it oc-
curs to her that everyone knows the feeling of being alone on your birthday and thinking that no one cares. But for Jessica, being alone wasn't just
a feeling; it was her reality. Once again, Ann is jarred out of the sadness
of the story into the more practical matter at hand: how to make it better.
Jessica needs to flesh out that moment, the moment she realized that she
was on her own.

"Be more specific," Ann suggests in the margin, keeping in mind some questions to ask Jessica in person. *Where do you live? How do you pay rent? What do you do when you get home from school, and you're alone? Do you cook for yourself? Do you do your own laundry? What does the room look like? Is it in someone else's apartment?*

The mental Post-it notes are piling up as Ann grabs her mug and goes into the kitchen to refill her coffee. Then she sits down at the dining room table and reads Jessica's essay again, this time more closely.

Dinner for Jessica

Sometimes, Jessica wishes that Harold would be more romantic. They have been going out for months, but all they ever do is study. He seems to take his cues from his plastic baseball folder, which declares in bold letters, GET IN THE GAME! Everywhere Harold goes, he carries a neatly typed list of the colleges and universities where he is applying, entitled "Harold's List of Private Colleges/Universities." There are nine in total, including Stanford. Jessica has a list of eight. When she was still living in China, she dreamed of going to one of the Ivies, like Harvard or Yale. Looking through her pile of college brochures, she sometimes imagines herself studying in quiet open spaces, or just hanging out with her new friends on the emerald-green lawns—"grasslands," she calls them. Lately though, Jessica has readjusted her sights to Tufts University, and the college counselor Joanna Yip has warned her that even that is a stretch.

Since school started, Jessica and Harold have been as inseparable as Bonnie and Clyde. Only, instead of robbing banks, applying for college seems to fan the flames of their romance. Their courtship started over the summer, when they took part in a volunteer program sponsored by a nonprofit group called Global Potential. Along with a bunch of their classmates, they went to the Dominican Republic to work in the *bateys*, basically shantytowns where Haitian migrants come every year to crop sugar. It was over the course of those six weeks—as they shoveled dirt to build a new study room for the migrants' children, hand-fed baby goats, and camped out on the beach with their fellow volunteers—that Harold and Jessica became close. They came from opposite ends of the world, but they found that they had a lot in common.

Like Jessica, Harold loves manga comic books, computer role-playing games, and action movies, though he prefers *Star Wars* to her all-time favorite franchise, *Indiana Jones*. Unlike Jessica who lives alone, Harold lives with his mother and two little brothers, but he waits for her every day after school, before going home.

By late fall, they have a routine. He walks her to the blue lockers on the fourth floor, and she trades in her glasses, her pencil case, and a worn copy of *The Outsiders*, by S. E. Hinton, for a bright orange folder labeled College Stuff. Once a week they attend meetings of the newspaper club together, typing their articles side by side. Sometimes they help each other fine-tune their college applications at the Brooklyn Library, or else head to Prospect Park and leaf through their pamphlets, poring over pictures of multicultural coeds smiling in their gowns and mortarboards. By the time they walk to the subway station at Franklin Avenue, the sky is often dark. They ride the express train together as far as they can, and then they head their separate ways.

The East River is sixteen miles long and flows between Brooklyn and Manhattan, past and present. Crossed by numerous bridges, tunnels, and ferries, the river, which is actually a tidal strait, connects the lives of millions of New Yorkers. "It avails not, neither time or place—distance avails not; / I am with you, you men and women of a generation, or every so many generations hence," Walt Whitman wrote in his celebrated poem "Crossing Brooklyn Ferry." "Just as you feel when you look on the river and sky, so I felt; / Just as any of you is one of a living crowd, I was one of a crowd."

More than a century later, Jessica is one of the crowd on the D train, sitting on plastic orange seats with beige trim and heading toward Manhattan. Through her smudged subway window, she gazes at the brackish waters dotted with ships and streaked with oil, iridescent as the feathers of a pigeon's collar. This view has become as familiar as the MTA subway map that hangs on her bedroom wall—the river a meandering belt of robin's egg blue, crisscrossed by green, yellow, brown, red, purple, and gray lines, like electrical wires fusing together time, space, and memory. Every day is the same. She and Harold ride the 4,5 to Atlantic, where he heads to Bed-Stuy and she transfers to the B or D. The total trip is about a half hour, the actual distance traveled only a few miles, but it might as well be thousands.

The next time Jessica is aboveground, it is a different world—faster, louder, and filled with ancient faces. After almost a year of living in Chinatown, she knows it well. Wearing her heavy black-and-blue backpack, Jessica weaves through the honking cars and disgruntled pedestrians at the intersection of Grand Street and Bowery, passing an old woman selling hair dye on the corner and an old man peddling mini pancakes in wax-paper bags. Deliverymen wheel their carts filled with sacks of rice and flour through clots of shoppers haggling for fish, herbal balms, furniture, and electronics.

Jessica is used to the human traffic jam. Rather than compete, she lets the aggressive old ladies shoulder past her, like life-sized windup toys. No one seems to notice Jessica, but she notices everything. She sees the way the vendors hide damaged fruit by putting the bruised sides down. She recognizes the bony man who squats on the sidewalk, repairing old shoes, his sun-blotched skin stretched tautly over his cheekbones like the hide of a tambourine. Day after day he grinds his hacksaw against broken soles, salvaging what he can from a pile of discarded pumps, sandals, and scraps of rubber. China might be thousands of miles away, but to Jessica it lives right here in this man: Nothing is wasted. Everything is valued.

Almost everything.

A year after arriving in the United States, Jessica is attuned to the little girls in her neighborhood. Her Chinatown is full of daughters who have been cast aside. "You can see the mother always holding the young son, and the girl walks by the side," she says. "You can feel that. I don't know why. Maybe we were born with it. You have this kind of concept for the rest of your life."

Jessica rounds the corner of Elizabeth Street. She walks past tables toppling over with cranium-sized cabbages, bags of garlic and dried mushrooms, stacks of salted fish, and spiky yellow-green durian fruits, stinking of rot. A few feet away a Malaysian jerky joint sells strips of dried meat behind a sweaty windowpane. Jessica lives in the five-story brick tenement building next door. The lock is jammed again. She presses her weight against the green metal door and jiggles the key until it opens. Her eyes adjust to the dark corridor, maroon and white, and smelling of smoked beef. Stepping over a shoe rack filled with someone else's sneakers, she lets herself into the first apartment on the left and goes to her room.

"I think every immigrant who comes here has a big story, especially people from China," Jessica once said. In some ways, her family's story ins't so unusual. It is the story of an ambitious father who left for a better life in America and a mother who hung all of her hopes on her only daughter to succeed, despite the odds against her. In 1979, the Chinese government implemented the one-child policy, forbidding urban couples from having more than one child. The law was intended to solve overpopulation, but it has led to other problems. In many cases, when a girl was born instead of a boy, it strained families who put great value on a male successor continuing the family line. In the worst cases, female fetuses were aborted and baby girls killed off, while little boys were pampered into early obesity, part of a phenomenon known as Little Emperor Syndrome. By the mid-1980s, China's cities and suburbs were dotted with propaganda posters featuring smiling older couples, hoisting cherubic babies in the air like trophies, and clear commands: CARRY OUT FAMILY PLANNING. IMPLEMENT THE BASIC NATIONAL POLICY. IT IS BETTER TO HAVE ONE CHILD ONLY.

In the shadow of these posters, Jessica was born on May 11, 1990, in Xiangtan, a small city in the southern province of Hunan that is the hometown of Chairman Mao. For almost as long as she could remember, Jessica had known two things. Number one: Her comfortable life in China was not permanent. Someday the Tans would move to America, if everything went according to the family's plan. Number two: There was no question in Jessica's mind that her father wished she had been born a boy. Why else would he be so strict with her, so hard? Sometimes he slapped her for no good reason—for not washing her hands before dinner, for asking too many questions, for not getting 100 on math. He punished her, Jessica was sure of it, for being a girl.

John Tan, Jessica's father, left for America on a foreign student visa when she was ten years old. The plan was that he would go to college and find work and a place to live before sending for Jessica and her mother. The first part went accordingly. Soon after arriving in the United States, Mr. Tan got a job as a waiter at a Japanese restaurant in New Jersey. He worked there for about six months, putting the money toward his tuition at the University of Bridgeport in Connecticut, where he enrolled in classes to earn a master's degree in computer science. Then September 11 happened.

Before the family's plan crumbled altogether, it cracked in unforeseen places. Mr. Tan had anticipated that it would take time before he and his family could be reunited in the States: three, four, five years, maybe more. But none of them could have anticipated how the terrible events of a single day—a day that didn't even seem to affect them directly—would change their lives. In China, Jessica and her mother had watched images of the planes crashing into the World Trade Center, the skies of New York City filling with smoke and ash. When the towers fell, so did their hopes of getting visas. Jessica's mother traveled twice to Beijing, entreating immigration officials to let her join her husband in America—and, twice she was denied.

Jessica has heard parts of her father's story over time, but it is so convoluted that even Mr. Tan seems to reel when recalling all the dashed hopes and disappointments that mounted up during his first years in America. The master's degree that he had earned in computer science turned out to be worthless because he couldn't find a job in his field, which was suffering along with the rest of the economy. He eventually took a position at a paralegal's office, thinking that his new employer would sponsor him for a work visa, and was devastated to find out that he wouldn't be eligible for such a permit because his new job didn't match his degree. (Federal labor law dictates that in order to sponsor a foreigner for permanent residence, the employer must prove the unavailability of U.S. workers qualified to fill that job.) As Mr. Tan saw it, he had two options: he could return to China—or stay in America and go back to school for another degree. There was a third option, of course. A former classmate told Mr. Tan that there was "a nice way" to get a green card—all he had to do was marry a U.S. citizen.

What transpired next is unclear. Jessica doesn't know the details of her parents' divorce—if, in fact, they did legally divorce. Mr. Tan insists that they did and also says that he would have gone back to China to try to make the marriage work if Jessica's mother had been willing. According to Mr. Tan, she wasn't. "She met somebody else, that's why," he says. "It's like a dream. My dream broke."

Later, it would seem to Jessica that her father had given up too easily. But through it all, Mrs. Tan's resolve never wavered. Someday Jessica would go to college in America, and someday she would become a U.S. citizen, enabling her to sponsor her mother as well. In the meantime, Mrs. Tan didn't want anything to distract Jessica from her studies, especially not boys. She made Jessica chop off her hair below her ears, as if under a rice bowl. She bought her lots of turtlenecks. She told Jessica that she was her only hope and sent her to boarding school in the countryside. Separated from her mother, Jessica plunged into her textbooks. From the time the sun rose to when it set, she memorized and recited lessons in Chinese, math, English, physics, chemistry, politics, geography, and biology, with a little time left over for music and gym.

Life went on. Eventually Mrs. Tan remarried, and five years after he had arrived in America with a very different vision for his family, so did Mr. Tan. His former classmate helped introduce him to a thirty-six-year-old garment worker who was on her way to becoming an American citizen, and he decided to get a green card "the nice way," just as his friend had advised. The same year they wed, Mr. Tan's new wife became a citizen and filed his paperwork. He got a job as a wholesale furniture dealer, and before long, his second wife gave him what his first wife could not: a son. Jessica was fourteen years old and still living in China when she heard the news that her first half brother had been born in America. That baby boy seemed to eclipse her in her father's heart and, two years later, Mr. Tan celebrated the birth of his second son.

Jessica doesn't blame her father for starting a new life without her. In fact, she wouldn't be here if not for Mr. Tan's second wife. Jessica's stepmother is the one who applied for her to come to the United States.

"That's the reason why he married her," Jessica says. "He stayed here for me to come. Our intention was for my father to come to this country and let the whole family come—me and my mom. But gradually he fell in love with his new family. In a Chinese family, if your wife born two sons for you, usually your husband will treat you differently. I just feel like my father so cares about his new family because of those two sons."

In 2007, Jessica got the news that she had been approved for a visa. Days later she was on a fourteen-hour flight to New York City. She was seventeen. She carried $6,000 in cash, two plastic sacks stuffed with clothes, an electronic Mandarin-English dictionary, and a digital camera filled with pictures of her mother. Jessica had no idea when she would see her mother next. But even though it had been seven years since she had seen her father, she knew he would be at the airport, waiting for her.

Tonight Jessica waits for her father. In the hours before his visit, she passes the time doing homework and playing computer games in her room, which she rents from a Malaysian hairdresser who also lives in the apartment with her seven-year-old son. Wedged between the kitchen and the entrance, Jessica's room is the first door to the left. It is only the size of a closet, but it is stocked like a fallout shelter. Her shelves are lined with Costco-sized provisions of Kleenex and Charmin toilet paper. A few paces away is a small desk and a computer loaded with action games like Torchlight and The Legend of Zelda. A week's supply of bottled water, bananas, Brisk lemon iced tea, and Doritos lies within arm's reach of her bed. Space is limited, but well used. When Jessica lies down and looks up at the ceiling, she sees her hanging wardrobe: a medley of pink things, fuzzy things, and heart-covered things that once made shadow monsters during a bad thunderstorm, scaring her awake in the middle of the night. Directly behind her pillow, a small wooden bookshelf is stacked with SAT and Regents guides for studying, and library copies of *Gossip Girl* and *Twilight* for fun. It could be worse. In one room, Jessica has everything she needs. And nothing. It is a shelter, not a home.

Home is a journal prompt that Ms. Ann gave in English class: "List adjectives that come to mind when you think of home." *Warm, happiness, satisfied, caring.* "List adjectives that describe "away from home." *Independent, lonely, disappointed, scared.* Home is thousands of miles away. Home is a tiny, crumpled black-and-white photo of her mother as a young woman with soft curls and painted bow lips that Jessica keeps in her wallet. Home is something that other kids have. For Jessica, home is something that once was, and was supposed to be.

For Jessica's father and his new family, home is a brick, prewar co-op with a doorman, mirrored walls, and a copper elevator. After Mr. Tan picked her up from the airport, Jessica moved into their two-bedroom apartment on the third floor. She spent her first night in America sleeping on a bed in the living room, which was separated by a partition from her half brothers' playroom, cluttered with toys and teddy bears. In fact, the whole apartment seemed to be a playroom for those two little boys, as well as a preschool, and a shrine. A foam-rubber mat of primary-color squares carpeted every inch of nearly every room, giving the place the feel of an inflatable bounce house. Crayon scribbles, stickers, and alphabet posters covered the walls. Jessica took in the Teletubbies, the Winnie the Pooh slippers, the high chairs, and baby bottles, the little-boy underwear hanging from the ceiling in the bathroom. She saw the framed studio portraits and snapshots of a happy family, complete without her. In one photo, Mr. Tan sat in an overstuffed armchair, holding his baby son in his lap, a tentative smile on his lips. His new wife towered several inches above him, her arm around his shoulder, her placid expression impossible to read.

In the college essay that Jessica later wrote about that first day, her father wasn't the villain. The villain was her stepmother. Moments after Jessica walked in the door, her stepmother went ballistic, screaming at her to get out. Then she redirected her rage at Mr. Tan. It was her stepmother who shouted at Jessica to get out of the living room when she tried taking a nap after the exhausting fourteen-hour flight from China, and her stepmother who blasted the television all day and all night so that Jessica couldn't sleep. It was her stepmother who disappeared days after Jessica's arrival, leaving Mr. Tan alone with his infant and toddler sons so he would understand just how much he needed a wife to take care of them. It was her stepmother who ultimately forced Mr. Tan to choose which he valued more: his wife and their two sons and the life they had built for themselves in America; or his daughter, and the life he had left behind.

Mr. Tan chose his wife and sons, and before the end of her first week in the United States, Jessica found herself suddenly adrift: a privileged girl dispossessed, jet-lagged, and halfway around the world from home. It all seemed so abrupt to Jessica, but, in fact, the idea of her coming to live in New York had been eating away at her stepmother for some time.

Before Jessica arrived, Mr. Tan and his wife had an argument. At the last minute she had said that she didn't want Jessica to come to the United States, let alone into their home. To this day, Mr. Tan doesn't know why his wife suddenly changed her mind; after all, she was the one who had applied for Jessica to come. At a certain point, though, Mr. Tan stopped wondering why his wife acted as she did and just came to accept it. "I never ask her, and she don't answer me this question," Mr. Tan says. "Before, I just think, 'Why? Why? Why?' Because time has passed, forget about it. I don't want to know the answers. I just want Jessica to live here, study good for her own future."

As Jessica sees it, her father failed her. But Mr. Tan feels that he did what he could to honor what little remained of their plan—without breaking up his new family. After his wife rejected Jessica, he brought her to one of the DOE's enrollment offices in Brooklyn, where a counselor referred them to the International High School at Prospect Heights. There, Jessica registered for the eleventh grade, despite the fact that the junior class was overcrowded, and she spoke a considerable amount of English. (Jessica had received years of language instruction at her boarding school in China.) During their meeting with the principal, Mr. Tan pleaded with her to let Jessica into the school, and believing that she only spoke Chinese, Alexandra found a way to squeeze her in. "I had no sense that she spoke any English," Alexandra later said, recalling how Jessica had barely said a word during their interview.

In the days that followed, Mr. Tan arranged for Jessica to move in with his wife's uncle and aunt, who lived in a home for low-income Chinese senior citizens and felt ashamed about the way that Jessica had been treated by one of their own relatives. Jessica spent one month sleeping in a small, cluttered apartment in the home known as Hong Ning Housing for the Elderly, a massive redbrick building on a quiet stretch of Norfolk Street on the Lower East Side.

Over time, Jessica came to recognize the wrinkled faces of the residents. Some tended to a little community garden in the back, where prized winter melons grew to be the size of healthy baby boys. Other people played mah-jongg in a common reading room that smelled of newsprint, ointment, and tea.

A few of the elderly residents came to recognize Jessica, too. At seventeen, she was the home's youngest tenant.

Jessica's ears perk at the clink of a key in the door. She pauses her computer game and waits for the familiar sounds. Sneakers coming off. Slippers sliding on. The rustle of a nylon jacket. Her father's voice. "Yuan Yuan," he says, calling her by the nickname he used when she was a little girl. "I'm here."

After living with Granduncle for a month, Jessica eventually moved a few blocks away. Mr. Tan began cooking for her in the cramped apartment on Elizabeth Street that she now shares with her Malaysian landlord and her son. Jessica never knows what days her father will come. He tries to make it three or four times a week, as soon as he can get away from work and before he will be missed at home. He usually arrives around four o'clock, carrying plastic bags full of groceries: tiny hot peppers in Christmas colors, Chinese celery, chicken, scallions, and whatever white fish is the freshest catch of the day. The kitchen is small and cluttered with other people's lives, and he dislikes being in the way. On the rare occasion that the apartment is empty, he cooks alone. Most days, when Jessica comes home from school, her father is already gone. But dinner is waiting for her, still warm.

Since he started cooking for Jessica last year, Mr. Tan has gotten into a routine. As soon as he walks in, he takes off his white New Balance sneakers and slides on the black leather sandals he keeps by the door. He throws his jacket on Jessica's bed. He spreads a pink towel on the linoleum floor under the stove. Then he puts on the rice. They can talk or not talk for as long as it takes for the meal to be prepared, but Jessica and her father never eat together.

Cooking is a meditation, a period of grace. For at least one hour, Mr. Tan is a man in control. His wife knows that he comes here, but she pretends that she doesn't. So, he leaves his cooking supplies in Jessica's cupboard the same way a lover might leave behind a toothbrush or a comb. He buys her the finest ingredients from the best stores in Chinatown, and over time he has taught her how to recognize the good vendors for herself. When he worked as a waiter at a restaurant in Times Square, Mr. Tan ate whatever they served to the staff, happy just to be getting a free meal. But he believes that Jessica needs to nourish her mind and her body with home-cooked meals; the sticky-sweet Cantonese takeout in her neighborhood won't do.

"Hunan people like spicy food," Mr. Tan says, whisking an egg with soy sauce and spicy green peppers. "Later, when she go to college, what she going to do? She don't like pizza or bagels."

Nobody taught Mr. Tan how to cook. He learned by watching. With a steady hand on his chef's cleaver, he minces garlic and ginger and slashes the celery. It's very important to control the flame—heat is everything. Chop, drop, hiss.

"She need good food for her body. I was a student also, I know," Mr. Tan says. "In my mind, I have to take care of her. I am her daddy. I so regret."

His eyes turn glassy. "Since I cannot live with her, I have to do something for her. I wish I can do more for her and make her happy. But this is what I can do. I can cook for her. The rest depend on her: to study, to make her future. I have no time. I have two other kids."

When the food is ready, he divides it onto several dishes. Every bite is a memory, a bittersweet reminder of home. Every plate is a penance, asking her forgiveness.

Before he leaves, Mr. Tan washes the pots and pans, while Jessica clears the Chinese newspapers and Transformer toys off the table. As he removes his slippers, she sits down to a Hunan-style feast of seared flounder, spicy chicken, and celery that will be her dinner for the next few nights.

"Taste it," Mr. Tan says, handing her a pair of plastic chopsticks.

Staring at her plate, Jessica tweezes a bite of fish and chews. "*Hao chi,* Pa," she says, "Delicious." Then she watches her father put on his sneakers and tie up the trash, before heading home to eat dinner with his new family.

Capturing Yasmeen

"Tilt your head this way," the photographer says.

Wearing a green-and-gold head scarf under a black smock and resting her arm on a faux Grecian column, Yasmeen Salahi lifts her chin ever so slightly to the right and grimaces. It's senior picture day, and she stands stiffly before a painted backdrop of a Mediterranean vista, complete with creeping rose vines and a window overlooking the sea at sunset. Even with her long, oval face semiveiled and her hair merely a suggestion beneath her shawl, anyone can see that she is beautiful. She has dark molten eyes, an almond complexion, thick black brows, a straight sculpted nose, and a naturally downturned mouth that can make her look like the happiest person in the world, or the saddest, depending on whether or not she is smiling.

"You can smile a little bit, you know," urges the photographer, a middle-aged guy with an endless supply of corny lines. "Pretend you're in Fiji or Malibu, or something. Pretend you're not in Brooklyn."

"Like I'm not at school?" Yasmeen asks. Invisible threads tug at the corners of her eyes and lips.

"There you go," he says. "One, two, three—GOTCHA!"

He pops the flash, and she blinks, temporarily blinded by the blaze, forever captured just as she is: nineteen years old with a faint smile on her lips and her back toward paradise.

When Yasmeen woke up this morning to go to school, she wasn't planning to get her picture taken. On one of her first days back since her mother died, she wasn't planning much more than making it through first period. That was before she saw the long line winding outside the cafeteria during lunch. She barely had a chance to peek her head in when Freeman shouted her name and a bunch of kids came running to hug her, attracting the attention of the photographer's assistant. A few seconds later the woman was pinning a black velvet smock around her head scarf. "Don't worry, we won't show your shoulders," the attendant said, as if reading Yasmeen's mind. "We do it all the time."

For the past few hours, students have been lining up to pose for their yearbook portraits. No one seems to care that the makeshift photo studio is actually a small storage room smelling of mildew and the occasional whiff of grease and overcooked vegetables from lunch. At least for one day, the space has been transformed into a glamorous atelier, with three different photographers at stations featuring three different backdrops: the Mediterranean vista, a marbled gray backdrop, and a third painted scrim showing shelves of leather-bound books. Like the sets and the formalwear options (tuxedo smocks attached with Velcro for the boys, and a black velvet smock and feather boas for the girls), the photographers' cheesy lines seem to have been dusted off from 1989—the combined effect being simultaneously archaic and timeless in the way that only a high school yearbook portrait can be.

"I'm gonna give you a rose," the photographer at the first station says, tossing a single stem at a giggling Dinice Liu, who raises it awkwardly in the air. "Don't hold it like a torch! You're not the Statue of Liberty!"

"Chin up, and say the word, 'YES!'" the photographer instructs a curly-haired Dominican girl as her boyfriend watches from the hall. "And . . . next potential graduate!"

"I feel like a king!" Freeman shouts, twirling around in a tattered tuxedo smock before taking his seat in front of the camera. He smacks his lips at a girl who walks by wearing turquoise eye shadow and knee-high black boots. *"Ai-ai-ai, caliente!"*

Today the blue-speckled linoleum floor outside the lunchroom might as well be the red carpet. In preparation for senior pictures, cheeks have been rouged, lips glossed, and hair sealed into place. "You want to see your hair? It doesn't move!" a photographer tells Ngawang's brother Lobsang, who brings to mind a Tibetan Spicoli with his beatific expression and styled surfer hair. A few feet away is a Chinese boy with serrated spikes sprouting at every angle from his scalp like an air plant on a host tree.

Despite all the primping, kids are still stressing out. A Bangladeshi girl named Mukta Mukta is a jittery mess over an argument she had with her boyfriend, Islam Fakrol, about how much skin she should expose under the requisite black velvet drape.

"He doesn't want me to show my shoulders!" she huffs at Yasmeen, before rushing off to the girls' bathroom and taking off her blouse anyway.

Dinice was late to first period because she was curling her hair. By the time she was satisfied with her wispy tendrils, she had another catastrophe on her hands—her nails. "They're round!" she whines, stamping her kitten heels while waiting her turn in line for the next shot. "I wanted them to be square!"

Behind her, Hasanatu still isn't happy with her yearbook smile, even after days of practicing. "I look fat!" she says, puffing her cheeks. "I'm not good at taking pictures."

"Say 'cheese,'" Yasmeen prompts her, just as Jessica Tan walks through the door.

"Chizz," Hasanatu says and peers into her compact mirror one last time.

In the past, students have had more than a little help when selecting a quote to appear next to their senior portraits. Last year the supervisor of the yearbook club surfed websites like BrainyQuote.com to provide some options. The resulting master list, which he photocopied and handed out to students, contained about fifty pearls of wisdom spun by everyone from Eleanor Roosevelt to Anne Frank, Confucius to Kanye West—and many more names that the students had never heard before. That helps explain the dearth of quotes by e.e. cummings and the motivational speaker John Mason ("You were born an original. Don't die a copy"), not to mention the occasional odd match, like the über-Christian Haitian boy who chose the words of the famous cross-dresser Harvey Fierstein ("Never be bullied into silence") or the Tibetan girl, a former yak herder, who will be forever remembered next to some deep thoughts from Les Brown. Her boyfriend, a Mexican wannabe rocker, opted for the words of John Lennon, which he coyly passed off as his own: "I still think that all you need is love."

No matter what happens, when the yearbooks come out in June, Yasmeen Salahi will be pictured alongside her classmates, sandwiched between a blacked-out box that says "Camera Shy" and a photo of a pale-skinned, chisel-jawed Eastern European boy who summed up his life's philosophy in three words next to his name: "Death before dishonor." But whether she will walk alongside her classmates at graduation is another story. Since school started, Yasmeen has strung up weeks of absences, alternately spending her time in mourning and taking care of two younger siblings. When she does make it to class, she is on autopilot, sleepwalking through her classes with a fistful of tissues and a weary smile. "She's not reflecting—she's reacting," Ann says. "It's hard to gauge if she even knows what's going on."

Ann isn't the only one who is worried about Yasmeen; all of the twelfth-grade teachers recognize the patterns. Every year kids drop out for different reasons. Some move back to their home countries. Some get pregnant. Some are pulled out of school by their parents to work. Some just give up. The school tries to preempt the problem, and more often than not their efforts work. According to data analyzed by the Internationals Network for Public Schools, International high schools have remarkably high graduation rates compared to other New York City public schools, and their English-language learner populations, in particular. At the International schools that were looked at, the four-year graduation rate was 73 percent, approximately double the graduation rate of

English-language learners at other New York City public schools. The graduation rate climbs steadily the longer some International students stay in school. (For those whose educations were either interrupted or never began in their native countries, it may take up to seven years to matriculate.)

At the International High School at Prospect Heights, the high graduation rate is thanks in large part to a built-in support system of dedicated teachers, advisors, social workers, and administrators. Still, sometimes there's no way to prevent kids from simply disappearing. They become an empty chair in the back of the classroom. A name on a manila folder left in a filing cabinet at the end of the year. A smiling face in the senior yearbook. By December, Yasmeen is in danger of becoming one of those kids.

"Relax! We're not pulling teeth today!" a photographer tells Jessica Tan. Wearing blue eye shadow, a pink feather boa, and a mortified expression, she slumps under the weight of her black velvet drape as if it were a lead X-ray smock, exposing every last cell in her body under the bright glare of the camera lights.

"Let your hair down," Yasmeen coaches her from the sidelines.

"Down?" Jessica asks, touching the back of her ponytail. "Will you help me?"

Weaving her way back to the front of the line, Yasmeen slips off Jessica's fluorescent-green elastic and runs her long nimble fingers through her hair, arranging the layered pieces in a pretty fringe around her face.

"It's so long," Yasmeen says, stepping back to admire her work. "Oh my goodness, you look beautiful!"

The two girls have been best friends ever since they met in the eleventh grade. A new student at the time, Jessica instantly was taken with the Muslim girl in the brown coat who sat down in front of her in English class and introduced herself as Yasmeen. Over time, Jessica noticed how Yasmeen was always the first to raise her hand to answer questions and everyone listened when she spoke. It was obvious that she was religious, but in some ways she was also more Americanized than her classmates. Not only was she a U.S. citizen—her English was stronger than most. She barely even had an accent.

She also was drop-dead gorgeous, Jessica thought. Most days Yasmeen wore a traditional black Islamic dress under a light coat or jacket. She covered her head with various silk and polyester head scarves, which puckered slightly above her eyebrow and were pinned just below her chin, creating an oval-shaped window for her face. In class, Jessica found herself staring at Yasmeen and wondering about her hair. How long was it? Was it curly or straight? Black or brown?

They started keeping a journal together. It was Jessica's idea. One day, a few weeks after she moved into her single room in Chinatown, she passed Yasmeen a spiral notebook with the first entry written inside. "In China, we called this 'exchange diary,'" Jessica wrote. "Basically, it's between friends, write down whatever they want expecially some troubles, sadness, conflicts. I believe this was a good way to express and improve writing skills. I hope you can join me with this 'Yemen-China-America' diary."

Jessica told her about the SAT classes she had started taking on the weekends at a Chinese-run prep school and warned Yasmeen against wasting her money on such courses, which she deemed overpriced and ineffective: "In the future, I'll try to avoid Chinese businessmen," she wrote. "They like to use bombast to tempt you." In the same entry, she unloaded about her father, about how he cooks for her but never stays to eat with her, as if he couldn't stand to spend even a minute in her company. "He has a new family with 2 healthy, cute boys," she wrote. "Remember last time I told you about the Chinese tradition about having boys was better than having girls. But anyway, I was his daughter. How could he treat me so indifferently?"

It took traveling across time zones for Jessica to realize just how much she missed her mother. They spoke almost every day on the phone—her mother always sounding strong, never complaining. But no phone call could bridge the distance between them, and no amount of assurances could conceal her mother's sadness at being separated from her daughter. "I envy you," Jessica wrote to Yasmeen, back when her parents were both still alive, "because you have a big and complete family."

Yasmeen responded immediately to Jessica with an ebullient five-page entry decorated in colored marker. She wrote their names perpendicularly under a cloud that said, "Friendship forever." In the lower corner of the page, next to a cartoon iPod, she scrawled the word, "College!" Maybe if Jessica had spent more time with both parents, Yasmeen pointed out, she would be happy to live alone. Yasmeen rarely spent time alone. She had five siblings, including two little ones who she looked after like a mother. Her mom was a traditional woman who had not gone to school and had mixed feelings about her middle daughter pursuing a college degree when she should be pursuing a husband instead. By the time she was seventeen, Yasmeen had received four marriage proposals, mostly from cousins back in Yemen who wanted a wife in the United States.

As for her dad, he was here and not here at the same time. He was ill. He had been living in the United States for almost forty years, working at a grocery store and eventually earning citizenship, which Yasmeen and her younger siblings inherited when they got to New York. Life in America was strict, but it was better than life in her village in Yemen, where she had been pulled out of school around the third grade. Compared to some other girls from her country, her parents gave her relative freedom. College was at least a possibility.

"I like your personality—optimistic. Keep it," Jessica responded to Yasmeen, a few days later. "And also, I really hope one day your mother will change her mind." In other news, Jessica wrote, "Today, I was 18 in China < China was 12 hour earlier than US >." Her father wouldn't be able to celebrate with her because in America her birthday fell on Mother's Day, and he would be with his new family. To make up for his absence, Mr. Tan visited Jessica the day before her birthday instead. He bought her two pairs of shoes, and they went to a restaurant, where they talked about *liang pi*, a Chinese noodle dish that they both missed. Back home, there was an older couple who used to stretch the rice dough by hand—thin, flat, gelatinous skeins that they served with a spicy broth. It only cost one dollar, and Jessica used to eat it every day for breakfast. "I miss that flavor. Did you miss the food in your country? Tell me!" Jessica wrote. "I can't believe I've been here for half year, time is going really fast."

In that time, Jessica had begun to relish her independence. Yasmeen didn't wander far from home without getting permission from her older brothers, but Jessica was free to roam wherever she wanted, whenever she wanted. She fell in love with movies, especially action films like *Batman*. Whenever she needed to remind herself of her own strength, she only had to recall the last line of *Iron Man*, which sent chills down her spine: "The truth is, I am Iron Man." Jessica recognized herself in those words and repeated them often. On the outside, she appeared to be an ordinary girl, but inside she was stronger than anyone knew.

When she wasn't watching movies, she began to meet Yasmeen and her little brother and sister to play soccer in Prospect Park. Away from her father, Jessica changed her last name to Snow, in honor of her boarding-school nickname, Little Snow, and in defiance of her father's new family, who were also named Tan. Away from her mother, she traded in the starchy school uniform that she used to wear for blue jeans and colorful cardigans and accessories; the more stripes, hearts, and smiley faces, the better. She also grew her hair long. By spring, it touched her shoulders, but it was still nowhere near as long as Yasmeen's. Jessica could tell by the lump in the back of her shawl. They were in the girls' locker room during gym one day when Yasmeen surprised her by taking off her *hijab*. Usually, she wore her hair tied up under her scarf, but she had taken it down, and the dark-brown waves fell almost to her hips. Jessica was speechless, and full of envy. Her best friend was even prettier than she had imagined.

"Do you ever stare at yourself in the mirror?" Jessica asked her, almost a year later.

"Why?" Yasmeen replied.

"Because," Jessica said, "you're beautiful."

"I do, but for a different reason," Yasmeen told her.

Six years since she left Yemen, Yasmeen explained, her life seemed unrecognizable. When she unpinned her scarf at night and looked at her reflection in the mirror, *she* was unrecognizable. Sometimes she thought about the little girl she had left behind, a girl who played in the shade of fig trees and dreamed of going to school. The girl from the village was gone.

In her place, Yasmeen sees a stranger with long, dark hair and deep mauve circles etched under her eyes. That young woman is a U.S. citizen; an English-speaking daughter who translated for her parents at the hospital when they could not speak for themselves. She is an A student who helps her little brother and sister with their homework and met with their teachers when their mother was too ill. She is a contradiction: an American girl who loves Big Macs but won't wear blue jeans; a believer who questions whether she has been punished too much, or not enough; a devout Muslim who will never take off her scarf in public, no matter how many times people ask her "Aren't you hot?" or call her a terrorist. When Yasmeen looks in the mirror, she sees a woman of marrying age who is not ready to marry. She is different from her Yemeni girlfriends, many of them unhappy young mothers who tell her, "Go to college! You see my life? I have no life!" And yet, at nineteen Yasmeen will do anything to keep her younger siblings together—even if that means getting married or dropping out of high school and moving back to Yemen. By the middle of her senior year, she doesn't seem to have many other options.

"I look at myself in the mirror to see, am I the person I used to be? I can speak English. I am in America, in high school," Yasmeen told Jessica that day. "Is that real? Am I living in reality or not? Who am I?"

"Okay, put your fingers here—*mira*." At the third and final station, the cameraman wraps Yasmeen's hand around a fake diploma fashioned out of what appears to be a PVC pipe tied with yellow ribbon. Behind her, a backdrop of painted books completes the image of a graduate who's going places. Wearing a white mortarboard over her head scarf and a wan smile on her lips, she stares ahead.

"Where are you from?" asks the photographer, a silver-haired man with inquisitive eyes.

"Yemen," she says.

He steps out from behind the camera to position a synthetic red rose in her hand. "You look like a princess," he says. "Do you want to be a princess?"

"No," Yasmeen says, a deep crimson creeping into her cheeks. "I want to be a doctor."

"What kind of doctor?" he asks.

"Kidney."

He pauses for a moment, his hand still on hers. "Somebody in your family have a problem?" he asks.

"Yeah."

With a deft touch, the photographer adjusts her cap over her shawl one last time, and rearranges her fingers in four straight lines across the prop diploma.

"Congratulations," he says softly. "You made it."

Part II

BETWEEN WORLDS

The Life and Times
of Mohamed Bah

> A diamond is a clear stone which look and feel greasy
> when you hold it. It is very hard to find but the only
> way you can find it is to go deep in the ground, which
> is risky sometimes.
>
> —"MINING DIAMONDS WITH MY FATHER"
> BY MOHAMED BAH

Every year, the principal encounters a handful of students that she cat-
egorizes as "the kids who will not *not* be known." Mohamed Bah is one
of those kids. Now a sophomore, he is a member of almost every school
club, from drama to science to the Gay-Straight Alliance. While most
teachers know Mohamed or at least know of him, few people understand him better than Mike Incze, his advisor and debate club coach.
Mike quickly learned three things: One, Mohamed's dream is to become
a doctor and someday return to Sierra Leone to help the people there.
Two, he is deeply committed to school and devoutly religious, and, unlike some of the other Muslim boys, he does not seem to have time for
girls. Not for lack of interest, for when the subject of girls does come up,
Mohamed turns from highly articulate to somewhat helpless, reduced
to claps and nervous giggles. Three, Red Bull and Bah don't mix. At one

of their first debate tournaments of the year, held at Rutgers University in New Jersey, Mohamed went berserk after drinking a single can. Later, Mike found him cracked out on the energy drink, lying Christlike on a conference-room table and staring at the ceiling while chatting up a couple of girls from another school. "You know, I'm going to be the president of Sierra Leone," he told one of the girls in a lusty Krio lilt. "You wanna be my first lady?"

A bit of a science geek with shaggy brown hair and a wide-open face, Mike isn't easily won over by what most people call charisma, but from the moment Mohamed walked into his classroom, he was impossible to ignore. For one, Mohamed's name was nowhere to be found on the roster. On paper, he wasn't merely absent; it was more like he didn't exist.

In person, he couldn't have been more present. Mohamed approached school as if his entire life had been just a prelude to the moment when he arrived in the halls of International High ready to conquer the world. Everything about the kid is intense. He has a serious face with small, flaring nostrils, skin the color of coffee beans, short loamy hair, a deep widow's peak, and a stare so penetrating it could bore holes into the earth. His voice is as gravelly as the diamond pits where he came from and so loud that it fills a room whenever he speaks. Which he does, a lot. In class, Mohamed often seems to be on the verge of an a-ha moment that threatens to explode in his face. Sometimes he talks so fast that he has to gasp for air, his breath whistling between words like a bottle rocket. As he has gotten older and more comfortable with standardized English, he has begun outlining his sentences with numbered points. In addition to helping him keep track of his thoughts, which seem to race around inside his brain like cars at a demolition derby, the habit lends him a certain erudite aspect that sets him apart from his peers.

Mike once described Mohamed as a "little statesman." Within months of his arrival, he ran for president of the African Club against two sophomore boys. Mohamed came prepared. He wore his nicest pair of True Religion jeans and carried eight index cards covered with a speech scrawled in pencil. After listening to his competition, he took his place at the front of the room and addressed the crowd, a mix of teachers and students, whom he would refer to throughout his speech as ladies and gentlemen, brothers and sisters.

"Well, my fellow students, as you all know, a country without a leader is a country without constitution," Mohamed boomed as his audience munched on the potato chips and sipped the orange juice that he had bought for the occasion. Surely they must be as worried as he was about the problems afflicting West Africa. In between glances at his cue cards, he rattled off a list: poverty, disease, starvation, illiteracy, joblessness, and the issue of child soldiers. Eyebrows raised. The other candidates mainly talked about helping their classmates with homework, maybe organizing a candy sale. They ended their bids with a halfhearted "Vote for me."

Mohamed, it seemed, wanted to do more than run African Club; he wanted to run Africa, and he needed their help. True, he said, they were just kids themselves. But they still could find ways to contribute: raising money for charities to build new hospitals and schools, for instance. They just had to band together. In his short time at International, he had seen enough to know that the only solution to their problems would be solidarity. "My own party will be AACP: All African Club Party," he said to scattered applause. They would work together, but in the end they needed to respect his rules and his word as final.

"Vote for me, once again, and there will be solutions to all your problems, complaints, and worries," he concluded. "This is the honorable Mohamed Bah speaking to you all."

Mohamed won by several votes and accomplished at least some of what he promised as president. He couldn't end genocide or hunger, but he helped his constituents with their science homework, and together they raised money for a school in Mali. Eventually he had to give up his position as president of African Club. He had too many other commitments, and other kids wanted a shot. But when it comes to his own country's presence at International, Mohamed is Sierra Leone's unofficial ambassador, a one-man board of tourism. When he speaks of home, he rarely mentions the civil war that devastated and displaced millions of people, including his own family. Instead, he talks about diamonds. "Hello, my name is Mohamed Bah—I'm from Sierra Leone," he once greeted a visitor to the school, all the while smiling brightly. "We are known for our riches!"

Cindy Chatman, the art teacher, was one of the first people at school to hear Mohamed's story about the day he went to work in the diamond mines with his father—a story that came out after he learned that his father had died in Sierra Leone. Mohamed got the devastating news in October, and the morning after receiving his brother's phone call, he had to be escorted to a social worker's office when he started crying in class. Various teachers came to Mohamed's assistance over the next few weeks, but Cindy was the one who later helped him write his essay, "Mining Diamonds with My Father."

At first she agreed to help out of sheer boredom. In addition to having Mohamed in her art class that spring, Cindy also saw him during a period known as Sustained Silent Reading, which was held in Mike's room when he wasn't teaching. Most days the quiet was so mind-numbing that she would have jumped at the chance to tie a kid's shoe, so when Mohamed told her he was working on a memoir, Cindy offered to be his typist.

That day, surrounded by posters of human body systems on the walls and linoleum block prints of cells that Mike had made on rice paper and hung over the windows, she sat with Mohamed at a computer near the back wall and typed as he began to talk. As the other students read to themselves, he told her about the mosquitoes that buzzed around the diamond pits, the smell of rusting water, and the sun that beat down on the workers as they sifted gravel through large sieves known as shakers. His father had spent years overseeing a team of miners in the Kono District, the heart of Sierra Leone's diamond industry, and had brought Mohamed along to observe how the work was done. "My father said he wanted me to grow up and become a responsible man who would replace him as a leader if he died," he told Cindy. "He was teaching me his job just in case I did not finish my education, and the job was to take care of my family so we would not struggle to survive." After only a few hours in the pit, Mohamed claims, he found a diamond so valuable his father said that it would feed the family for an entire season. Mohamed remembers that day at the mines as being one of the best days of his life.

Until then, Mohamed hadn't talked much about the family he had left behind in Africa. He didn't even have a photograph to remember their faces. But as he sat with Cindy, a clear portrait began to emerge. "My father's name was Amadu Bah. His tribe was Fulani," Mohamed began, piecing together memories like clues in a police sketch of a missing person. "He had a cocoa complexion, small eyes, black hair, small chin, round head, long neck, normal ears, and he was a normal size person."

"He prayed a lot and went to work every day," Mohamed told Cindy. "His favorite color was white, and he was an indoor person. He didn't like pork meat, and didn't like watching television. He hated looking people in the eyes."

In his sixty-three years, Amadu Bah never went to school. "He got married to four wives and had twenty-five children," Mohamed said, "and the one he liked most was me."

Mohamed's story about the day he spent at the mines opened the floodgates for an ongoing narrative about his life, which began pouring out in journal entries and essays as well as in conversations with his advisor, Mike Incze. "It was a bit of a catharsis," Mike says one day after school in his science classroom, where a detached skeleton hand—the bathroom pass—rests on his desk. "What do you do when you lose somebody? You grab something and pin it down, and that is instantly what he did."

But while Mohamed seems to have pinned down some of his personal history successfully, other details have been lost in transit: mixed up, embellished, or blocked out altogether. Occasionally he speaks to Mike about the refugee camp in Guinea where he lived after fleeing Sierra Leone. He talks about kids playing soccer and standing in line for rice and bulgur. Mike tries to visualize it, but he can't. "There are big spots missing on that canvas, like, 'What was your daily life like in the refugee camp?' 'What were *you* doing?'" Mike says. Sometimes Mohamed claims that he spent almost three years at the camp; sometimes it's "half of my life." And yet, the picture that he paints of the camp seems generic and unfinished. It is the portrait of hundreds of refugee camps and millions of refugees—not of a single boy, not of Mohamed. (Strangely, the UN Refugee Agency school ID card that his older half brother keeps in his care in Sierra Leone, and insists is Mohamed's, pictures a much smaller boy with a different name. "There was a mistake in the age and name," his brother has said.)

Mohamed's recollections about his early childhood are also muddled. He has written extensively about his small village, Motema, located in the Eastern Province of Sierra Leone—a place that he now refers to as The Remote Village Where I Am From. He describes the mud-brick hut where he grew up, surrounded by trees, mountains, and streams, with painstaking precision. Other times, his imagination seems to get the better of him. Though he dismisses the witch stories that sometimes circulated his village as "nonsense stuff," as of the beginning of his sophomore year, he still believes in the power of the Koran to cure disease and bestow special powers like the ability to predict the future or be immune to bullets. One of his more recent memories is of a bunch of villagers spearing an anaconda from a nearby forest and eating it for dinner. Never mind that he had recently seen the movie *Snakes on a Plane* or that encountering an anaconda in Sierra Leone is as likely as seeing a spear used as a weapon in the twenty-first century. It *is* possible that he saw a python stabbed with sticks, which could help explain Mohamed's strange answer when asked if there is anything besides pork that he can't eat as a Muslim. After giving it some thought, he replied, "I don't eat snakes, dogs, or cats."

For the most part, Mohamed portrays life in his village as peaceful and idyllic. However, every once in a while, a very different picture emerges. Not long after he finished "Mining Diamonds with My Father," he wrote a story called "Victim of a Child Soldier," about the day a young rebel soldier held Mohamed's family hostage in their own home. He recalls being around seven at the time.

I was looking at the boy thinking to myself, why is he holding a gun and why is he telling my father to kneel down. In sierra Leone a young boy is not allowed to disrespect an elder person, if you do you will be badly beating by that elder or they will tell your parents and your parents will punish you for that. My father actually kneel down for him, he took his foot and put it on top of my father's back and he pointed the gun toward my mother, my grand mother and the other wives of my father . . . They were afraid that the young boy is going to kill them. I was behind the door trembling and I was afraid that I am going to lose my whole family. The village was a disaster people are crying and shouting for their family. The rebels were shouting up and down. The animals were no longer under control. The village that once seen to be in peace was now under fire. Back to my family, the boy was still pointing the gun on my family; he said that if they move an inch they would be sorry.

Mohamed's family survived the attack on their village, but they fled their home, and in the years following the war, his mother sent him to live with his older half brother in Freetown. In Sierra Leone it is not uncommon for parents to ask friends, relatives, or even strangers to raise their children, basically as an informal kind of foster care with benefits on both sides. In Krio the practice is known as *men pikin: men* meaning "mind," as in minding the store, and *pikin* meaning "child." Minding the child. Parents living in the village might send their child to an acquaintance in the city, where there are better schools, and in return the child might help out with domestic chores. A man might pay for his friend's son's school tuition, if the boy is bright and likely to become successful in the future.

Children are seen as assets, and the underlying expectation is that, someday, the "fostered" child will be able to offer assistance in return. But sometimes the arrangement is abused, and the child may end up being maltreated or exploited, doing work that borders on slavery, while the other children in the family are going to school.

Nedda de Castro was in Dariana's office when she first heard Mohamed's story in the fall of 2007. From what Dariana had described, he was living with a group of African men who were not his relatives, and they were making him work for them, illegally burning CDs and DVDs to sell on the street. Dariana was upset. She had been on the phone looking into social services for Mohamed, who was a freshman at the time, when Nedda came in. "This kid needs a home," Dariana told her.

As an assistant principal with a background in social work, Nedda is often one of the first people to hear about students in need. In her years at International, she has helped kids struggling at school because of a fight with their parents, an unexpected pregnancy, or immigration problems. She has heard about older kids, like Jessica Tan, who are living on their own, or who have been evicted and left homeless along with their families. But she had never encountered a situation quite like Mohamed's. "He was only fourteen," as she recalls. "He was over-the-counter, a brand-newcomer, and he was here totally alone. He had little to no communication with his father or mother. He had not a single relative in this country—not a single one. Even for our school, that's unusual. When a fourteen-year-old in our school is without their parents, they're with Auntie—blood relatives, frequently. He was really, really by himself."

Thousands of miles away from Freetown, Nedda had never heard of *men pikin*, but after hearing about Mohamed's dilemma, that's essentially what she had in mind. Someone needed to mind this child—someone who could put Mohamed in the way of success, but someone who would benefit from the relationship as well.

Cindy doesn't remember the first time Nedda talked to her about becoming Mohamed's guardian. It was before she had him in art class during the spring of his freshman year, before she even really knew who he was. Since then, Nedda has brought up the idea so many times that Cindy can't keep track. In her mind, it all just blurs together as one question, which makes the answer seem more like a done deed: "So," Cindy recalls Nedda saying, "when are you going to adopt Mohamed Bah?" She says it as casually as she might ask, "So, do you want to get a burger?"

Teachers and students living together isn't exactly encouraged in the

Chancellor's Regulations that the principal has handed out at staff meetings. But Nedda hasn't exactly been searching for approval. She has been searching for a home for Mohamed, and from the start she knew exactly where to look. Within minutes of hearing about his situation from Dariana, Nedda thought of Cindy, who lived alone in a two-story house a few blocks from the school, and had wanted to adopt a child at one point in her life. As Nedda remembers it, she didn't suggest the possibility of Cindy adopting Mohamed, but rather floated the idea of her "helping him out."

Nedda and Cindy have been close friends for more than twenty years, having met in a graduate course on classroom management at Medgar Evers College in Brooklyn in the late 1980s. Back then, Nedda sported Doc Martens and a spiky crew cut. She still wears a lot of black, but these days her Gothic leanings are channeled into a professional uniform of dark fitted blazers and sensible heels, her obsidian hair in a low ponytail, and black-frame glasses on the bridge of her nose.

Cindy hasn't changed much since her late twenties, at least not physically. A forty-seven-year-old black woman with shoulder-length tight curls and a girlish, cheek-splitting smile, she is still the same artsy chick from Washington, D.C., who fell in love with New York City during a stint at Parsons and decided to stay.

After grad school she and Nedda were roommates in the Park Slope neighborhood of Brooklyn. The experience nearly killed their friendship. "We fought like two *bitches*," says Cindy, whose colleagues aptly describe her as shooting straight from the hip. "We're both hardheaded, and we locked horns a lot."

That was before Nedda got married and started a family, and before Cindy seriously began to consider adopting a child. After rooming together, Cindy taught art to middle schoolers and Nedda got her master's degree in social work. When Cindy expressed interest in becoming a parent, Nedda was the one who helped her look into her options. Cindy was open to becoming either an adoptive parent or a foster parent, but she had been adamant about one detail: she wanted a little girl.

Cindy eventually completed all the coursework to become a foster parent with the intention of adopting a child, had a home study done, and got certified. She went as far as combing through photos of children five and under in hopes of finding one to take home. She never did make a match. There were too many applicants, too few baby girls, and most of the older children had siblings and couldn't be separated. The only ones left were teenage boys. "But who wants these grown-ass boys?" Cindy recalls thinking. "Who's *that* crazy? There were kids who looked older than I did."

The older she got, the more it began to seem like she might never become a parent. Sometimes she joked about it in the teachers' lounge at International. "I ain't birthing no babies. There are some things that are not going to happen on this Earth—and that's one of them," Cindy told a group of her colleagues over lunch. In more private moments, however, she has expressed concern for the future, if not exactly regret for the past. "It's not as if I had a burning desire to have kids. It's just something I always thought I would do, but then I didn't. I do worry about going through life without making an impression or mattering to somebody."

After Nedda brought up the idea of helping out Mohamed, Cindy wouldn't think about it for several months. The seed had been planted, left to either germinate or die. Nedda knew that Mohamed wasn't exactly what Cindy had been envisioning all those years when she had wanted to adopt. He was, after all, "a grown-ass boy." By his sophomore year, he would be slightly over five seven, 140 pounds and still growing, not to mention fully formed in other ways: He is a Muslim; Cindy is an atheist. He grew up in a remote African village that wasn't visible on most maps; she was born and raised in Washington, D.C. They would be an odd match, and Nedda's training as a social worker had taught her the importance of not forcing the issue. "He's a good kid in a bad situation, and he needs some help," Nedda told Cindy. "Maybe you can do something for him, or not. I'm just letting you know that this is a kid who has a need, and if you're curious about it, why don't you check him out? Get to know him."

*   *   *

Cindy eventually took Nedda's advice and got to know Mohamed, but he was also good at making himself known. Occasionally, Cindy gives an assignment called Secret Mission, in which students have to go on a James Bond–style mission to an exotic locale of their choice and track down a villain who has claim to some coveted, secret power. Most of the kids draw space aliens or celebrities. Mohamed was different. Using colored pencil, he drew a portrait of Foday Sankoh. The leader of the rebel army known as the Revolutionary United Front (RUF), he was nicknamed the Butcher of Sierra Leone. For ten years, Foday Sankoh's fighters burned, raped, and killed. They used machetes to chop off the hands, feet, ears, lips, and genitalia of innocent civilians, including children. To his followers, Sankoh was known as "The Lion," in part because of his full, bristly beard. To the impoverished young soldiers whom he recruited and forced to murder their own mothers and fathers, he was simply "Papa." A stroke helped kill the real, flesh-and-blood Sankoh, but he lives on in the drawing, which Mohamed later gave to Mike. It now hangs over his desk, attached to the peach wall by two pieces of blue tape. In a flash of inspiration, Mohamed drew Sankoh wearing olive-green fatigues and standing next to a giant missile, which is labeled "Sierra Leone" and aimed at the village where he grew up. In the frozen colored-pencil scene, the sun never fully sets; it bathes the sky in an eerie red and orange glow behind the humps of grassy green mountains. There are no people in the bunkers, and the missile never launches. But day after day after day, Sankoh smiles sinisterly from behind his bristly black beard.

Mike tried asking Mohamed about the drawing and what it is supposed to mean, but at the time he seemed more interested in talking about his improving art skills. Mike recalls that when he pointed to the man in the picture, Mohamed simply said, " 'Oh, it's the king of Sierra Leone.' He didn't really care about the content that much. He was more like, 'Look at how I did this—you see the sunset back there?' "

The drawing is the perfect metaphor for Mohamed's stories, which often blur the line between reality and fantasy. Just as the missile in the drawing never launches, in his stories about the war, no one ever dies. It is difficult to tell where Mohamed's memory falters and at what point the desire to remember, or the need to forget, takes over. But by the winter of his sophomore year, he has stopped writing, and his autobiography seems less like a work in progress than an abandoned draft in which many important chapters are missing—and none more conspicuously than the story of how he came to America.

Illegal

The immigration lawyers who sometimes visit the International High School have a saying: "No human being is 'illegal.' They're 'undocumented.'" The quote is adapted from a deeper sentiment expressed by Nobel Prize–winner and Holocaust survivor Elie Wiesel. "Human beings can be beautiful or more beautiful, they can be fat or skinny, they can be right or wrong, but illegal? How can a human being be illegal?" Wiesel asked. "That is a contradiction in terms."

At International, the students embody those words. Poor and middle class, Christian and Muslim, hailing from the snow-capped mountains of eastern Tibet, the arrondissements of Paris, and the sun-scorched deserts of Mauritania, they are class flirts and class clowns, cricket players and soccer stars, aspiring actors, doctors, zoologists, and flight attendants. And yet, as immigrants in America, they are divided into one of two categories: Legal or Illegal. The new haves and have-nots. The kids with documents plan for college and careers. Those without documents take the same college-prep classes. They learn how to apply for the same financial aid. They network with the same professionals in the fields of their choice. But whether they will ever get the opportunity to follow through with any of it is largely dependent on the fate of a bill known as the Development, Relief and Education for Alien Minors (DREAM) Act, which would create a conditional path to citizenship for high school graduates who arrived in the United States before they were sixteen and have been here for at least five years, in exchange for completing two years of college or military service. Despite support from advocates such as New York City Mayor Michael Bloomberg and Senator Harry Reid of Nevada, the legislation has failed to be enacted by Congress after several attempts to pass it. However, as of the 2008–9 school year, many administrators and teachers at the International High School still feel optimistic that the bill could grow new legs with the election of President Obama, who has supported the DREAM Act since he was a senator in Illinois. In the meantime, students of every status drop by Dariana's office with immigration questions. They ask her about social security numbers and passports (most of the Tibetan kids don't have them because Tibet is not recognized as its own country), and how to apply for green cards. Often they are seeking answers for a parent, an aunt or uncle, or a distant friend in their home countries.

In response to the great demand for counsel on all matters immigration, Miguel Antunes, the parent coordinator whose job it is to process new students, has helped organize the year's first PTA meeting. Actually, "PTA" is a bit of a misnomer. Past meetings of the Parent-Teacher Association have lacked parents; many don't show up because they work late shifts or are needed at home, or simply because they don't speak English. Student-Parent-Teacher Association might be a more accurate description, considering the large number of kids who come to serve as translators for the few parents who *do* attend—as well as to glean information for themselves. Despite poor attendance in the past, Miguel and Dariana are hoping that tonight's topic, "Legalization and Citizenship," will reverse the trend. In preparation for the event, they wallpapered the halls with photocopied signs like so many concert flyers and invited two lawyers to come in and answer questions from parents and students.

One of those students is Mohamed Bah, who, like many of his classmates, is here illegally. When he was fourteen years old and living in Freetown, the capital of Sierra Leone, he says he won a school history competition sponsored by a group of Christian missionaries. In October of 2006, Mohamed entered the United States with a travel visa good for approximately five weeks and went to Farmington, Connecticut, where the group's church was based and a host family was waiting for him.

After that, the story goes off the rails. Mohamed says that he no longer remembers the name of the church ("Something Christ?" he once offered) or the names of the missionaries themselves. But much more puzzling is the information that he does provide. Mohamed has told several of his teachers about the day he got lost at the Empire State Building while on an outing with members from the church. He says that he was eating lunch with some "Christian white ladies" in a restaurant when he got up to go to the bathroom and couldn't find his way back. The next thing he knew, he was outside on the street, headed toward the great neon blaze of Times Square. Mohamed's teachers aren't sure what to make of his account, which seems to collect new details and grow more outrageous with each telling. Even among the amazing stories in the school, "Mohamed's story is particularly amazing. Like, *what*?!" Mike Incze says. "It's wrought wild. You don't know where those things come from—whether they're from his own chaotic experience that he's had over the last couple of years, or if he's concocted parts of the story, to hide other things, and now he sort of believes them. It's difficult to figure out because everything he says is with such conviction that the story itself is somewhat plausible."

Somewhat.

"Mohamed has a million stories of how he got here. No one really knows for sure," says Dariana Castro. "Sometimes I just wish I could go to Africa to meet his family and find out how this kid ended up here in the United States, in Brooklyn—in my life."

A couple of hours before the PTA meeting, Mohamed finds Dariana in the student-government office, as she is organizing flyers into neat piles on the long conference table.

"Today I discovered I was Pisces," he booms, pulling up his baggy jeans, which have begun their downward descent, before sitting beside her. "Intelligent, Thoughtful, Clever, Strong, Confident, Humanitarian. It totally described me!"

"Did it also say Arrogant? Prideful? Slightly Irritating?" Dariana asks with a cold smile.

She is not pleased with Mohamed at the moment. Last week Dariana arranged for him to see an attorney from The Door, a nonprofit organization that provides legal and immigration services to disadvantaged kids in New York City, and he missed the appointment.

"Your lawyer is going to be here tonight, and she's going to ask you why you stood her up," Dariana says.

"Are you blaming me for that?" Mohamed squawks, nearly jumping out of his seat. "You didn't tell me, Miss, I swear to God! I didn't know about it. Plus, I had a severe common cold."

She laughs, eyeing Mohamed from behind her cat's-eye glasses. " 'A severe common cold.' What, did you get that from a commercial or something?"

In a school echoing with strange malapropisms—"Chill down, dude," for instance—Mohamed's vernacular is among the strangest. His teachers came up with a name to describe his peculiar brand of pidgin: Fubahnish, a hybrid of the West African language known as Fula, English, and a third tongue that only can be described as Bah-nese. A distinguishing characteristic is Mohamed's inability to pronounce his *r*'s. He has gotten his fair share of dirty looks at restaurants for asking the server for a *fahk* and knife. Another feature is hyperbole. In distress, Mohamed often sighs, "Oh, my life!" No one knows where he learned the expression, but it fits into a bigger lexicon of dramatic exclamations and catchphrases that he has amassed in the two years since he landed in America. "Life is a crazy jah-ney," he likes to say, shaking his head.

He outlined the contours of that journey for Camila Sosman Palmer, his lawyer from The Door. A slim blonde in her thirties, she represents teenagers in immigration limbo. The first time Mohamed met Camila in her office in lower Manhattan, he told her how he came to live with four young Sierra Leonean men, all of whom he calls Uncle as a sign of respect and not one of whom is family. During his first year in New York, Mohamed didn't go to school. From the time he woke up to when he went to bed, he worked for his roommates, who run an illegal pirating business out of their apartment in Bedford-Stuyvesant. For a while Mohamed crashed on a couch in the living room, but now he shares a bed with a bootlegger in his midtwenties, who taught him how to use the duplicator machine that they use to burn CDs and DVDs for resale on the streets.

The lawyer was the first person Mohamed heard give it a name: labor trafficking. His roommates could call it whatever they wanted; they saw it as payback for letting him stay. But the facts would speak in court: Mohamed was a minor working for no wages in an illegal business run by undocumented immigrants. Camila explained that there were a couple of paths he could take to get a green card. He could apply for Special Immigrant Juvenile Status, an option for children for whom reunification with one or both parents is deemed not viable due to abuse, abandonment, or neglect. (A court must also find that it is not in the child's best interest to return to his or her home country.) Or he could apply for a T visa, a temporary status for victims of human trafficking who agree to assist law enforcement in investigating the crime. If Mohamed wanted a shot at obtaining a green card the first way, she said, he needed to find a new place to live, and, if possible, someone willing to become his legal guardian.

"So, where are you living these days?" Camila asks. She smooths her pale-gray suit and takes a seat across from Dariana's desk.

"Same old place," Mohamed says, digging his fists into the pockets of his pine-green hoodie.

"How desperate are you to get out?"

Mohamed shrugs. He doesn't say more, not now, not yet. But anxiety is written onto his face, as plain as a cheat sheet: the clenched jaw, the creased brow, the way he keeps swatting at the back of his ear as if trying to shoo away a swarm of mosquitoes.

"One concern is that the people you're living with could get into a lot of trouble," Camila says.

"Because the slightest mistake," Mohamed says, "they might take me back to Africa?"

Mohamed would never tell her, but he is not fully convinced that Camila can win his case, even though she assures him repeatedly that he doesn't need to worry about being "sent back to Africa." Lately he has been watching a lot of Court TV. He especially likes Judge Lopez and Judge Judy. He has started imagining himself on the stand so that, should he ever end up there, he would know what to do.

In debate club, he has argued sides of many different topics: Recycling and Alternative Energy, for instance. In court, the lawyers would do the same, only their topic would be, What to Do About Mohamed Bah. He knows Camila will try her best. He is worried about her opponent.

"He's in the country illegally!" the prosecutor might tell the jury, brandishing a copy of the Constitution to back up his argument. "He shouldn't be here!"

"Okay, I totally agree with you," Mohamed would say, addressing the prosecutor directly. "But this is a situation where someone is fighting for his future. Like, for example, *I* am fighting for my future."

But was he not in the country illegally? "Yes, I totally take the blame for that," Mohamed would explain, "but there are reasons. For example: One, I want to finish my education. Two, I want a better future."

In his courtroom reveries, Mohamed always concludes with a plea to the jury. "I didn't mean to do evil things. I came here in a good way to help the United States if I grow up and become a doctor. I might be here for a certain time helping the American people, then later go to Africa and help my own people."

That's where the fantasy ends. The jury never deliberates, and the courtroom never adjourns.

Outside Dariana's office, Livenski Talcius and Mesbah Uddin wait for Mohamed. Now in their sophomore year, the three boys are inseparable. They are in the same after-school clubs and they have an identical list of dream colleges: Harvard, Yale, Princeton, and Columbia. As of early December, they have started their own techno/R&B band, called The Intellectuals. Tall and lanky with sharp angles, wide-set eyes, and a protruding Adam's apple, Livenski is Haitian and the ladies' man of the group. Mesbah, a short Bangladeshi boy with leftover baby fat, is the producer, improvising beats on the computer in the science room.

Mohamed wrote their first song. For the past few days he has been wandering through the halls testing out the lyrics, which sound remarkably similar to "Angel" by Shaggy. "Angel, my love, yes you mean a lot to meeee," he sings in a croaky voice. "You are the queen, and I'm the kiiiiiing."

For a while, the three boys each toyed with the idea of becoming presidents of their respective countries. Livenski jokes about replacing René Préval as the head of Haiti. Mesbah wants to rule Bangladesh. Naturally, they would join forces to invade Sierra Leone when Mohamed became president. In the meantime, they put aside their political differences to attend the PTA meeting.

"You guys are like a gang," Dariana says, taking a seat among the boys at the conference table scattered with empty juice cartons.

"But we're the opposite of the Crips and the Bloods," Livenski says.

"Yeah," Mesbah says, "we rob knowledge out of people."

Tonight they have come to rob knowledge out of the lawyers whom Miguel has invited to speak on the subject of Legalization and Citizenship. By the time the boys walk out of the student-government office a little after five o'clock, the hallway is buzzing with parents. Some look old enough to be grandparents, others young enough to enroll in the school themselves. Their faces range from smooth to sun-creased. Several men have come straight from work in sweat pants or steel-toed boots. The women jiggle babies in their arms or trail young children as they thread through the clumps of students loitering in front of the blue lockers. Near the girls' bathroom a dark-skinned Dominican boy tries to kick Odanis in the ass and slips in the act, landing with a thud on the linoleum floor. "*Mira! Mira!*" Odanis yells, a few feet away from Hasanatu, who is practicing how to tie a tie on a cute boy. Other students have volunteered to translate for the night and help direct traffic to the end of the hall.

Every few minutes the elevator doors open to deliver another family to the throng of people headed to Room 418, where Alexandra Anormaliza, dressed in a sharp gray suit, stands in the doorway. "Hello! *Hola!* How *are* you?" she greets each new face.

Mohamed, Livenski, and Mesbah head to the back of the room as tentative parents settle into plastic chairs, glancing at their surroundings like timid freshmen. Near the window, a table is set with refreshments that only the students and teachers dare touch.

Standing with her hands folded in front of the whiteboard, Alexandra waits for silence. She is always present at PTA meetings, but this one is different and particularly resonant for her. Alexandra was nine years old when she joined her parents in New York City, where they were living illegally. Her father, who had been a bus driver in Ecuador, was the first to arrive in the late 1970s, seeking financial stability and a better life for his daughters. Over the next five years, he sent for his entire family. In 1981, traveling with a visa for vacation purposes, Alexandra and her grandmother landed in JFK Airport, not knowing a word of English. Their flight arrived early, and when they deplaned, no one was waiting at the gate. A young couple who had traveled on the same plane offered to walk around the airport with Alexandra, looking for her parents, while her grandmother waited. After a few laps around the terminal, Alexandra spotted a woman who resembled her mother, if her mother had been ten to fifteen pounds heavier. Maybe it was her mother. It had been two years since they had seen each other, and she wasn't sure, so Alexandra did the logical thing and asked, "Excuse me, are you my mother?" Indeed, she was. They hugged and kissed and said each other's names out loud, just to be sure. Later, Alexandra's mother told her that she had seen a young couple circling the terminal with a little girl who looked a lot like her daughter, but decided it couldn't be; she was too small. After two years, she thought Alexandra would be much bigger.

Tonight, standing just over five feet in heels and looking out at the small crowd that has gathered in Room 418, Alexandra sees families whose stories aren't so different from her own. "We were the working poor," Alexandra has said. "When we applied for visas at the American Consulate, we were precisely the kind of people consular officials suspect will come to stay. They weren't wrong." The Anormaliza family overstayed their visas, becoming undocumented aliens within months of their separate arrivals. It wasn't until around her senior year of high school that Alexandra was legalized under the Immigration Reform and Control Act of 1986, which granted amnesty to certain undocumented immigrants who had been living in the United States since 1982. IRCA helped make it possible for Alexandra to go to college and become an American citizen.

When the students look at their principal, petite with a broad face and inky black hair, she wants them to see what is possible for themselves. As for the mothers and fathers in the room, Alexandra imagines that they want for their children what her parents wanted for her—a chance. Several families in the room are learning about high school requirements for the first time. Alexandra takes a moment to explain Regents exams and class credits before handing the reins over to Miguel, who introduces the attorneys. Joining Camila Sosman Palmer from The Door is Zachary Sanders, a Brooklyn-based immigration lawyer. Wearing glasses, a slightly crumpled suit, and a black tie, he stands with Camila at the front of the room, next to an American flag and a calendar featuring Barack Obama's face under the banner, MR. PRESIDENT.

In between the murmurs of toddlers and the sporadic, jazzy rings of cell phones, the lawyers deliver their presentation in short bursts of English and Spanish. For the better part of an hour, they dispense advice on everything from the different ways to get legal status to the importance of keeping pay stubs and paying taxes in order to document a physical presence in the United States in case of a raid. With the election of President Obama, they hope that Congress will finally do some heavy lifting on immigration reform, but Zachary tells the mothers and fathers, aunts and uncles, and sisters and brothers who sit scattered throughout the room that they may not be able to prevent a visit from Immigration and Customs Enforcement, or ICE. Just in case, they should know their rights.

To drive home the point, he passes out visual aids: illustrated, photocopied packets bearing the headline WARNING! PROTECT YOURSELF FROM IMMIGRATION RAIDS! The drawings look like they were torn straight out of the Sunday comics, only they feature ICE agents with holstered guns and black shades and dark-haired mothers and fathers with closed mouths and sweat beads jumping off their foreheads. In one sketch, a buff, square-jawed agent leads away the man of the house with his hands shackled behind his back. Another illustration shows a roomful of husbandless women wearing institutional uniforms and sitting on cots, above the caption: "Some people who are not United States citizens have been arrested or detained by the U.S. government. Learn how to protect yourself if this happens to you!"

"I don't want to alarm you," Zachary says, "but there have been a lot more home raids lately. They come in the middle of the night and in the morning. Sometimes they bang on the door and say that they're the police. This is very important: Don't give them permission to come into your home, unless they show you a warrant. One of the most important rights you have in this country is to remain silent."

Camila continues after blowing her nose, which is red and raw from a cold. "Another thing we've been seeing, with students who have been visiting colleges, is that Immigration has been coming on Amtrak trains and Greyhound buses and into the airports and doing random searches. The police in New York City are not supposed to ask about immigration status, but if you end up at Rikers and you have no documents, they *will* find you."

She directs her attention to the back of the room, where Mohamed is jabbing Mesbah with his pencil eraser. "You guys in the back not listening? This is very important. Something as simple as jumping a turnstile can get someone who's undocumented into a lot of trouble."

"Does anyone have any questions?" Miguel jumps in, puncturing the uneasy silence in Room 418.

Mohamed jabs his index finger in the air. "Is it true that the undocumented are eligible for scholarships?"

"You can get a scholarship," Camila says. "You're just not eligible for financial aid."

"Immigration status is irrelevant when you're applying for college," Zachary adds. "It's paying for it that's hard."

Camila scans the room for signs of life. A little girl with black pigtails plays with a plastic wrapper at the refreshment table, and her mother shoos her away.

Mohamed's finger shoots up again. "What if you have a green card, and you get in trouble?"

"That's important for all the young people in the room to hear," Camila says. "The federal government hates drugs. Anything more than thirty grams of marijuana can get you deported."

A Haitian girl standing against the wall raises her hand, but before she can get her question out, Mohamed's voice booms again from the back of the room.

"What about a citizen?" A dozen heads turn to look at the boy in the green hoodie, finger jabbing. Along the wall, a couple of teachers snigger.

"No, but you could go to jail."

"And if you're illegal?"

"'Undocumented,'" Camila corrects him. "No human being is illegal."

"If you're 'undocumented,' and you want to ship something back home in the mail, will they ask to see your papers?"

"They shouldn't," she says with a vexed smile.

"What about if you're shipping cars?" Mohamed asks.

"Well . . ." Camila's eyes narrow. "Cars, maybe, but now you're getting into trade."

Two seconds later Mohamed is jabbing the air again, using his other hand to support his tired arm. Camila calls on other people. The Haitian girl asks about a friend of hers who wants to apply for permanent residence. Dariana asks about college applications and whether Immigration is permitted to read private forms in order to glean information about a person's status. Still standing in the back of the room, Mesbah clears his throat. His voice cracks anyway.

"If someone is a citizen, but was not born here," he asks between vocal spasms, "what is the highest post he can get?"

"Keep dreaming!" Mohamed shouts, knowing exactly where Mesbah is headed.

"Well, he can't be president, if that's what you're asking," Zachary says, to a few chuckles. "You have to be over thirty-five, too."

In the remaining minutes, Mohamed moves closer to the front of the room as the questions pile up in his brain like dirty dishes on a busboy's tray, wobbling and crashing and sloshing around until he can't take it anymore. He has to unload. He forgot to bring up one of the most important points, a question that has followed him ever since he arrived in the United States two years ago, wearing a jean jacket, brand-new black FUBU sneakers, and a small gray backpack, empty except for a green-and-gold Republic of Sierra Leone passport and two pairs of underwear.

This time he doesn't wait to be called on. "If I'm undocumented and I want a house or a car," Mohamed asks his voice rising a key, "can I have those things?"

A few seniors leaning against the wall laugh. But Camila hears the urgency behind the question.

"Yes," she tells Mohamed. "You can own things in the United States."

Guardians

For one reason or another, many kids at International have either lost their parents or lost touch with them. But all of the students are able to find extra emotional support through their advisories. Almost every teacher is an advisor and has an advisory, a handful of kids whom they get to know over the course of anywhere from one to four years, through class time, home visits, and field trips. "Guardian" would be a better label than "advisor," and in some cases even "guardian angel." All advisors are advocates for their students, speaking on their behalf in meetings with other teachers and staff and, depending on the kid, an advisor also may take on the role of an in-school parent, counselor, or cultural attaché. When Jessica found herself suddenly stranded during her first week in America, her advisor called homeless shelters looking for an empty bed. When an African girl complained that her religious Muslim father wouldn't let her go to prom, her advisor was the one who negotiated the terms of her big night out. Chit Su might not have tried ice-skating or her first bite of cranberry sauce if not for her advisor, Suzannah Taylor, who took her students to the rink at Rockefeller Center one day and another day hosted Thanksgiving dinner in class.

Just as there are a million different ways to parent, the same is true when it comes to advising. Some advisors coddle while others make threats. Some use a reward system while others resort to raising their voices. James Rice, a twelfth-grade social studies teacher, has tried all of the above to get his advisees to take their college application deadlines seriously—to no avail.

"Your applications should be done already!" James yells one day in early January, his voice booming within the four thin walls of Room 407. A light-skinned black man with a bald head, James has a hard time hiding his emotions, which play across his face like a laser-light show on a planetarium dome. The blood is already rushing to the tips of his ears and staining the taut skin of his freckled head a bright scarlet. It's just past 2 PM on a Thursday, and the group of about a dozen kids who make up James's advisory sit around a conference table in a small room on the fourth floor in various states of stupefaction. Bags of animal crackers and cartons of apple juice are scattered across the table, but no one reaches out to take one. The door opens, and the assistant principal who shares her office lounge with James and his advisees every Tuesday and Thursday during sixth period slinks by unnoticed.

All eyes are on Mr. Rice and his reddening face. Even his eyebrows and goatee, normally a light ochre, have taken on a fiery glow, lending his fat orange freckles the appearance of hot embers. For the past few months he has been stressing the importance of submitting a Free Application for Federal Student Aid—otherwise known as FAFSA—to the college counselor Joanna Yip. Despite multiple warnings from teachers and administrators, several of Jame's advisees have missed the first deadline, drastically reducing their chances of receiving financial aid. "If you don't want the money, that's fine," James says, grinning maniacally. "You're just competing against fifteen million other students. The money will be *gone*."

Steepling his fingers against his lips, he explains the protocol one more time, making eye contact with every student in the room. "Whether you're documented or undocumented, you need your tax information or a letter from your parents saying how much they make," he says as the heat bangs on and a gust of warm air reanimates the remnants of someone's chicken lunch in the trash can. "Where does the money come from?

I don't care if it's off the books. Someone must work—you gotta eat! Who has already given that information to Ms. Yip?"

A few hands go up. A Tibetan boy blinks to stay awake, his thick body swaying ever so slightly like a blade of sea grass on the ocean floor. "Lobsang, you're so lazy!" James yells, clapping his hands, and scaring the boy awake. "I'm just going to *reiterate*—which means repeat—get it to Ms. Yip ASAP."

"A-S-A-P," Angie Sherpa says, flicking a piece of metallic nail polish off her finger.

"What is that?" asks a Chinese boy with black-frame glasses.

James lets out a deep sigh and rolls his neck. "As. Soon. As. Possible."

He isn't the only one feeling the stress of the coming months. All of the twelfth-grade teachers are working with urgency to get their students on the right track to college. Sixth period has been devoted to preparing for Regents testing and filling out forms for scholarships and financial aid. Every day Joanna Yip's office is packed with students putting the final touches on their college essays and applications to schools ranging from the City University of New York (CUNY) and the State University of New York (SUNY) to prominent universities and artsy liberal-arts colleges, such as Syracuse, Tufts, and Bard. On top of that, they also have Portfolio, a culminating, cross-discipline project that includes research papers, book reports, science experiments, and an oral presentation that students in every grade must complete at the end of each semester.

All the work doesn't leave much time for hanging out, but that's important, too. Most of the kids in James's advisory have known each other since they were freshmen. Ever since the students walked into his classroom, James has been collecting snapshots of them. Near a sheet of easel paper bearing his advisees' names and birthdays is a blank patch of wall where he is planning to post a gallery of their greatest moments, their own photographic version of the kind of montage typically found in romantic comedies. There's Mr. Rice making a funny face and pretending to sneak off with a prized rose during a field trip to the Brooklyn Botanic Garden. There's Mr. Rice, again, wearing a party hat and making a kissy face as he hugs Dariana. There's Maria Mendez in a white crop top and jeans squatting down in the front row for a class portrait, and there's one of the first pictures of Maria's son, Edwin, who was born during her sophomore year.

Spread out on the conference table, the snapshots are more like time-lapse photography, showing the evolution of an American teenager from the various molds of their ninth-grade selves: fuller-faced kids with shorter hair, not-as-cool clothes, and an arsenal of cheesy poses from peace signs to gangsta shrugs. "You're going to be adults soon, and we haven't even finished putting our pictures on the wall," James says, tapping a pile of construction paper that he brought to decorate the bulletin board.

"Joe," he says to the Chinese boy with the black-frame glasses. "I need you to help me for a few minutes today."

"I can't do it," Joe says with a sheepish smile. "I have dance class."

"You have dance?" James squawks. "I didn't know you take dance class! Come on, shake it!" Tucking his elbows into his sides, James does a little chicken dance, swishing his hips with a nasty smile on his face as the class cracks up. "Come *ON*, shake it, Joe! We're waiting!"

"Shake it, Joe!" shouts Maria, a stocky Guatemalan girl with a broad face and a mischievous giggle. "*Como* Beyoncé!"

"You're going to fail dance if you're too shy to shake it," James says, resting a hand on Yasmeen's shoulder as she covers her mouth. "Yasmeen, show him how to do it."

Yasmeen laughs. "Oh, my goodness—you're crazy, Mr. Rice."

For the most part, Yasmeen plays the straight man to James's flamboyant foil. It is hard to imagine two people with less in common than James, who, on his Facebook page, describes his political views as "Extreme Left" and his religious views as "ALL," and Yasmeen, a nineteen-year-old from Yemen who watches Al Jazeera at home and lives by the words of the Koran. Nevertheless, they have one of the closest advisor-advisee relationships in the whole school. He helped talk her into coming back to school after her father died in September and again when her mother passed away a couple months later. When she began to consider dropping out and moving back to Yemen, he was the one she told. "I love that child," James says. "I feel like we are a family."

*   *   *

In essence, advisories are a kind of "school family," with the advisor acting as the head of that family for sixty-five minutes of classtime, twice
a week. Of course, after the period is over, students go home to their
real families, where their voices aren't always as clearly heard. Every year
there are kids who face outside pressures to drop out for any number
of reasons—to go to work, take care of siblings and tend house, or to
move back to their native countries. Many times an advisor will step in
to encourage a student to push on to the finish line, when a parent may
not be as supportive. "They need to hear, 'I am behind you.' It takes
that extra *umph* to make it through," says Nedda de Castro, who created
and oversees the advisory program at International. "Imagine you're in
a marathon, and you're thirsty, and you only have a little bit to go, and
someone's saying, 'You're really tired, aren't you? You really want to sit
down. Maybe you shouldn't continue. You don't have to finish this race.'
Our job is to say, 'You can do it.' And sometimes we have to say, 'Don't
listen to your dad right now.'"

Ever since Yasmeen started the ninth grade, James has been working
on her family to allow her to go to college. In the beginning, it didn't
seem likely. Yasmeen was pulled out of school in Yemen and spent her
first years in the United States helping out around the house when she
should have been attending middle school. Like many International
students, she had an offputting experience at her previous school, M.S.
390 in Brooklyn. Post 9/11, some of her classmates called her Terrorist
and The Taliban for wearing her *hijab*. After another student heckled
her about what age child brides get married off in her country, Yasmeen
began showing up to class only once or twice a month, "just so I wouldn't
make trouble, or ACS would call," she says, referring to the city's Administration for Children's Services.

Eventually, a Lebanese teacher at Yasmeen's middle school told her
about the Internationals Network. However, even after Yasmeen enrolled
at the International High School at Prospect Heights as a freshman,
there were times when her mother seemed ambivalent about her daughter pursuing her education. "I think the mother was conflicted between

what she knows, and what's possible," James recalls. "She was new to this country. When we started to talk about college, her mother was like, 'I don't know, I don't know.' That just wasn't in her realm of possibilities."

James put the possibility squarely in her realm when Yasmeen's mother came in for the last parent-teacher conference of junior year. "Look, she's going to college," he told her mother, whom he remembers as a somewhat heavy woman with cloudy eyes. "She's bright, she's a resident, it's not going to cost a lot of money. This is what she wants."

It was a tense moment. "Yasmeen wasn't cringing, but she was totally silent because she'd been hesitant to broach this with the family," James says. "It made her very nervous, but I said, 'We're going to bring it up because I want to know that you have your mother's support.' The last thing her mother said at the conference was, 'Whatever she wants. I want her to do whatever she wants.' That was the closest she'd come to saying yes, which was kind of a confirmation, a stamp of approval."

James never saw Yasmeen's mother again. She fell ill a few months later. In the aftermath of her death, there are now limits to what James can do. He can call Yasmeen's older brother to get permission for her to tag along on an advisory field trip to see *Slumdog Millionaire*, followed by cupcakes at Magnolia Bakery. But he can't prevent her relatives from sending her back to Yemen. He can help Yasmeen fill out her applications for CUNY and SUNY. But he can't stop her family from trying to marry her off and potentially destroying her chance of going to college altogether. The best James can do is remind Yasmeen that despite everything—despite losing her parents, the newfound responsibility of raising her siblings, and her brothers' plans for her—she still has options. She is a citizen. She can go to school, work, and take care of her siblings.

"You don't have to go back to Yemen. You don't have to get married. This is a new time," James tells her one day in January. "You have a voice, and you're doing yourself a disservice if you don't say something. You have to stand up for yourself. What do *you* want?"

If James had asked Yasmeen what she wanted last year, college would have been at the top of the list. But as of early January, her priorities have changed. Her new priorities are her own flesh and blood. They are ages nine and eleven. Their names are Ahmed and Amani, but she calls them The Boy and The Girl. As in, "The Boy talks a lot." Or, "Me and The Girl sleep in the same room." They are her little brother and her little sister, and much more. They are the last vestiges of her parents, and, depending on how things go this afternoon when Yasmeen officially files a petition for guardianship of her siblings, they could be more like her son and daughter. At nineteen, Yasmeen is old enough to be a legal guardian to both of her younger siblings, but whether she is fit for the job in the eyes of the court is yet to be seen.

Yasmeen left school early today to pick up both kids on the way to the Children's Law Center, a nonprofit legal firm in downtown Brooklyn that provides representation to minors. On the way to the office, she stops at McDonald's to buy dinner for her little brother and sister, and to pick up the family's caseworker, a plump, curly-haired Palestinian woman from the Arab-American Family Support Center who has worked with the family for years.

Every once in a while, sitting in the waiting room of the Children's Law Center, the caseworker strains her neck toward the hallway, where a lawyer should be appearing any minute now to lead them to a conference room for an interview to begin the child-custody proceedings. Until then, her job is to help Yasmeen and the children bide their time.

"You're still president of your class?" the caseworker asks Ahmed, a skinny boy with huge brown eyes and a bouncing knee.

"No," he says, "vice president."

"Oh, so you stepped down," the caseworker says, winning a laugh from Yasmeen.

"Too much responsibility," she says.

Yasmeen combs Ahmed's hair with her fingers. She picked out his outfit two days before. Wearing a festive red-and-green flannel shirt under a gray argyle sweater vest with tan corduroy pants, he looks the part of a well-adjusted all-American boy, and that is no accident. Yasmeen re-created his look, item by item, off a boy model she saw in an advertisement for the kids' clothing store The Children's Place. She liked how the boy looked "professional." As for The Girl, she chose her veil herself, a sky-blue scarf that gives the impression that her head is in the clouds. Amani looks just like her sister, only swaddled in baby fat and sporting a few raggedy front teeth that are still growing in. "Come here," Yasmeen says, wiping the remnants of a McDonald's fried-chicken wrap off her chubby cheeks. "That's better."

"So, how do you feel about Yasmeen being your guardian?" the caseworker asks Amani.

"I feel good," she says.

In the corner of the room, a black boy with a shaved head rams a Tonka truck into a pygmy Christmas tree, sending little plastic passengers skidding across the carpet with sound effects of doom and destruction. *Woo-woooooo! Ppppppccccchhh!* A little girl explores a pile of presents wrapped in paper with candy-cane stripes. Someone clearly has tried to warm the place up. Children's crayon drawings plaster the walls and the ceiling, and the floor is strewn with games, toys, and stuffed animals. At least for the holidays, the waiting room feels more like Santa's workshop than a place where families come when children have been abused, neglected, or suddenly orphaned.

The distractions work. Minutes after taking their seats among the other children, Amani and Ahmed seem to have forgotten why they're here. As Yasmeen rubs her temples, The Boy plays monkey-in-the-middle with two kids around his age. The Girl hasn't stopped babbling since she walked through the door. ". . . and the school counselor? He was talking to us about respect? And he said his mom is sixty-eight—no—eighty-six this month, and if he disrespects her? She has a broomstick and she'll hit him with her broomstick . . ."

Yasmeen shuts her eyes, bleary from not sleeping. She spent the night at the hospital with her three-year-old nephew, who is recovering from tonsil surgery, and whose mother—Yasmeen's older sister—is pregnant and couldn't stay overnight. The little boy didn't want to sleep in his crib, so Yasmeen had a restless night shushing and holding him in her arms. The father was supposed to come early in the morning to take her place so that Yasmeen could make it to school by second period, but he was late, and she didn't leave the hospital until around eleven o'clock. Breakfast was coffee and a bagel scarfed down on the B45 bus. She didn't have time to go home first.

Less than twenty-four hours since she left the hospital, Yasmeen sits in another waiting room. It's amazing how much time she has spent in waiting rooms, and how similar one is to another, with their controlled thermostats creating some sense of stability in the absence of weather and the outside world. The décor changes from place to place. It's the faces that are the same, and the smells: the sweet sulfur of dirty diapers mixed with the lingering trace of french fries that someone ate hours before. The hot-dust smell of a pocket filled with lint after going through the dryer, or the coach section on a crowded airplane, of idle bodies and sterilized surfaces, at once grimy and antiseptic, like a pair of used rubber gloves.

Over the past few months, Yasmeen has become familiar with the white linoleum floors, long wooden benches, and panels of fluorescent lights that buzz like electric hives in the waiting rooms of Family Court, where the lounge smells like disinfectant and Cinnabons. Like many of her classmates at International, Yasmeen's proficiency in English has made her a valuable asset to friends and relatives who need help navigating the city's many bureaucratic services, from health care to child care. Her nephew got his tonsils taken out at the same hospital where her father died. In a twist of fate both cruel and convenient, that hospital happens to be located across the street from another hospital where her mother spent her final days in a coma. Yasmeen spent the summer shuttling between the two parents, translating on their behalves and occasionally finding time for herself. Her favorite place is the concrete courtyard between the two hospital buildings, where she used to take her lunch breaks under a row of trees. "It was amazing just to have some peace," she says.

Despite the cheerful décor of the waiting room inside the Children's Law Center, there is no peace now. The toys and games that seem to be working so well on her siblings do nothing to soothe Yasmeen's nerves. Sensing her anxiety, the caseworker tries small talk instead.

"Have you read *A Thousand Splendid Suns*?" she asks, knowing how much Yasmeen loved *The Kite Runner*.

"No," Yasmeen says, chewing her nails.

"I have it—you can borrow it."

"Thanks."

In between the caseworker's stories of her own two little boys, they talk about Amani. Lately she has been getting bullied at school, and Yasmeen needs to meet with her teacher about it.

"She'll ask for a pencil sharpener, and no one will give it to her," Yasmeen says. "Girls are mean. They talk about her behind her back. I went through that same thing, so I know how it feels."

There is a brief lull in conversation, and the caseworker changes the subject to what's happening in Palestine, where she is from. Israel has been bombing Gaza, and images of women and children covered in blood and corpses in the middle of the road have been permeating the news.

"I've been waking up at three in the morning to watch Al Jazeera," the caseworker says. "How can I watch? How can I *not* watch? Oh, she's cute," she says, swiftly turning her attention to a baby girl dressed in pink. "It's more fun to dress girls. I mean, how many pairs of jeans can you buy? But girls, you have little skirts . . ."

She is still talking when a young lawyer walks into the waiting room and asks Yasmeen and the caseworker to follow her down the hall.

Yasmeen does her crying at night, after the children are asleep. But lately she has started wondering how she makes it through the day. "I keep asking myself the same question over and over: 'What keeps me going?'" she says. "I have no idea." From the time she leaves her family's apartment in Crown Heights in the morning to when she returns after school, Yasmeen lives in a world of ghosts. In the months after her parents' deaths, she feels their presence everywhere. She sees her mother scooping olives from the garlicky bins at Fertile Crescent, a Middle Eastern grocery store on Atlantic Avenue, every time she does her shopping. Only months ago, Yasmeen and her mother browsed the aisles together, passing the large glass jars and shelves filled with pumpkin seeds, rainbow sprinkles, shelled almonds, leathery strips of marzipan, Turkish delight, and plump dried dates as big as Florida cockroaches.

Now Yasmeen goes to the market alone. Giving her order in Arabic to the halal butchers who work in the back of the shop, she buys enough ground beef for several burgers, which she stuffs in pita-bread pockets for her younger siblings and cousins: Big Macs, Yemeni style. Once in a while, she takes a detour to the Islamic bookstore upstairs. Amid the framed pictures of Mecca, electronic prayer timers, and a single belly-dancing costume, a copy of a poster she once bought for her mother's hospital room is still there, even though her mother is gone. "*Allah Jalla Jalalahu*," reads the gold script on a black velvet background. "Allah's splendor be glorified." Downstairs, behind the cash register, the same woman always nods hello. After Yasmeen's mother died, the cashier was one of the women who helped wash her body at the mosque before burial.

Other landmarks are notable for no reason other than the fact that her parents were once there. Riding the B41 bus through downtown Brooklyn one day, Yasmeen points out the building where she and her mother went to apply for Supplemental Security Income. Nearby is a fabric store. "We bought curtains there," she says. Ironically, she has trouble remembering important details about her mother. It's the mundane memories that crowd in on her every day, like the times they went out to eat at the Atlantic Center Mall. Her mother lives on in random places like the Chuck E. Cheese where they used to bring Yasmeen's younger siblings, a place that she now avoids because, she says, "Remembering is just too painful."

There aren't many places where Yasmeen feels free, but she once said that she feels the *most* free when she finds herself visiting anywhere that her parents never went. "It's only two places," she recalled. "The Brooklyn Bridge and the movie theater." As of this afternoon, she can add the Children's Law Center to that very short list. While there are no memories here to haunt her, it is hardly a happy place. Yasmeen has been under the impression that the attorney from the Children's Law Center would be representing her in the child-custody proceedings. But minutes after they sit down in the conference room, the lawyer explains to Yasmeen that she is representing her brother and sister only. This is unnerving. It means that Yasmeen and the children are on two different sides. Suddenly it is up to her to convince her siblings' lawyer, a woman whom she has never met before, that she is ready to be their guardian, even though she is still in high school. When the lawyer leaves the room for a moment, the doubt creeps in.

"Should I get an interpreter?" Yasmeen asks, her cheeks flushed.

"You speak perfect English!" her caseworker says, moments before the lawyer returns, sipping coffee from a Styrofoam Dunkin' Donuts cup.

With feverish eyes, Yasmeen takes in the wall of leather-bound law books, the maroon office chairs, and a blank yellow legal pad, which will soon be filled with her answers to the attorney's questions. "When did your parents pass away?" "Were they unexpected deaths?" "Are you getting counseling?" "Have you ever had an alcohol problem?" "Have you ever had a drug problem?" "Have you ever been convicted of any felonies?"

Throughout the interrogation, Yasmeen holds her own. When she misremembers the exact date her father died, the caseworker quietly corrects her. When the lawyer asks how the city's Administration for Children's Services got involved with her family, the caseworker fills in again. "That was when Mom was sick, so Amani had to stay home because Yasmeen was always at the hospital and couldn't take her to school," the caseworker says.

Everything else Yasmeen answers herself. She knows the dates of her siblings' last physicals and dentist appointments, and she has the records in her bag to prove it. Rent, food stamps, cash assistance—she knows all the information by heart.

"Describe your typical day for me," the lawyer says.

"I wake up at seven to make breakfast for me and them, send them to school, and then I go to school," Yasmeen says.

"What grade are they in?"

"Amani is in sixth, Ahmed is in fourth."

"Do they have health insurance?"

"Yes, HIP."

"Any medical issues?"

"No, not really. Amani has high cholesterol, but it's not dangerous or anything."

"Where are you getting your income from?"

"My brother, he's supporting us."

"What does your brother do for work?"

"He works in a grocery store."

"Does he live in New York?"

"Yes, he sleeps with us."

"If he's supporting you, and living with you," the lawyer asks, reading her notes, "why isn't he on the petition?"

Yasmeen exchanges a glance with her caseworker. It's a logical question, but the answer comes out sounding more emotional than anyone in the room could have anticipated.

"No, it's not *about* that," Yasmeen says, biting her words. "I understand them more. *I* help with their homeworks. *I* make them dinner. *I* take them to the playground."

The lawyer scribbles in her pad and takes another sip of coffee. "What if you need help with babysitting—what do you do?"

"I take them with me."

"Who goes to the parent-teacher conferences?"

"Yes, that's me."

"How do you punish your siblings when they're misbehaving?"

"Take away their game, or TV."

"Do you ever punish them physically?"

"No."

Finishing her coffee, the lawyer explains what Yasmeen will need for court. Report cards, school attendance and medical records—she needs to get her hands on as many documents as she possibly can to show to the judge.

"They might scrutinize you because you're so young," she tells Yasmeen. "It's a big responsibility for an adult, let alone a teenager. You're only nineteen. Do you think you can handle it?"

Yasmeen's cheeks redden. The room is warm, and she never took off her winter coat. "Yes," she says and nods. "I've handled a lot already."

When the questions are over, Yasmeen is consumed by doubt. "What will happen if the judge says no?" she asks the lawyer on the way out.

"If they start missing school or there's abuse, then ACS will investigate," the lawyer replies. "I don't see why they shouldn't give you guardianship. You seem very competent."

Despite her assurances, Yasmeen can't seem to shake the feeling that she could lose her siblings at any moment. She is caught off guard when the lawyer asks to speak to Amani and Ahmed, separately and alone. Both children have been prepped for the moment when they might be called upon to answer some questions themselves, but Yasmeen never thought that the questioning would happen behind closed doors, when she was not in the room. They don't fully understand the importance of this day. She has been trying to protect both children from knowing too much. But what if they don't know enough? What if they say the wrong thing?

The Boy is the first to go. Before he gets up, he hands Yasmeen his Nintendo DS, still playing the theme music from his favorite game, Colonial Marines. Running her thumb over the buttons, she watches the lawyer give Ahmed a small cup of water from the cooler, and a big smile, as they head down the hall. There's nothing left to do now but sit in the waiting room, and wait.

When Ahmed finally came out of the conference room, his cup of water was empty, and he had a sticker of a red apple on his hand that hadn't been there before. "How did it go? Was she friendly?" the caseworker asked Ahmed, moments after the lawyer led Amani down the same hall. "She gave me a sticker from the sticker box!" he said excitedly, thrusting his hand under Yasmeen's nose and getting a meek smile in return.

It wasn't until the subway ride home that Yasmeen got the chance to ask both children about their interview with the lawyer. By the time they got on the train, crowded with passengers, she was shaking. In the absence of seats, she directed both kids to hold on to the pole and steadied herself by gripping their shoulders. "What did she say?" Yasmeen asked them, crouching down to hear their every word. "What did you say?"

As the train screeched and lurched underground, Ahmed and Amani told her about their interviews. Yasmeen probably could have predicted most of the questions. The attorney asked her siblings who else lives in their house, where the two children sleep, and what they do if they're hungry: Do they ask for food or simply get it themselves? Do they feel free at home? "Then she said, 'What are your three wishes?'" Ahmed added. Before their interviews were over, the lawyer asked a version of a standard question often used by child advocates, almost as a verbal Rorschach test: "If you could have any three wishes, what would they be?"

"The Boy told me his first wish was to get a good job. The second wish was, 'I wish all the people who are sick get better,'" Yasmeen recalls the next day in Room 407, her voice catching as she repeats her brother's answers. "The third wish was to finish college. That was really touching."

As for The Girl, she wished for an A in math class and a high score on her English language arts exam. Her last wish was about Yasmeen and Ahmed. "I wish that we stay together," she said.

The lawyer never asked for Yasmeen's three wishes, but if she had, she might have been surprised. Aside from raising her siblings and finding a career for herself—her first and second wishes—Yasmeen's third and final wish is more childish than anything her younger siblings said. After all, despite everything they have been through, they are getting the chance to have a childhood, and that is mainly thanks to their big sister, who sacrificed hers a long time ago.

"The third wish," Yasmeen says, "is to go to Disney World with Jessica."

Hope Day

One morning in December, thousands of students wake up to white skies and brittle winds. Shortly before school started, a sleet storm began to blow through the city, turning Brooklyn into a shattered snow globe. By midafternoon, thin, glittery coats of ice grip the fallen branches and power lines along Prospect Park West. Banks of white powder pile on every street corner like Styrofoam hills, slowly melting with each passing dog. Despite the quiet, a few brave vendors trudge through the slanting snow-rain with their metal carts to sell hot dogs and pretzels, trying to make the most of a slow morning by listening to the radio, with its news about Obama's upcoming inauguration and staticky reports of subway delays.

Across the city, thousands of prayers had gone out for school to be canceled, and as usual, students took to their Facebook pages to vent with messages like: "F-ck Bloomberg for making us have school tomorrow!" "I want a snow day!" But they had no such luck, and when the wide double doors of the Prospect Heights campus open a little after 3 PM, revenge takes the form of snow fights. Gloveless hands grab snowballs and then snow bricks and then entire snow shelves still retaining the grit of the sidewalks and the shape of the curbs from which they were taken.

After a restless day inside, most kids head home, but not Mohamed. Along with Mesbah and Livenski, he trudges through the snow to Five-Myles art gallery, where Cindy is hosting an exhibit of her students' drawings and paintings. Mohamed doesn't have any artwork in the show; he is going for another reason. A little more than two weeks ago, Cindy told Mohamed that she wants to be his legal guardian, and since that day in the art room, Mohamed has been visiting Cindy every morning around lunch to talk about their plans. He's also helping her get ready for the exhibit's opening night.

Inside the gallery, the room has been transformed since Mohamed saw it last. Near the entrance, a table of refreshments has been set up, and Ann Parry and some of the other twelfth-grade teachers mingle and sip ginger ale, passing time until they can head over to Franklin Park, the bar a couple of blocks away. Despite the weather, the place is packed and echoing with voices bouncing off the exposed brick and putty-gray walls. "Where is that?" Ngawang asks, peering at a snowy landscape of a bridge surrounded by bare trees and tall buildings. "Central Park?" someone guesses. A few feet away, Chit Su's advisor, Suzannah Taylor, studies the paintings of sunflowers and penguins in between discussing with her husband which one they should buy.

Standing around awkwardly with a camera around his neck, a gangly Senegalese junior tells Mohamed's crew that he wants to take their picture for the school newspaper. He zooms the lens as they nonchalantly pass by a portrait of a Muslim girl in a bright-green dress sitting against a background of robin's egg blue. "Look interested," the boy directs his subjects, "like you're talking about the painting." Wearing a giant black puffer coat, Livenski slinks over to his red, white, and blue self-portrait, which bears an uncanny likeness to the Barack Obama poster for "Hope," and poses for posterity, smiling across the room at Cindy.

With the exception of a few of Mohamed's friends and Cindy's colleagues, most people don't know about their arrangement. It's not a secret, but it's not being advertised, either, and if the principal had known about it sooner, it might be happening a little differently, or not at all. In fact, Alexandra didn't learn about Cindy's offer to be Mohamed's legal guardian until after it had been made and his immigration lawyer was involved.

Cindy has heard snippets of gossip about how the principal disapproves of the idea, but it's more complicated than that. Alexandra knows that Nedda didn't mean to keep anything from her. "I think she just saw an opportunity, and the social worker in her took over. She didn't really stop to think about any of the legal repercussions. You know, these kinds of things can be misinterpreted very easily," Alexandra says. At the same time she recognizes that, in many ways, Nedda's instinct to find the best possible home for a child in need is simply an extreme example of everything that the school stands for. "It's very hard, when you have a school that functions as more of a secondary family, to put on the brakes," Alexandra says. "I tend to err on the side of being cautious, without letting that stop our school from functioning at another level, because it's easy to let legalities take over, and then you suddenly end up with a school that's less about the people and more about following the rules. So, I would have advised caution and checking with the DOE, but I think I would have supported it, nonetheless."

Until someone comes knocking on her door saying that she *can't* go through with her plan to let a student live in her house, Cindy is moving forward with Mohamed. On the surface, they are all business, using their lunch periods to discuss when they should meet with his immigration lawyer and how exactly to tell his African roommates that he is moving out of their apartment and in with his teacher. Cindy already has a room ready upstairs. For the past few years, she has made it available to strangers from around the world, through www.couchsurfing.org, a website that connects travelers to local hosts. Couch-surfers from Israel, England, Australia, Argentina, Korea, and Russia have all rested their heads in her home. Currently there is a Japanese foreign exchange student renting out her basement, and in a few days a girl from São Paolo will move into the upstairs room, staying there while she takes a film course for six weeks. As soon as the film student moves out, Mohamed can move in. Some of Cindy's friends outside of school already have expressed their doubts: "Ooh. A sixteen-year-old boy—aren't you worried?" But the truth is, the whole idea hasn't really sunk in yet. "One day I'm going to be like,

'Oops!'" Cindy jokes. "Believe it or not, I haven't given it much thought. He's just going to be another person who lives in my house. I really don't think it's going to change my lifestyle."

And yet, it already has. This time there is no coursework to complete, no certification to get, no album to thumb through looking for the right fit. There is simply a hyperactive sixteen-year-old African boy who is bounding through an art gallery, tripping over his True Religion jeans and flapping his elbows like a pterodactyl, bellowing, "I CAN FLY!"

On the other side of the gallery, Cindy has been talking to a friend of hers, who is sporting a fleece vest and a peace-sign button and belongs to the same working artists coalition in Red Hook, Brooklyn. Wearing a nubby red sweater and a black skirt with tall matching boots, she watches Mohamed suck tortellini salad off his paper plate that has been doubling as a chin rest. She is still talking to her friend when "Thriller" comes on, and Mohamed extends his arms and knocks his head around in a bad impression of a zombie. "Like the dead people from the video!" he shouts, nearly scattering a stack of cups.

Finally Cindy breaks out of her conversation to give Mohamed some assistance, and in her absence Mesbah and Livenski step in to offer Cindy's friend their opinions about the phenomenon of brain drain in the developing world. "Well, that's neat that you want to go back to your own countries to be president," the man says courteously as Cindy leads Mohamed back to the snack table.

"Do you have enough food, darlin'?" she asks, handing him a fork and a napkin. She picks over a selection of ham wraps and puts a turkey one on his plate. "Here, this is safe. No pork."

Other than filing for guardianship, there are no formal steps Cindy needs to take to be a parent. It just happens. It's in the way she calls Mohamed "darlin'" and "baby" when she calls his friends by their first names. It's how she listens patiently as he tries out new words—words that he learned from her. For months Cindy has been correcting Mohamed's grammar and telling him to pull up his pants, but lately she has started paying close attention to his health. A few weeks ago she noticed a constellation of dull pink spots around his mouth, and she is already planning to take him to the dermatologist.

As Cindy and Mohamed pass pencil drawings and acrylic paintings of water birds, wolves, a medieval castle, and a portrait of a girl cloaked in an aqua-blue head scarf, Mohamed presses his nose up to each canvas, and before long Cindy realizes that he might need glasses, too.

"What's this?" Mohamed asks, stopping in front of an abstract water-color of swirling blue and gray.

"It's a water tower with a stormy sky. Can you dig it?" she asks, and he shrugs, apparently unimpressed. "Come on, I want you to feel it, baby."

Leaning in for a closer look, Mohamed wobbles the frame on the wall ever so slightly. He steps back quickly, but a few of his fingerprints cling to the glass.

"They should have No Touch signs," he says, "because I'm touching everything."

Sure enough, Mohamed has touched nearly every painting in the room by the time he is ready to leave. Outside, the snow is still falling sideways, and the sky looks like TV static. Soon the entire city will be glazed with ice. Ann Parry puts on her coat and leaves with a bunch of teachers going to Franklin Park to kick back some beers in honor of Friday night. They invite Cindy along, but she has to stick around and close up. She is hanging out in a small office near the front of the gallery when the boys come to say good-bye.

"Okay, Miss Cindy," Mesbah says, tapping the wall. "See ya when I see ya."

"Does that even mean anything?" Mohamed says, scrunching up his face.

"Yes," Mesbah says. "I learned it from Matt Damon. Didn't you see *Ocean's Thirteen*?"

"Oh. Bye, Miss Cindy. See ya when I see ya," Mohamed says, and fills one more plate with tortellini salad for the road.

Around the time when Nedda first brought up the idea of adopting Mohamed, Cindy expressed a major concern right off the bat. "He's not an orphan," she said. "He has a family." At the time she didn't know the whole story, but it has emerged piecemeal ever since. Like everyone who has heard Mohamed's tale about getting separated from a group of Christian missionaries at the Empire State Building, Cindy is incredulous. "How do you just 'get lost'? I don't believe it for a minute," she says one day in Dariana's office. "This isn't the Amazon jungle. This is New York City. You don't get lost unless you want to get lost."

No one at the school really knows what happened from Point A to Point C—Mohamed leaving Freetown and arriving in Brooklyn. All they know is that, for a few weeks in between, he lived somewhere in Connecticut.

That somewhere was actually Farmington, Connecticut. Located about ten miles west of Hartford, Farmington is an affluent, postcard-perfect New England town, with rambling driveways and manicured lawns as soft and green as old money. The face of the dollar bill himself, George Washington, passed through Farmington several times during the Revolutionary War and is said to have called it "the village of pretty houses." At the time there were no megamansions like today. In 2003, 50 Cent took over a 50,000-square-foot, multimillion-dollar residence once owned by Mike Tyson. Most of the homes, however, follow a strict code of understated Connecticut charm. In the fall, pumpkins on porches and piles of just-raked leaves on sidewalks lend a down-home Norman Rockwell feel to the otherwise imperious colonials. Rows of trees help to sequester some of the stateliest houses. But when it comes to prime locations, the white farmhouse where Mohamed spent his first weeks in America is hard to beat. It is just around the corner from one of Farmington's main attractions: the First Church of Christ–Congregational, whose slender white steeple pierces the sky.

Founded in 1652, the church has a unique place in history. One of its earliest ministers, Samuel Hooker, was the son of Thomas Hooker, who founded Hartford. Another pastor, Noah Porter, began America's first foreign missionary service in the parlor of his house. His son, Noah Jr., became president of Yale, while his daughter, Sarah, stayed closer to home and, just down the street from her father's church, opened Miss Porter's School, an all-girl preparatory school whose famous alumnae include Jacqueline Bouvier Kennedy Onassis and many other elite young women with names like Vanderbilt, Rockefeller, and Bush. The people of

Farmington are proud of their heritage and their church, a historic Colonial meetinghouse. But among all of the town's notable roles in world history, one stands out.

In 1839, Portuguese slave merchants illegally captured a large group of African adults and children from the Mende tribe in what is now known as Sierra Leone and sent them to Havana, Cuba, a bustling center of the slave trade. There, two Spanish planters purchased the surviving fifty-three Africans and put them aboard the schooner *Amistad*—Spanish for "friendship"—for passage to a Caribbean plantation. Led by a rice farmer named Sengbe Pieh, the captives overtook the boat days into the journey, killing the captain and the cook, and forcing the planters to sail toward Africa. At night, however, the Spaniards altered their course and headed toward New York. The *Amistad* was seized off Long Island, the planters were freed, and the Africans were charged with murder.

Those who hadn't died at sea were imprisoned in New Haven, Connecticut, as the U.S. government grappled with the next course of action to take. President Martin Van Buren argued to extradite the Africans to Cuba, while Northern abolitionists rallied to raise money for their defense. Eventually the case went to the U.S. Supreme Court, where former President John Quincy Adams defended the right of the Africans to regain their freedom. In 1841, they won that right; but, upon their release in New Haven, they still needed passage back to Africa.

Enter Austin Williams, an abolitionist and lawyer who was part of the Africans' defense committee and who had strong ties to the First Church of Christ in Farmington. For eight months, Williams and a coalition of abolitionists and church members provided shelter to the Mende people who made it that far, while parishioners also raised enough money to sail their guests back to Sierra Leone. Their destination: Freetown, which British philanthropists had established as a settlement for former slaves in 1787 and which is today the capital of Sierra Leone.

It is hard to think of two places on earth more different than Farmington and Freetown, the latter of which is one of the poorest cities in the world. But more than a century and a half after the *Amistad* revolt, friendship between the two communities is a major part of the ideological foundation upon which the church stands, although of the church's

eight hundred members, there have been only a handful of Sierra Leonean parishioners more recently. Over the years, the church has hosted
several of Sierra Leone's past presidents and heads of state, who have
come all the way to Farmington to tour *Amistad* sites, including the town
cemetery where one of the original passengers is buried. Cultures are
woven together in the chapel, where pews lined in red velvet meet a communion table that was crafted by a local cabinetmaker and parishioner
with iroko wood from Sierra Leone.

In the summer of 1998, the church wove its kinship with Freetown
even tighter when members helped to resettle a Sierra Leonean refugee, Jael Williams, along with two of her children. Her husband came to
Farmington the following year. Jael and her family inspired a group of
parishioners to form the Sierra Leone Ministry Team, and Jael, formerly
a secretary at University of Sierra Leone's Fourah Bay College, introduced the group to her brother, Professor Victor Strasser-King, who was
living in Freetown. In 1999, Strasser-King was principal of Fourah Bay
when an army of drugged-out rebels set half the campus on fire and continued their raid in the city and surrounding suburbs. His own mother-
in-law was burned alive inside her house. Thousands of other civilians
were murdered, raped, mutilated, or dismembered in the rebels' second
surge of terror, known as Operation No Living Thing.

It was Strasser-King who pressed the First Church of Christ about
the need for aid. Soon after, the congregation sent Fourah Bay College a
forty-foot container packed with clothes, medical supplies, and 125 com-
puters. In April of 2004, Jael and the Ministry Team chair, an occupa-
tional therapist named Marilyn Ostreicher, went to Freetown as guests
of the college, together with volunteers from the organization Freetown/
New Haven Sister Cities Inc., to make sure that the supplies they had
sent were meeting the needs of their recipients. In addition to visiting
the students at Fourah Bay College and meeting the president of Sierra Leone, Jael and Victor brought Marilyn to a nearby refugee camp
crowded with displaced women and children, and on the street Marilyn
encountered beggars missing arms, legs, hands, and feet.

As far as the eye could see were the remnants of the eleven-year war:
shanties made of junkyard scraps; roofs that were no more than rotted-

out mattresses, or missing altogether; people forced to squat and defecate in the street. Dogs ran wild, but running water was scarce and often limited to the pails that barefoot children carried atop their heads. The poverty was endless and stunning.

Years later Marilyn returned to the same slum with the church's senior minister Ned Edwards. They passed a shanty with its main room open to the road, a single candle burning on a wooden table inside. The flickering light was enough to illuminate the four little brown feet underneath. That's when Marilyn realized that there were children sleeping under those tables.

Mohamed Bah lived just down the street. He was eleven years old when his older half brother Abdulai, the first of their father's twenty-five children with multiple wives, took him to Freetown. In the years following the war, life in the village had been hard. Their father was abusive. Once, he beat Mohamed's mother with a belt so hard that she collapsed on the ground. After that, she moved out for three months, leaving her children to their own defenses. When she finally returned, it wasn't hard for Mohamed, her oldest son, to convince her to let him go to Freetown with Abdulai, who worked as a vendor selling cans of soda in the street.

Mohamed's mother had given him up once before. Shortly after he was born, she passed her baby son on to her own mother to raise until he was around seven. Now it was Abdulai's turn. Tall and skinny with full lips and a sly smile, Abdulai lived with his wife in a shack made of tar paper, wood, and corrugated metal. Located off one of Freetown's main roads in the largely Fula area known as Fula Town, it faced a primary school called Hope Day, an unlikely name for the dilapidated shack where, soon, two very different paths would cross. Mohamed was in the sixth grade when Marilyn Ostreicher visited his school, accompanied by Jael Williams and Professor Strasser-King, one of Hope Day's most famous graduates and chairman of the school's board of governors.

Hope Day, once held in respect, was in dire straits. In 1985 the school had relocated to a timber shack at Number 1 Gerber Lane. When Jael and Marilyn toured the site in 2004, the small lopsided shanty constructed out of wooden boards and scraps of metal was so corroded with dirt and

rust, it was like a tetanus infection waiting to happen. Its single classroom, wide enough to fit six small children, had attracted the interest of
nearly two hundred. Jael wouldn't go inside for fear that the structure
would collapse if one more person entered. But during her visit, dozens of kids who couldn't afford the $40 tuition lined the perimeter, beg-
ging for admission. Mohamed was considered lucky: In addition to the
help that he got from his brother, he earned money for books by selling
candy and cookies in the streets. Along with the other pupils, Mohamed
received lessons inside the tilting classroom that smelled like shit. All
the time. Students from other schools had more than one nickname for
Hope Day, which was located near a latrine that constantly overflowed
with human waste. *"Kaka na well!"* they yelled in Krio as they passed by,
holding their noses. *"Kaka bokits!"*

Back in Farmington, Marilyn and Jael helped organize a new mission for the church. They needed to build a better primary school in
Freetown. Initially, they had hoped to collect $60,000. The congregation
eventually raised around $140,000, enough for construction of a brand-
new three-story building featuring a nursery and a computer lab—a sum
that doesn't include money later spent on textbooks, school uniforms,
teachers' salaries, scholarships, and solar paneling for the roof. In the
coming months they shipped over more containers of supplies.

As the church progressed with their plans for the Hope Day School,
Freetown/New Haven Sister Cities, Inc. decided to sponsor a contest
that would signify the rekindled friendship between the two communities: an oratory competition for the sixth grade celebrating the leader of
the *Amistad* revolt, Sengbe Pieh (better known to Americans as Joseph
Cinqué). The prize would be a certificate of merit signed by members of
the Hope Day board of governors.

Around the same time, the First Church of Christ in Farmington
wanted to find a way to celebrate their own historic relationship with
Freetown. They volunteered to host a teacher from the Hope Day
School for a few weeks in Connecticut, the idea being that a stay in the
United States would familiarize the chosen educator with the American
school system. They also opened up the invitation to include a student,
and Hope Day only wanted to send the best, an exemplary child who

could be an ambassador to Farmington and an inspiration to Freetown when he returned.

Finding the right student turned out to be a simple task, as there was one obvious child, one boy who made himself noticed above all the rest. Mohamed Bah was awarded first prize for his speech about Sengbe Pieh and chosen as Hope Day's ambassador to Farmington.

Choosing the right student was the easy part. It was arranging the travel plans that proved difficult. As church member Patricia Reville waited for Mohamed's flight to arrive at Boston's Logan Airport months later in October of 2006, it occurred to her that a lot could go wrong. A freckled blond mother of four who coordinates art education events at Wesleyan University, "Pat," as she is known, is not a worrier, but there had been problems from the beginning. The church had had trouble securing visas for Mohamed and his chaperone, a third-grade teacher named Salamatu Jalloh who taught at the Hope Day School. The American embassy in Conakry, Guinea, which borders Sierra Leone to the north, does not give travel visas easily, knowing the likelihood of a permanent "overstay." After many failed attempts with the embassy, the church eventually used its clout to sidestep the piles of red tape that often prevent such visits. Pat got in touch with Connecticut's Republican congresswoman Nancy Johnson, while Marilyn, the head of the Sierra Leone Ministry Team, made another connection that was even closer to home. Down the street from the church, at Miss Porter's School for girls, there was a student whose father just happened to be the ambassador to the Republic of Sierra Leone, Thomas Hull. He had visited the church and was happy to help the congregation's African guests secure their visas. With the help of both Congresswoman Johnson and Ambassador Hull, a flight was booked.

Neither Mohamed nor Salamatu had ever traveled on a plane before, let alone taken a twenty-four-hour journey that involved a complicated network of stopovers in several different countries. From Freetown, they had caught a ferry upriver to an airport in the coastal town of Lungi, where they boarded a flight to Dakar, Senegal, connected to London, switched airports from Heathrow to Gatwick, and boarded the final flight to Newark.

After many hours, security checks, and a rerouting to Boston, Mohamed and Salamatu arrived at Logan Airport jet-lagged and bewildered.

When Pat spotted Salamatu and Mohamed walking out of the gate, her first thought was that they were going to be cold. Thick and sturdy as she was, Salamatu looked like she had picked out her light jean jacket with a balmy night in the Bahamas in mind, not New England. Mohamed was thin and smaller than Pat had expected. He also wore a jean jacket and carried a deflated gray backpack, but nothing else. Autumn had arrived, and they would need coats. In fact, they would need everything.

Over the next few days, friends and neighbors would drop by the Donaldsons' house—Pat's kids had taken the name of their father, David Donaldson—with armfuls of clothes for Mohamed. But he and Salamatu spent that first night at the house of Jael Williams, the Sierra Leonean woman whose family the church had helped to resettle in Farmington years before. The Williamses had been looking forward to the visit for weeks, and Jael made a traditional West African dinner of stew and rice, which she hoped would make her guests feel more at home. Only Jael's home was nothing like Abdulai's. There were three bedrooms, each large enough to fit an entire family from Freetown. At the front door, Jael asked Mohamed to take off his shoes, the black FUBU sneakers that his brother had bought him as a going-away present. When he stepped barefooted onto her white carpet, it felt like sinking into a cloud. Then he saw the TV. In Freetown, Abdulai's TV played only recorded movies. Mohamed had never seen an actual television show. As familiar smells of simmering onions and meat wafted from the kitchen, he watched in amazement as a bucktoothed, square-shaped, yellow cartoon sponge man danced across the screen to a chorus of funny voices.

The church had expected that their guests would experience a fair amount of culture shock, and they were right. Even though he would be spending the rest of his stay at Pat's house, Jael was the first person to show Mohamed how to live like an American. The daughter of a stationmaster in Sierra Leone, she had grown up with privilege, attending Pitman's Secretarial College in London before moving back to Freetown to work as a secretary at Fourah Bay College. During dinner, she cut her meat with a fork and knife, while Mohamed shoveled his with a spoon.

She knew that other modern amenities like toilets and showers, though familiar to her, would be foreign to her guests, who were used to latrines and buckets baths. Anticipating that they might not have packed personal hygiene items, she stocked the bathroom with extra toiletries like toothpaste and lotion.

Jael hadn't anticipated that Mohamed would arrive without a single change of clothes. Less than twenty-four hours after landing, he and Salamatu were supposed to go to church, but Mohamed had nothing suitable to wear. On the way to Sunday service the following morning, Jael drove Salamatu and Mohamed to Walmart, where they bought trousers, shirts, and shoes. They arrived late to church because Jael's car wouldn't start in the parking lot, but at least when they walked in, Mohamed looked sharp. Jael wanted her guests to make a good impression. They weren't just representing Hope Day—they were representing Africa. "Comb your hair," she ordered Mohamed, before he went home with Pat Reville. "Fold your clothes."

In those first few days, when Mohamed didn't like what Pat cooked for dinner, Jael made large batches of *fufu* and a brothy stew, which she stored in the freezer and often brought over to the Donaldsons' house for Mohamed to eat when the rest of the family was having chicken marsala or vegetable pot pie. Other things Mohamed adapted to himself. In the village, he had grown up eating with his hands, yet he never asked anyone how to use silverware; he simply watched and learned.

The first night that he spent at the Donaldsons' house was the biggest test. Mohamed's father always said that coming into contact with a dog is *haram*, forbidden. The Prophet Muhammad himself was said to be denied a visit from the angel Gabriel for keeping a house dog, a creature that, in addition to scaring away holy spirits, later became synonymous with uncleanliness. In the case that a dog's hair—or worse, saliva—touched his skin, Mohamed knew that he was supposed to wash and scrub himself on the contaminated spot until he bled. Otherwise, he was told, Allah wouldn't listen to his prayers for as long as he lived on earth and he would be plagued with bad luck until Judgment Day.

As it happened, the Donaldsons had two dogs: giant German shepherds named Theo, after Theo van Gogh, and Pacem, Latin for "peace."

Almost as soon as Mohamed walked through the front door of the white farmhouse, Theo and Pacem jumped on top of him, sniffing and slobbering and licking his hands as he stood motionless, catatonic with fear. Seeing the look of shock on Mohamed's face, Pat held the dogs back, but the damage was done.

Later, when he was alone, Mohamed would inspect his jean jacket for dog hairs, deciding that none had touched his skin. Just in case, he took a shower. To be clean. To be pure again.

Soon after he arrived at Pat's house, Mohamed asked to use the telephone. He needed to call Freetown to let Abdulai know that he had made it safely to Connecticut.

"Brother! I'm in the United States! It's so cool!" Mohamed said excitedly, switching to Krio, when he heard his brother's voice. He told Abdulai that, in America, the streets were full of white people—"*waytman*"—everywhere you turn.

Abdulai put his wife on the line with his little brother. She wanted to know about America, too. What was it like? How were the houses? "Well," Mohamed said, "*den na bod os.*" They were board houses.

"*Bod os?*" she scoffed and told Mohamed to talk true. She had expected better. They had houses made of wooden boards in Freetown. In America, she thought the houses would be built with finer materials, like glass. Mohamed agreed. On the outside, the houses in America were "*wowoh*"—ugly—but they were pretty on the inside, he said.

Mohamed still hadn't completely taken in the Donaldsons' white farmhouse with its latticed, light-green porch overlooking a gingerbread-cottage tree house and blueberry bushes. But his eyes only got wider as he got the full tour. Inside, peach wallpaper decorated the living room, where elephants paraded on a red armchair near a black Steinway upright piano and various string instruments. Electric candles offset either side of a pearly overstuffed sofa and art was everywhere. Over time, Pat had accumulated a collection that covered the walls of nearly every room, including the kitchen, where she kept the big turquoise doggie bowls belonging to Theo and Pacem.

There was so much space, and yet every inch of it was covered with clues to the people, and animals, who lived there. Pat's art books lined the shelves and lay in teetering stacks on coffee tables and ottomans. Her husband displayed his gold trophies for platform tennis and various racquet sports in the TV room, not far from where their son Henry's lacrosse sticks marked an X against the wall. A year and a half younger than Mohamed, Henry had already accumulated more stuff than Mohamed ever could have dreamed of.

Even rooms that had been evacuated by their occupants still kept their things. One of the reasons why Pat decided to host Mohamed in the first place was because she had two spare rooms. She put Mohamed in her daughter Cynthia's bedroom, just down the hall from Henry.

Mohamed would not meet Cynthia, a sophomore at the University of Massachusetts Amherst, but on his very first night at the Donaldsons' house, he moved in with the ghost of her teenage self. Her checkered shirts, piles of Converse and Vans, hoodies in various shades of rain, and two billion vintage T-shirts still filled the closet, its door markered with Shakespearean verse. Her walls, painted sky blue and spangled with silver stars, still bore the proof of high school celebrity crushes. After the door closed and everyone else had gone to bed, Mohamed inspected the magazine cutouts of Jake Gyllenhaal, Sean Penn, and Johnny Depp wearing a white tank top, his bare arms bronzed and tattooed.

On that first night, it bothered Mohamed a little that he was sleeping in a girl's room, but he got over it pretty quickly. Not only did he have a room and a bathroom of his own, he had running water and endless electricity. Abdulai owned a generator in Freetown, but in the village, electricity came only once a week, sometimes once a month. After brushing his teeth, Mohamed got into bed and listened to the sound of the farmhouse shifting its weight in the wind like an old arthritic woman. Other than the creaks and cracks in the walls, it was quiet. Too quiet. Even though the Donaldsons lived in a village of sorts, there was no sawing of cricket legs, like in Motema. No whir of mosquito wings. No little brothers breathing close by. Many hours passed before Mohamed finally dozed off under a ceiling of stars, with the light on. Over at Marilyn Ostreicher's house, Mohamed's chaperone Salamatu slept with the light on, too, but for a very different reason. Salamatu was afraid of the dark. Mohamed was simply, and irreversibly, in love with the light.

One night after dinner, Pat gave Mohamed a spiral notebook and an assignment. "You really should be keeping a journal," she said. Over the next few weeks, he would be meeting a lot of different people and seeing a lot of new places. He should write it all down so that when he was back in Sierra Leone he would remember his time in America. Later that night, Mohamed sat on his bed and wrote his first entry in the notebook, re-creating the day he went with Henry to an elementary school playground in the neighborhood.

> *Henry took me with his bicycle to the children play ground I played with some children and the asked me some question, and the said What is my name, and where do I come from How old I am and the we come home.*

Home. Less than two weeks in, Mohamed was adapting remarkably well to life in Farmington. At the Donaldsons' house, he began to sleep with the lights off and try strange foods, like meat in sliced form called "cold cuts." He discovered that he loved cheeseburgers from McDonald's, but he just wasn't "a grilled-cheese guy," as Pat said. The Donaldsons adapted, too. They started eating white rice with every meal, and once in a while Pat would come home to find Henry and Mohamed at the stove, cooking up a batch themselves, when they weren't wrestling. Even though Mohamed was older by about a year and a half, he was skinny and light. Once, Henry strong-armed Mohamed to the ground and just sat on him until they both laughed.

Mohamed began going to Irving A. Robbins Middle School with Henry later in October. But it was Farmington High School—where Henry's older sister Chloe was a junior—that really caught his eye. The first time he saw the sprawling redbrick building adorned with decorative stone pilasters, he thought it looked like a palace. Wearing Henry's clothes and carrying a peanut-butter-and-Fluff sandwich in his lunch bag, Mohamed watched the boys and girls in tight designer jeans, their social status as clear as the stitching on their back pockets for Citizens of Humanity and True Religion. He was there just long enough to get a feel for school spirit made manifest in shades of maroon and gray, but not long enough to figure out what exactly the teachers and students were saying.

People had a hard time understanding Mohamed, too. Several times when he was talking about his day at school over dinner, Pat had to ask Mohamed to "slow it down." It was amazing how the same language could sound so different depending on who spoke it. Pat's English was refined and elegant. Mohamed's English was muddy at best. If she listened hard, Pat could pick out the words she recognized, but otherwise she would have had better luck tuning into a radio station broadcast from the backwoods of Louisiana. He never betrayed the slightest hint that he was having trouble himself, until one day Pat asked Mohamed point-blank, "Is it difficult for you to understand us?"

"Yes," he whispered.

Mostly, when Mohamed needed someone to talk to, he called his older brother Abdulai, who offered support and advice from the other end of the world. Before Mohamed left for America, Abdulai had explained that Christians and Muslims weren't really so different in their beliefs. "The only difference is that they call their religion Christianity, and we call our religion Islam. But we worship the same God," Abdulai had said. Despite being Muslim, Mohamed started going to church on Sundays. He didn't just attend services, he guest-starred in them, wearing his Hope Day ceremonial uniform, a festive hot-pink shirt with a pine-green vest and matching pants.

The first time he went to church, Mohamed was terrified. Later, he recalled what was running through his head on that Sunday and the many more that followed: *What's going to be the consequences of me going to church every day, if I'm a Muslim? God is going to be really mad at me probably.* At the same time, Mohamed remembered what his brother had said, that Muslims and Christians worshipped the same God, and he wanted to please the members of the congregation. "Since they brought me to the United States," he explained, "I have to follow their rules."

As senior minister, Ned Edwards went to great lengths to make their guests feel at home. There was a visiting preacher from Ghana that first

Sunday, and before he took the lectern, Pastor Edwards publicly welcomed Mohamed and Salamatu to Farmington. "Hello, I am glad to be here," Mohamed said shyly, looking out at the sea of smiling white faces in the pews and the children who had gathered on the floor. Then he and Salamatu led the congregation in a Krio song that the students sang at the Hope Day School in Freetown called "Tenke God."

Within weeks of his arrival, Mohamed became a minor celebrity. Neighbors recognized the charismatic boy who had spoken at church or rung their doorbell on Halloween, wearing a rainbow-colored poncho and sombrero and calling out, "Trick or treat!" In late fall, he and Salamatu visited schools in the area, talking to students of all ages about life in Sierra Leone. Third-graders at the elite Renbrook School in West Hartford wanted to know what kind of food he ate (cassava and rice) and what his house looked like (the one in the village was made of mud bricks). At one of the schools, a boy asked Mohamed if he wore clothes in Sierra Leone, and at the end of October, a reporter from the *New Haven Register* interviewed him and Salamatu for a feature article entitled, "City Schools Welcome African Visitors."

After the article came out, Pat bought Mohamed a Mavis typing program, one of many gifts that Mohamed received from the people of Farmington. Polly Hincks, a white-haired parishioner who zipped around the church in her cherry-red scooter, bought Mohamed his first CD player. Slowly, Cynthia's room filled with Mohamed's things: piles of blue jeans, a pocket-sized digital camera, books, and a brand-new soccer ball. In November, he started showing off his soccer skills for a town team. A bunch of Henry's friends from middle school played on the upper field outside Farmington High and invited Mohamed to kick the ball around at practice, when Henry wasn't around. At home over dinner, Mohamed talked up his game. But at school, Henry heard a different story. One day in the halls, he asked his friends if Mohamed was any good.

"Yeah, he's really good," one of the guys said. "But he's really dirty when he plays."

"That's because he never played on an organized team—he just played with his friends on the streets," Henry said, coloring a little. "There were no real rules."

He defended Mohamed that day. But in the days that followed, Henry noticed that the problem wasn't just on the field. At one point, as Pat recalls, Mohamed told Henry that he never played checkers before. But the first time they played a game, Mohamed won. A few nights later, the same thing happened with backgammon. Henry moped around all night. At first, Pat thought he was just jealous. Mohamed did have a way of stealing the show. She told Henry to get over it and not to be so uptight. Mohamed was just a quick learner.

As time passed, Pat would see it differently: Henry had been hustled.

Sierra Leone was far away, but for Mohamed it never seemed to be far behind. For Salamatu, Sierra Leone was every single moment of her waking life. Months before coming to Farmington, she had buried her son in her yard after he fell ill and died in the backseat of a taxicab. She said nothing about it until a few weeks in. One day when they were out shopping for gifts for her family, Salamatu calmly told Marilyn her story, in between eyeing shoes at Payless and browsing cosmetics in a dollar store in Bristol, Connecticut. Marilyn was bowled over. She didn't know what to do, except encourage Salamatu to call her husband every other night.

One evening Salamatu got off the phone sobbing, tears streaming down her face. Her two best friends had both died in childbirth. The news was shocking, but according to the World Health Organization, in 2005 Sierra Leone had the highest maternal mortality rate in the world. Five years earlier in another report that surveyed 191 countries, Sierra Leone ranked last in "healthy life expectancy," with an average projected life span of less than twenty-six years. Sierra Leone was death. And hunger. Toward mid-November, the Ostreichers began to notice that Salamatu was eating less and less. Marilyn assumed it was grief that cut off her appetite, until Salamatu explained that she was shrinking her stomach to get ready to go home. In Freetown, where she lived on a teacher's salary of $750 a year plus whatever she could earn at the market, she ate only one small meal a day. The rest went to her husband and remaining four children.

The church began preparing, too, to say good-bye. Soon their African guests would be flying back to Freetown. Shortly before Thanksgiving, Marilyn and two other women from the church took Salamatu and Mohamed to Boston for the day. At the Boston Museum of Science, he was mesmerized by a demonstration of the dissection of a fetal pig, an activity that was in conjunction with the traveling Body Worlds exhibit. Afterward, they rode the T to Faneuil Hall Marketplace, where Marilyn offered to buy Mohamed a souvenir. Weaving through the pushcarts selling Beantown trolley tours, airbrush tattoos, and Pillow Pets, she pointed out a stack of T-shirts. He asked for a sweatshirt instead.

"You can't wear a sweatshirt over in Sierra Leone," Marilyn said. "It's too hot!"

But Mohamed persisted, pointing out a plain hoodie.

"Oh, you have to get Red Sox," Marilyn cooed, "We're all for the Red Sox!"

Years later, Marilyn would remember buying Mohamed the plain sweatshirt, anonymous as a passing cloud. Mohamed insists that he actually got a Red Sox sweatshirt. The lenses of memory are cloudy, but they agree on one detail. Before they left, Mohamed picked out a baseball cap in a brown-and-green camouflage print. Marilyn didn't think anything of it at the time.

Back in Connecticut, members of the congregation hosted a farewell ceremony for their African guests, followed by a dinner of turkey and *fufu* in the church's newly built $5.5 million Amistad Hall. A few days before their flight back to Freetown, Salamatu and Mohamed stood for the last time at the lectern in the meetinghouse, the morning sun throwing hexagons of light across the red-velvet pews and smiling white faces, once so foreign, now so familiar. Mohamed shone that day, brighter than ever before, and it wasn't just because of the hot-pink-and-green ceremonial outfit that he wore, despite making huge protests against it earlier that morning. When he spoke, it was with a hubris beyond his fourteen years. In a voice loud and clear, Mohamed announced his plans for the future. He was going to go to college, he said. He was going to become a doctor.

After the astonishment wore off, Pat didn't know whether to laugh or cry. When Mohamed said he wanted to go to college, she knew he meant in the United States. She also knew that was about as likely as Mohamed becoming the president of Sierra Leone. They had talked about both possibilities many nights at Pat's house, with varying degrees of seriousness. Behind closed doors, Marilyn's husband, Gene Ostreicher, offered to pay Mohamed's tuition at Freetown's Fourah Bay College, if he got that far. There were also rumblings in the church about sending Mohamed to a prep school in West Hartford. But the whole purpose of the trip to Farmington had been for Mohamed and Salamatu to return to Freetown and share their experiences of the American school system. Their five weeks were almost up; it was time to go home. "Well," Pat said one evening when she stopped by Mohamed's room, "you'll have to go back to Sierra Leone and apply."

"No," she later recalled him saying. "I'd rather stay."

That day at church, watching Mohamed hold court in his hot-pink-and-green outfit for the last time, Pat realized just how much of a joke this whole plan really was. She had worried from the start about plucking a kid from the depths of poverty in Africa and dropping him into one of the wealthiest zip codes in America. Later, she would compare it to dangling a child over the Yellow Brick Road, giving him directions to the Emerald City, and then taking it all away.

In Search of a New Life

A little more than two years since he told the people of Farmington that his plan was to go to college and become a doctor, Mohamed sits at a blue Formica table in the school cafeteria, straining to hear Livenski's question over the din of screaming voices. It's 11:45 AM on January 20, 2009, and soon, on Capitol Hill, Barack Obama will be sworn in as the forty-fourth president of the United States—an event that hundreds of students and staff have packed into the lunchroom to watch live. Near a bulletin board decorated with a pyramid of the five basic food groups, a projector screen has been wheeled in just for the occasion. The cafeteria ladies are nowhere in sight, but in their place, teachers hand out the special boxed lunches that normally are reserved for field trips. Fourth-period classes have been canceled to make time for Obama's inaugural speech, and in the minutes before he takes the podium, it is hard to tell which is more exciting: the fact that America is about to get its first black president, or that lunch has been extended indefinitely.

"Obama is my husband!" someone screams, banging the tabletop.

"Obama is my father!" another voice counters.

"Hello, I am President Obama," says a mustached Yemeni sophomore in a "Change Has Come" T-shirt, shaking the hands of the other boys at his table.

"Does anyone else smell weed?" Suzannah Taylor asks a cluster of teachers hanging out by the double doors. She sniffs the air. "I think it's coming from the hallway."

As she investigates, Livenski peers into the viewfinder of a small digital video camera that he got on loan from the documentary club and repeats his question. "Yo," he says, zooming in on Mohamed's face. "How do you feel about Obama's inauguration?"

"Well, it's great," Mohamed says, resting his chin in his hand and shifting his jaw back and forth. "He's the first black president. This is historical event, and no one want to miss it."

"Thank you," Livenski says and moves on to the next table. "Yo, how do you feel about Obama's inauguration?"

"It's good, man," says a big-boned junior sporting a black jacket and a gold baseball cap. "Obama, he from Africa! KENYA! He gonna be our president, nigga!"

"This is history, man," another boy cuts in. "Love your mama, that's why you vote for Obama!"

"Obama '08!" shrieks a girl in a purple silk head wrap.

"Dumbass!" her friend scowls. "It's 2009."

"Thank you," Livenski says, and turns the camera on a light-skinned kid eating a beef patty. "Yo, how do you feel about Obama's inauguration?"

"Dude!" Mohamed shouts. "Ask a different question!"

Standing in front of the room, the principal Alexandra Anormaliza taps the mic. "Students! I know you're excited," she says. "I'm excited. This is a great time to be alive, right? But you need to be *silent*." She raises her hand in the air. "The teachers want to hear. I want to hear. You have to be quiet."

After passing the mic to Nedda de Castro, Alexandra walks over to the Mac computer where several teachers and a technology coordinator have been trying to find an Internet connection and failing. For weeks the chancellor of New York City schools, Joel Klein, has been promoting a citywide initiative to stream in live feed of the inauguration via the Internet, and Alexandra took heed. Last night she sent out an email to the entire staff outlining the procedure. Plan A was to watch the inauguration on a screen in the cafeteria. In case there were any technical difficulties, Plan B was to relocate to the fourth-floor hallway and project the footage onto a wall. That was before the system crashed altogether. "I think we have a one-in-three chance of this happening," Ann Parry tells a disgruntled group of teachers who have been watching the technical meltdown and checking their cell phones for the time. "This sucks."

In fact, there is a Plan C: to go to the auditorium. A little before noon, all of the floor seats have been claimed by students from the three other schools inside the Prospect Heights Campus, but at the eleventh hour, approximately four hundred more bodies are herded into the balcony, overlooking a giant screen bordered by two dusty-red drapes. There are just enough rows there for the kids, and a few teachers sit on the steps, their eyes glassy before the address even begins. When Obama's face appears on the screen, the entire room explodes with cheers and whistles and more than a thousand voices chanting, "Oba-MA! Oba-MA! Oba-MA!"

When he puts his hand on the Bible and says, "I, Barack Hussein Obama," a group of Yemeni boys sitting in the balcony chant his name again. Moments before in the cafeteria, Yasmeen had been running around snapping pictures of her advisory with a digital camera to commemorate the day, but in the auditorium she sits alone, watching the screen intently. "We are a nation of Christians and Muslims, Jews and Hindus, and nonbelievers," Obama's voice echoes throughout the auditorium. "We are shaped by every language and culture, drawn from every end of this Earth."

Behind Yasmeen, Chit Su stares at the screen, her eyes following the tear-streaked faces of spectators in red earmuffs and fur coats, hoodies, cowboy hats and Tuskegee Airmen caps as if they were characters in a silent film. A few rows ahead, a group of African boys erupt in a burst of Fula when the broadcast pans to a scene of barefoot revelers dancing and waving American flags in the dusty village of Kogelo, Kenya, where Obama's father grew up.

As applause ripples through the auditorium and the crowd of millions that has gathered around Capitol Hill, Mohamed listens as Obama reminds the world that America is a nation built by risk takers and doers—and by generations of immigrants. "For us," Obama says, shaking his fist, "they packed up their few worldly possessions and traveled across oceans in search of a new life."

Obama didn't mention the risk takers and doers who pack nothing; who show up out of nowhere; who seem to belong to no one. Their stories aren't often heard, at least not in presidential addresses. But about a week later at The Door, the nonprofit organization that provides youth with legal and immigration services, Mohamed takes the first major step toward applying for Special Immigrant Juvenile Status: writing his affidavit.

"Your affidavit is your story," says the social worker whose job it is to interview the details out of Mohamed this afternoon, the first of two sessions it will take to complete the task. She sits in an office decorated with pictures of Che Guevara and Frida Kahlo, and a book called *Slavery in New York* rests on her desk. Wearing a yellow ski hat and blue trousers, Mohamed's advisor, Mike Incze, is also in the room, while Cindy talks to the lawyer in another room.

In order to apply for a green card this way, the social worker explains, a child must be deemed unable to return to one or both parents due to abuse, abandonment, or neglect. "You know 'neglect'?" she asks.

"Yeah," Mohamed says, still wearing his black-and-olive North Face jacket from the brisk walk over. "Not care about."

"And that's by the standards of *this country*," she adds. "Your parents aren't financially supporting you? What about emotionally?"

Mohamed shakes his head. Later, when the lawyer asks how to spell his mother's name, he doesn't mention that she is illiterate or that he had been the one to show her how to write R-a-m-a-t-o-l-a-i on a small slate board. He doesn't know her address, because she doesn't have one. She still lives in a mud-brick hut in the Remote Village Where He Is From.

Holding Mike's red bicycle helmet in his lap, Mohamed simply tells his story, the same one he has been telling for years. He talks about going to school in Freetown and winning a trip to the United States to live with a group of "Catholic people" from "Something Christ Church." Though the social worker asks for more information, no one challenges his story about getting separated from members of the group, whom he refers to as his "teachers," at the Empire State Building in November of 2006. Nor do they counter his claim that he first met his African roommates, who he has said sell DVDs and sneakers on the street, while "roaming around the Empire State Building" the same night. After recognizing the men to be Sierra Leonean, Mohamed has said that he introduced himself in Krio, and explained that he had gotten lost from his group and didn't have their phone number. "The place was getting dark, so they decided to take me home with them," he says.

Mike has heard parts of Mohamed's story before. But toward the end of the interview, he notices a discrepancy among the dates. "Wait," he says, after it comes up that Mohamed's sixteenth birthday is just a few weeks away. "Weren't you born in 1992?"

"Yes," Mohamed says.

"Then you're going to be seventeen."

"I'm seventeen?" Mohamed bellows, his voice echoing down the halls. "I can't believe it!" (In Sierra Leone, Mohamed never once celebrated his birthday, he would explain later: " 'Happy Birthday' doesn't exist in our language. My mom doesn't even know when she was born.")

In a matter of minutes, Mohamed has aged a year and gained a new potential guardian. Shortly before he leaves the social worker's office with Cindy, they all agree on a plan. Applying for Special Immigrant Juvenile Status is just the first step of what could be a long and winding path toward citizenship, in the best-case scenario. But the sooner he moves in with Cindy, the better it would look in Family Court once they begin the proceedings. With that in mind, Cindy sets the move-in date for February 4, about two-and-a-half weeks before Mohamed's seventeenth birthday. There is just one problem: He hasn't told anyone yet—not his mother, brother, or his roommates. "I'm scared," he admits. "It's going to be very hard for me, going up against four guys. They might not let me go."

For most of the interview, Mike has sat silently in the corner with clasped hands. But when Mohamed leaves the room for a minute, he gives the social worker some unsolicited advice.

"He is a bit of a storyteller," Mike says. "I would press him to give thorough answers to those questions because what he says is conflicting."

As Mohamed and Salamatu's departure date approached, the church's task force had been trying to think of fun things to do with them before they left. Polly Hincks, the widow in the red electric scooter, suggested that they go to New York City. Back when she was an art student at the Parsons School of Design in the late 1940s, Polly had worked at *Harper's Bazaar* and lived in Manhattan. To her, there was no more exciting place in the world. In the days before the outing, she talked up the city whenever she saw Mohamed or Salamatu. They would go to the top of the Empire State Building, which Mohamed had seen in the movies, and drive down Broadway at night to see all the theater lights. Along with Pat, she made plans to pick up Mohamed and Salamatu one morning in mid-November—just a couple of days before their flight back to Freetown—so that they could spend the whole day in the city and still get home in time to pack.

Polly had shown up at the church in her dark-blue Ford Windstar minivan at 8:45 AM sharp. Diagnosed with polio when she was pregnant with her second child, Polly had a leg brace and a lot of moxie. Her van had a special lift in the back for loading her Jazzy Scooter, red and shiny as a candy apple. Mohamed usually loved anything with wheels, but the morning of the trip, he seemed a little quiet. It was raining out, which was disappointing. Polly hoped the heavy clouds wouldn't put a damper on their trip.

Mohamed had seen New York in the movies, but in real life it was even more like a dream. Through the foggy windows of Polly's van, he and Salamatu watched a succession of small towns and suburbs whir past, each similar to the last, until gradually the blur of trees along the Merritt Parkway gave way to traffic jams and exit signs for the George Washington Bridge. Polly wanted to drive down the West Side of Manhattan because it had the best views of the Hudson River.

Around Thirty-sixth Street, Polly found a spot in a parking garage, and, with Mohamed's help, unloaded her scooter from the back of the Windstar as Pat and Salamatu walked ahead. It was only a short distance to the Empire State Building, but in the blocks around the parking garage and the world's tallest skyscraper, the beginnings of a small pan-African nation shifted into view. Years later, Mohamed says that he doesn't remember much about the surrounding area, only that, for the first time since he left Africa, he saw "a lot of black people." On corners and side streets near Herald Square, men from Guinea, Senegal, Burkina Faso, South Africa, Zimbabwe, and Sierra Leone had set up shop on rickety metal tables, piled high with handbags, baseball caps, belts, wallets, backpacks, cell-phone holsters, flash drives, and USB cables. Everything was for sale, and everyone was a salesman. Strains of French, Fula, Krio, and Wolof wafted down the sidewalk, but when it came to dealing with customers, the men spoke a common language.

"CD's? Perfume? Sneakers?"

"Let's go, let's go, let's go! Ten dollars on the bags, ladies! Ten dollars!"

"You lookin' to do some shopping, Ma? Follow me."

Shifty-eyed and standing in the doorways of old office buildings, young men invited tourists up flights of stairs to dingy rooms filled with faux designer sunglasses, Louis Vuitton purses, and bootleg DVDs. Hidden under dashikis and crocheted prayer caps, North Face jackets and G-Unit sweatshirts, they stood in clumps, smoking cigarettes, eating halal, jabbering on Bluetooth headsets, and pushing knockoffs onto potential customers.

The next time Polly turned around on Thirty-fourth Street, Mohamed was gone. Her heart froze. Then she saw him about fifteen feet behind. *Poor thing*, she thought. He was just standing there, completely dazed, and no wonder, with all the crowds and buildings and honking horns. She briefly considered holding his hand the rest of the way. "Mohamed!" she said sternly, motioning toward her scooter. "Come up here! Look at all these people! I don't want to lose you."

Pat and Salamatu were already at the entrance to the Empire State Building. From the sidewalk, it looked like an infinite slab of granite disappearing into an infinite sky. One push through the revolving glass doors, and the chaos of the street disappeared. Instead of honking yellow cabs, there was the din of awe in dozens of different languages, tourists taking in the art deco lobby with its marbled floors, golden-hued walls, and brilliant medallion of the Eighth Wonder of the World silhouetted against a shining sun. Even the janitors mopping the lobby wore bow ties.

Neither Salamatu nor Mohamed had ever been on an elevator before, much less an express elevator that reached the eighty-sixth floor in the span of a minute. The trip up to the second floor was enough for Salamatu, who refused to see *NY Skyride*, an IMAX-style attraction simulating a turbulent helicopter flight over New York City. She waited in the lobby while Mohamed went with Pat and Polly. Pat had bought the $20 tickets thinking that Mohamed would love the ride, but when they "landed" back in the black-box theater and the lights came on, he seemed a little shaken up.

"What'd you think?" Pat asked Mohamed as they walked out. "Was that fun?"

"Yeah," he mumbled. "It was great."

As Pat, Polly, and Salamatu followed the throngs of tourists headed up to the observatory on the eighty-sixth floor, Mohamed grew even quieter. Pat had expected more of a reaction and wondered if he was overwhelmed. The elevators, the crowds, the heights—it was all so new, so vast. Polly thought he was disappointed. On the promenade, the fog was so thick they wouldn't have been able to see two feet ahead if they had ventured outside. On a clear day, she would have pointed out all of the important landmarks—the Statue of Liberty, Ellis Island—but they saw none of that. In the time since they had parked the car, a heavy mist had settled over Manhattan, as if a watercolorist in a deep Ambien haze had painted the world's most famous skyline. Here and there, a cloud shifted to reveal rooftops in daubs of rust and gray, a glimmer of a golden dome, a smear of yellow suggesting a cab, before another cloud came and blotted it all away.

Earlier that morning, Pat had reminded Mohamed to bring his camera, but he had left it in Polly's car, which was just as well. There was nothing to see. Digging his hands into the pockets of his hoodie, he took one last look at the view: an entire city wrapped in fog, hunching its shoulders against the coming rain.

Polly wanted to drive around the theater district at dusk when it would be lit up, but it was still afternoon and they had some time to kill before it got dark. So they decided to get lunch. Pat suggested Macy's, only a few blocks away. The food options were a little inglorious, but at least Polly wouldn't have a problem with stairs, and they could hang out as long as they needed to if it rained. Near the entrance, the window displays were already up for Christmas: scenes inspired by *Miracle on 34th Street*.

Inside Macy's, Pat led the way down a wide crimson carpet as Polly, Salamatu, and Mohamed followed close behind. From Handbags, they walked through Jewelry, passing chandelier earrings and pearl chokers in gleaming cases, to the brightly lit galleria of Cosmetics and Fragrances. The scent of Chanel No. 5 lasted all the way to the elevator bank.

Au Bon Pain was on the eighth floor. Polly zipped into the first elevator. On the second floor the doors opened, and more shoppers squeezed in, causing Pat and Polly to exchange a concerned look on Salamatu's behalf. On eight, they got out and headed for the café.

Almost two years later, Polly doesn't remember what she or anyone else ate that day or what they talked about. She just remembers that, at a certain point, Pat and Salamatu excused themselves to go to the ladies' room, and a few minutes after they left the table, Mohamed put down his dessert and said, "I think I should go to the men's room now."

What a cutie, Polly thought. He sounded so formal and grown-up. Getting there was a little complicated, she explained. From the restaurant, the closest elevator bank was around the corner near women's coats, and the closest men's room was a full floor below. "Go down to the seventh floor," she told Mohamed, "and ask." From her scooter, Polly watched Mohamed head toward the elevators, his dark-blue hoodie bobbing through the crowd.

He never came back.

*   *   *

The day Mohamed disappeared, the sky broke over Manhattan. For days, a system had been brewing up and down the East Coast, unleashing stiff winds and downpours from the Carolinas to Ontario. By the time night fell in New York, the storm had arrived. The sky was graphite with streaks of white, as if someone had tried to erase it. Lightning cracked like a ruler over the hand of a punished child, and rain pounded the windshield of Polly's Ford Windstar until Pat's vision was as blurred as the taillights of the cars ahead of her on the West Side Highway.

Polly wasn't fit to drive. Sitting in the passenger seat in clothes soaked through from the rain, she slowly came undone. She tried to stop all of the horrible thoughts, but they spewed out anyway. She was convinced that Mohamed had been abducted by a child molester. New York was full of sleazeballs, and he was such a lovely-looking young boy. He must have gotten lost on the way from the bathroom, and he just asked the wrong person. "Goddamnit!" Polly wailed. "Why did I tell him to ask?"

"Polly, calm down," Pat said, keeping her eyes on the road. "Child molesters don't go shopping for children at Macy's. I just don't think that's a phenomenon." Once in a while she glanced in the rearview mirror. In the backseat, where Mohamed had sat only hours before, Salamatu had curled herself up into a ball, silent and still.

Over the course of their nearly three-hour drive back to Farmington, Pat and Polly went through every possible scenario, playing the events of the day over and over again in their minds like a horror film on a shoddy projector. To this day, no one is quite sure what Mohamed was wearing that afternoon. Polly remembers a sweatshirt with a Red Sox logo. "You don't see too many black kids in Red Sox sweatshirts, especially in Yankees country," she would observe. But that directly contradicts Marilyn's recollection of the afternoon she took Mohamed shopping in Boston, and he opted for the camouflage cap and the plain hoodie. It dawned on her later, she said. "Every boy who wants to hide himself puts a hood up, right?"

It is impossible to splice together so many flawed flashbacks without creating an equally glitchy story, but one memory remains unchallenged.

Years later, Polly would tell Henry Donaldson that his mother was "the strong one." Calling her husband from the security office, it was Pat who first uttered the words aloud: "Mohamed's gone." When Pat and Salamatu returned from the restroom, they waited at Au Bon Pain for ten minutes before Polly checked her watch. "Where's Mohamed?" she asked.

Fifteen minutes passed, then twenty. The other people they had come into the café with were clearing their trays. After half an hour, Pat talked to a salesperson who alerted security. At first they were told, "He'll come back." Almost an hour went by before they were rerouted to the security office on the 1½ Floor. Walking there, Pat felt she was entering another dimension, some liminal world beyond time and space. Floor 1½? Seriously? It sounded like Platform 9¾, the secret portal in *Harry Potter* that magically appears when students need to catch the Hogwarts Express. In fact, the security office was just past Hosiery, with its severed hips in nude stockings and Technicolor can-can of disembodied dummy legs. Pat officially reported Mohamed to the Lost & Found department.

About two hours after Mohamed had disappeared, Macy's began to take the case more seriously, and a radio message went out to the walkie-talkies of the store's nearly two hundred security guards. They were put on alert for a black teenage boy wearing a Red Sox sweatshirt, hat, or T-shirt. Polly couldn't remember for sure, but a couple of hours later when the police showed up, they received a similar description. Most of the security guards were detached at best, but there was one guy, Polly recalls, a young black officer, who seemed genuinely concerned. "I'm sorry," he said again and again. "I'm so sorry."

A little after 3 PM, Pat left Polly and Salamatu behind in one of the interrogation rooms of the security office to go with a Macy's store detective and look for Mohamed. The more Pat walked under the acres of fluorescent lights and exit signs stretching out one after the other, the stronger she felt that Mohamed was definitely *not* in the store. But the detective persisted.

"Kids," he said with a wink, "they love electronics. Maybe he just wanted an iPod."

A few minutes later, the detective was ogling plasma TVs and Play-Station games at J&R Express in The Cellar.

"Maybe he's up in Bedding," he suggested next. "You know, in Africa, they don't have good beds. He probably went to sleep."

On the sixth floor, as Pat followed the detective past phony bedroom displays, her soles suddenly ached. Hours had passed. Every second was a fissure, every minute another chasm separating her from Mohamed. Pat checked her watch for the thousandth time. *How do you know when to stop looking?* she asked herself.

It was around 7 PM—several hours after Mohamed went to the bath-room—when Pat finally collected Polly and Salamatu from the interro-gation room and left Macy's. At one point Polly had called her oldest son, a psychotherapist who lived in Northampton, Massachusetts, and he was concerned enough to call his younger brother and drive the distance to Farmington. When Polly got home at 10:30 and saw her sons waiting for her with a glass of bourbon and some food, she burst into tears.

Pat's son was waiting up for her, too. "I should have told you, Mom," Henry said, his face hardening. "I never trusted him."

Salamatu boarded a plane to Freetown approximately forty-eight hours later, just as scheduled. But in the fraught days and nights after Mo-hamed's disappearance, the Sierra Leone Task Force continued their search in Farmington, following an emergency committee meeting at Polly Hincks's house, just uphill from the church.

Led by the senior minister Ned Edwards, they reached out to the State Department and the American Embassy. They left no stone unturned, contacting the National Center for Missing & Exploited Children, send-ing out All Points Bulletins, and involving the Farmington police after the NYPD claimed that the case was out of their jurisdiction. Later, as Pat Reville recalls, the Farmington department made the same claim. On the other side of the world in Freetown, Strasser-King contacted Mohamed's parents and older brother Abdulai, who seemed surprised at the news of Mohamed's disappearance. At one point Pat called a friend of a friend who happened to be a former deputy director of Homeland Security. After explaining how Mohamed had escaped their oversight, she braced herself to pose the question that had been dogging her since

Friday. "Is Mohamed going to have to live the rest of his life as a fugitive?" she asked. He simply laughed and said, "His life is going to be so much better than it ever was."

Around the second day, they got a break after Pat's husband got hold of some phone records. Over the course of his stay, Mohamed had made numerous calls; not just at Pat's house, but at the residence of Marilyn Ostreicher, who participated in the hunt for Mohamed all the way from St. Louis, where she had planned to celebrate Thanksgiving with her family. Strangely, on Marilyn's phone bill, there was an area code listed for Washington, D.C.

For the first few hours after getting the call that Mohamed had vanished, Jael Williams, like Polly, thought he had been abducted. But gradually a new theory emerged. Before boarding the flight back to Freetown, Salamatu was the first person to say it out loud: "I think he ran away," she told Jael through her tears. The more Jael thought about it, the more obvious it seemed. She remembered a day not long before the trip to Macy's, when Mohamed and Salamatu had eaten dinner over at her house. "You'd better get used to this again," Salamatu had said, washing their dishes by hand, even though Jael owned a dishwasher.

"I'm not going back to this again," Jael later recalled Mohamed saying in response. Jael remembered another conversation that her brother, Professor Victor Strasser-King, had shared with her. Early on, before Mohamed was officially selected to go to Farmington, there had been some concern about his religion. The First Church of Christ was open to the idea of hosting a Muslim boy, but Mohamed's older brother had seemed overeager.

Looking back, the clues seemed to be there. Jael was determined to find Mohamed, if it meant watching every last minute of Macy's surveillance videos. Instead, she recruited her son Henderson, who had grown up in Freetown and spoke Krio, to follow up on the phone records that Pat's husband had gotten from the police.

To this day, Pat and Marilyn remember Henderson's involvement as a moment of levity during a terrible trial. It was like watching an episode of *CSI*. Within minutes of receiving the records, Henderson was retracing the calls Mohamed had made, dialing random numbers and chatting up whoever happened to answer the phone as if they were old friends. Within hours, Henderson had learned that Mohamed was staying in Brooklyn. At a certain point they were also told that he would be headed toward Washington, D.C., and they even got an address.

Within weeks, the Sierra Leone Task Force had serious grounds to suspect that Mohamed had run away, but no proof. Even if they had proof, then what? If they found Mohamed, would they support him, or report him? The church was divided. Consumed with shame and anger, Jael was dead set on sending him back to Sierra Leone, while Gene Ostreicher, Marilyn's husband, privately told Pastor Edwards that he would fully support Mohamed's decision to stay in the United States, legally or illegally. Another congregant complained that the church wasn't doing enough to locate Mohamed and posed the question of whether they would be acting with more urgency if he had been a teenager visiting from California rather than Sierra Leone.

Meanwhile, the clock was ticking. In the final hours before taking an official position as a church, Pastor Edwards led the committee in a recitation of a verse from the hymn, "O Come O Come, Emmanuel," a request for guidance.

A few days later, Pastor Edwards posted a letter in the mail to the address in Washington, D.C., explaining Mohamed's relationship to the church and their concern for his well-being. "We are not looking to locate or identify Mohamed or anyone else. We merely want to confirm that he is safe, and we would be most grateful for this assurance," he had written in all capital letters, before concluding: "If this is not something you can assure us, I would ask you to please pass this letter on to someone who can."

Ned Edwards never got a response to his letter. When it came to Mohamed Bah, there seemed to be a lack of answers—just endless questions. *Who knew?* Pat asked herself. *Who knew this little person would be that brave?* Sometimes, it felt as if he had never existed. He didn't die, but the church mourned his loss. Pat called it "a little death." Other times, reminders of the radiant fourteen-year-old boy who had walked in and out of their lives without so much as a glance backward were too painful to bear.

After Mohamed vanished, Pat boxed up his clothes and books to send to the children at the Hope Day School in Freetown. Cynthia was coming home from UMass for Thanksgiving and would be reclaiming her room. In the days before her daughter's return, Pat got rid of as much as she could, but a few traces still linger to this day: Mohamed's handwriting on the pages of his journal, the Colorado Rockies jacket that he used to wear, hanging in the basement. Once in a while, when she's looking for a greeting card among the stack of old photos and mail that she keeps in the kitchen drawer, Pat comes up against a single snapshot of Mohamed playing on the front lawn with Theo, who died not long after the picture was taken—a double heart clench. Her reaction is always the same. She smiles back at Mohamed, remembering how scared he was of the dogs at first. Her hand slides to the back of her neck, and she has to look away. It still stings. She felt the same wince of sadness after her father passed away, going through his things. She chastises herself for not having put the photo away a long time ago.

Then, for the millionth time, she asks herself: "But where does it go?" It doesn't belong in any of the family albums, but it doesn't belong in the trash, either. So, she keeps it in the drawer for now. It is a bookmark in the narrative that she has since created for herself, the story of "What Happened to Mohamed Bah." Unlike Polly, Pat never thought that he was kidnapped at Macy's. She remembers all the times he asked to use the phone, and then she thinks of all the times that he didn't ask. She imagines Mohamed coming home from school and hiding in the bedroom to make his calls. He must have been getting reassurances from whoever was on the other end of the line that everything was going to be okay. He didn't just walk off the edge of the world that day. There had to have been someone waiting on the other side.

Negotiating

In a school of English-language learners, a lot can be lost in translation. Sex education is one subject that gets everyone's attention, especially when it is taught by today's guest, a young black public health advisor with a stash of free condoms and a shock jock's supply of dirty jokes. Wearing a red hoodie and a five o'clock shadow, he is visiting International from a city program that dispatches counselors to public high schools to talk to students about sex and its consequences.

Having eaten lunch, Ann, Vadim, and about forty of their students are gathered in the school library to learn about sexually transmitted diseases, their sweaty bodies adding a sharp, glandular tinge to the dry-rot smell of old pencil shavings and paperbacks. Half of the senior class already attended an earlier presentation before lunch, but the room is still packed and buzzing. As the counselor sets up a laptop and projector, students thumb through tabloid magazines and copies of the *New York Post*. On the walls, posters for the American Library Association feature celebrities peering into the pages of their favorite books. Spike Lee flips through *The Autobiography of Malcolm X*, not far from where Denzel Washington muses over *Green Eggs and Ham*, under the banner READ. In the window, a typewritten sign reminds students to use "Library Voices Please," a rule that is promptly forgotten as soon as the counselor projects a photograph of a giant black penis onto the screen.

"This," he says as a collective gasp spreads through the room like the Wave at a Yankees game, "is what gonorrhea looks like."

He points out a pearl-sized drop of discharge oozing out of the top of the head. "Please do not pay attention to the color of this man's penis," he says with a perfect poker face. "Gonorrhea does *not* turn your penis black."

Sitting in the front row, Jessica Tan stops writing, her brown eyes a little wider than usual behind her checkered glasses. Beside her, a poster of a nondescript bridge fades alongside an equally nondescript tagline, EDUCATION IS THE BRIDGE BETWEEN INEXPERIENCE AND WISDOM. Behind her, Odanis and Eduardo howl with laughter. "WOOOOOO! Oh, shit!"

At least for the first few minutes of the presentation, Jessica takes copious notes with her aqua mechanical pencil. As the counselor introduces new words like "nut sack," "balls," "scrotal," and "pre-cum," she jots down the important points in her yellow legal pad. She continues to listen attentively when he projects a diagram of a vagina several feet high onto the screen. "This is the female reproduction system," he says, pointing out the ovaries, uterus, and fallopian tubes. "Well, it's not the *actual* size."

Eduardo and Odanis nearly fall out of their seats at that one, but Jessica seems unfazed, at least until the counselor starts talking about all the ways they could contract any number of horrible, pus-producing, rash-spreading, genital-inflaming ailments, if they aren't careful. "It's not really for *us*," she whispers to the Haitian girl sitting next to her, moments after the counselor defines fecal-oral transmission as "doo-doo in the mouth," to the delight of a few dozen teenagers and the horror of their teachers. "Most of us aren't sexually active yet."

Actually, most of Jessica's classmates would probably disagree with her. The past twenty minutes have been illuminating, and not just in terms of teaching the kids the best prevention tips against contracting gonorrhea, chlamydia, and herpes. (Tip #1: Abstinence. "If you don't have sex, you can't get an STI!") Whether they wanted to or not, everybody in the room now has a much clearer view of who is having sex, who's not, and who wishes they were. Some information was already common knowledge. Anyone who has ever attended a school dance in the cafeteria knows that the Dominican boys don't lack for female company. "Oh, my God—I don't even do that in my own bedroom!" one office administrator screamed at the holiday dance, her mouth agape as she watched two sweaty Haitian girls grind on two smiling Dominican boys as they lay on their backs on the dirty linoleum floor. That "dance" is so popular at school functions that the staff came up with a name for it: Body Rocking. "We call ourselves the Body Rocking Police," another administrator said. "Basically, it's like sex on the dance floor. It's like, 'Guys, we don't want any babies tonight. Keep it easy.'"

It's also common knowledge that many of the Muslim girls have never held a boy's hand, let alone seen a diagram of male genitalia. After attending the first presentation a couple of hours earlier, Yasmeen was scandalized. "They showed male parts and female parts with boys and girls in the same room!" she said, standing in line for lunch. "If I knew, I wouldn't have gone." Until today, she has managed to skip out on every sex ed class in four years, citing religious reasons.

Glancing at the clock, the counselor clicks on the mouse and gives the class a few minutes to read a bullet-point list of commonly held myths about safe sex—everything from pulling out to having sex in a pool to wearing two condoms.

"Anybody know what 'pulling out' means?" he asks over the tittering.

"Yeah," says Daisy Dessources, a prim-looking Haitian with deep dimples and a crown of curls. "Putting it in and pulling it out."

Leaning against one of the low wooden bookshelves, Ann drops her head into her hands as the room explodes in laughter.

"Okaaay . . . anyone else?" the counselor asks. "Maybe be a little more specific?"

"Oh, I know!"

Thirty-nine heads turn to see Dinice Liu, blushing in the back row. "Um, is it when a boy and a girl is having sex and the boy thinks he's going to cum, so he pulls out?"

"Yes, exactly," the counselor says. "Pulling out doesn't work."

"It doesn't?" Daisy asks.

"No, and who knows why two condoms doesn't work?"

Sitting with her chin in her hand, a petite Bangladeshi girl in a lime-green sari frowns thoughtfully. "I have no idea," someone else sighs. A few rows up, Owen Zhu twists the flash drive on a cord around his neck and narrows his eyes behind silver, wire-rim glasses.

"Because friction fawce?" he mumbles to himself, his eyebrows raising in question like furry black parentheses.

"That's right, Owen," Ann coaches from the sidelines. "Speak up!"

Adjusting his glasses, he smiles to reveal a mouthful of metal braces, and stands.

"FRICTION FAWCE!" he shouts, spraying a few threads of saliva and winning a spattering of applause from his teachers.

"Yeah, Owen!"

In the remaining minutes of the period, the counselor opens up the floor for questions about sex and STIs. A dark-skinned Haitian girl raises her hand. "What happens if a male has really big testes?" she asks, biting down a smile. "But, like, really *really* big?"

"Well," the counselor says, "maybe they just have really big testes, or maybe it's elephantiasis, but it doesn't mean that they have a sexually transmitted disease."

The girl nods. But when the class is over, she turns to Jessica and tells her how they diagnose elephantiasis in her country, where the parasitic disease that is medically known as lymphatic filariasis infects a sizable percentage of the population in different ways and is commonly believed to be the result of a voodoo curse.

"In Haiti, we burn the feathers of a rooster," the girl says, crossing her arms. "If it hurts the boy, *then* we know."

A few minutes before the seniors are dismissed from the library, the counselor passes out brown paper bags packed with supplies for confidential STD testing. "Here are your cupcakes, Slim Jims . . . no, really, this is the important part. This is a pee cup," he says, holding up a plastic cup the size of a shot glass. "We're offering you the opportunity to take a test that you don't even have to study for! We're testing for chlamydia and gonorrhea. All we need is one ounce of urine. A half a cup is okay. We don't need a whole cup," he adds, pretending to hand off an overflowing plastic cup. "Guys, do not come out of the stall and say, 'Hey, mister!'"

"Hey, mister!" a group of spiky-haired Chinese boys repeats, cracking up as they pretend to hand off their overflowing cups to one another with wobbly hands.

"If you need free condoms," the counselor says as the kids walk out the door, "talk to your school nurse—or if you can't find any condoms, come on down to my clinic with your backpack and fill 'er up!"

In the lounge outside the social workers' offices on the fourth floor, there are stacks of safe-sex pamphlets and brochures that are there for the taking. They have titles like "Safer Sex Better Too" and "Abstinence & Self-Esteem," and feature soft-focus photographs of multicultural faces with expressions of beatific awareness, simultaneously evoking United Colors of Benetton ads and promotional literature for the Latter-day Saints. "It's cool to take charge to protect yourself and your partner," reads one brochure picturing a guy with a white tank top and a pocketful of condoms on the cover. "Knowing how to be sexy with a condom can spell Romance with a capital R."

Cheesy as the graphics are, these packets provide good information, but other questions about sex are much harder to answer. Already a complicated issue in any high school, sex is even more complex at International, where the students represent a confluence of ideas, superstitions, and traditions from around the world, and often have to negotiate for themselves what it means to be "normal." No one ever authored a pamphlet for the West African girls who were circumcised before they got their first periods. Nor has anyone written a primer called "Cousins Marrying Cousins," but that's exactly what is on Yasmeen's mind. In Yemen, it is not uncommon for first cousins to marry each other, and the tradition has traveled thousands of miles to the United States, where the exact terms of such a union are being negotiated for Yasmeen by the beginning of the New Year.

One day, Yasmeen stopped by Dariana Castro's office on the fourth floor to break the big news. "I have to tell you something," she said, taking Dariana's hand in hers. "I'm engaged."

"What?! I thought you didn't want to get married!" Dariana gasped. "What are you doing? Do you know him?" Yasmeen explained that, over Christmas break, her aunt made the proposal on behalf of her son, Yasmeen's first cousin, Saif, who was working as a grocer in California after dropping out of school. If she accepted, he would move to New York to take care of Yasmeen and her siblings, and they wouldn't have to return to Yemen.

That day in Dariana's office, Yasmeen tried to seem at ease with the decision—after all, it had been made—but she also had her doubts, and questions. "Why do people think it's so weird?" she asked. Before she left, Yasmeen and Dariana googled "cousins marrying cousins." One of the results that came up was an article by the sex columnist Dan Savage that put to rest some fears. They found out that it's not illegal in most states for first cousins to marry, and it's not uncommon, either. In the U.S., twenty-six states allow first cousins to marry, and worldwide first cousins make up an estimated 20 percent of all couples. In other words, Dariana said dubiously, "There's nothing 'wrong' with marrying your first cousin."

Since that afternoon, Yasmeen has started visiting Dariana almost every day during lunch. The window from 11:00 to 11:35 is a busy time for Dariana, whose office becomes a waystation for teachers who want to use her microwave to heat up their leftovers and students who just want to chat. There are a million distractions a day, but as long as there is an empty seat, it belongs to Yasmeen. Minutes after she sits down this morning to talk about her senior internship, Dariana has to interrupt her to deal with a Tibetan freshman, a smiley girl dressed head to toe in Pepto-Bismol pink, who has come to inquire about joining the school's cleaning squad.

"So," Dariana asks the Tibetan girl, "you want to clean the cafeteria?"

"No, the bathroom," the girl says, and mimes a gushing stream from the general area of her hips. "Many girls have menstruation, and they leave—"

"No!" Dariana interrupts, putting up her hand. She uses the staff restroom, which requires a separate key, but everyone knows the state of the girls' bathroom. Despite daily upkeep, the floors often end up covered in bloody maxi pads, balled up tissue paper, and tumbleweeds of hair weave.

"You can't do that!" Dariana says. "You can't pick up—no, no, no. You can't clean the girls' bathroom."

"But"—the Tibetan girl protests, her eyes blinking rapidly—"in India, I clean my school, I clean the bathroom. It's my behavior!"

"You *can't* clean the girls' bathroom," Dariana says again, this time more firmly. "You can join the cleaning squad and clean the cafeteria. You'll get community-service credit." As an afterthought, she adds, "and gloves."

After the girl leaves, Dariana exchanges a look with Yasmeen, who has been silently listening to the whole exchange with cocked eyebrows and a curled smile. Only at International would a student beg to be a bathroom janitor. "Maybe she just wants to take care of her school, and she doesn't like to see it dirty," Yasmeen says. "Maybe she feels lucky to be here."

Dariana removes her glasses and squeezes the bridge of her nose. Months after Harold helped her organize various folders into a small metropolis of black plastic crates labeled, "To Be Filed," nothing has been filed. On a corkboard, her "To Do" list from September has many items that have yet to be done. Finding internships for the seniors is number one—not talking a kid out of doing volunteer bathroom duty.

Ann Parry describes Dariana as the person who provides everything that the students will remember about high school. Every year she organizes after-school clubs, student government, field trips, and food festivals. She is the one who makes donated dresses and suits materialize out of thin air for prom, and who decorates the auditorium stage with roses for graduation day. "She's probably the most underappreciated member of our staff in terms of the number of hours she puts in and the amount of vacation she gets," Ann says. "She does this job solely because she loves working with these kids. But she also knows exactly what they're going through. She came to this country and learned English perfectly, and she's really the success story of our school. The kids look at her and say, 'This is the person I could be like.'"

Fifteen years since she left the Dominican Republic at the age of ten to immigrate to Brooklyn, where her mother owns a hair salon, Dariana is enough of an outsider to relate to the students, but enough of an insider to dispense important, real-world advice about life after high school. And at least at the beginning of the spring semester, nothing seems to be more crucial to Dariana than helping the seniors think about their career goals. Pajama Day is cute, but they can live without it. Internships are crucial: valuable opportunities for her kids, many for whom the term "work experience" has meant washing dishes, cleaning other people's homes, or painting nails, until now. "It's easy for our kids to get jobs—sometimes it's easier for them than it is for kids of privilege," Dariana says, "but our students' exposure to work is often to jobs where they are exploited. Maybe only five kids get jobs in their field after the program is over, but those five kids aren't going to just work in a Chinese restaurant somewhere in Indiana and sleep at the boss's house. Internships open a door, and chances are they might not otherwise open that door for themselves."

Earlier in the year, Dariana led an internship class during sixth period for a select group of seniors. In one exercise, she took the kids to a reception in honor of Hispanic Heritage Month at Gracie Mansion, where they networked with professionals in their desired fields: everything from engineering to acting. In addition to collecting business cards—which they used to invite their new contacts to Career Night in the cafeteria—the students posed for pictures with Mayor Bloomberg. Another day, they learned about basic interview etiquette. "Does anyone come from a culture where eye contact is not always a good thing?" Dariana asked, prompting a windy explanation from Mukta on when it is appropriate and inappropriate to meet someone's eye in Bangladesh. "Well," Dariana said when Mukta had finished, "when you go on an interview, yes, you give eye contact. It's a cultural thing, and this is what American work culture looks like."

Since then, Dariana has been collecting applications from all of the seniors, who have been answering questions like, "What careers have you been thinking about exploring?" and "What activities do you enjoy most?" All of the responses have been eye opening, and a few have been flat out jarring. Not bothering to proofread his form after hastily filling it out, Freeman wrote that his hobbies include "guitar, raping, basketball, swimming." (He meant "rapping.") After considering a career in fashion, Kalsang decided that she wanted to be an "air hostess," and Dariana has started calling travel agencies on her behalf. Several of the Chinese kids told Dariana that they don't want to end up working at restaurants or nail salons like their parents. In response to a question about why he wanted to have an internship, one boy in particular answered with heartbreaking candor. "I fells like I'm useless," he wrote.

Other kids know exactly what they want. Many students seem to take to heart International's motto, "Opening Doors to the American Dream," unconventional as their American dreams may be. Last year a Chinese senior who worked as a manicurist in his family's salon harbored a dream to become either a pop-and-lock dancer, or the next Dog Whisperer, like Cesar Millan. (Dariana got the boy an internship as a professional dog groomer in Manhattan.)

This year Freeman dreams of becoming an actor/zoologist. Not an actor *or* a zoologist, but an actor-slash-zoologist. At the last minute, Dariana managed to get Freeman and another aspiring thespian, Ngawang, auditions at the famed Stella Adler Studio of Acting in Manhattan, which runs a workshop for teens. The day of the first round of tryouts, Freeman spilled apple juice all over the front of his shirt and Dariana had to come to his rescue with a Tide to Go pen, which she turned into an impromptu lesson on interview preparedness. "This should be your homework," she said, thrusting the stain stick in the air. "Everyone should buy this so if you have an interview, and you get dirty, you can take care of it!"

Unfortunately, the same preparedness didn't extend to Freeman and Ngawang's actual auditions, perhaps the weirdest that the acting instructors at Stella Adler had ever seen. Instead of reciting a monologue from a popular Broadway show or teen movie like the majority of the drama kids who showed up for auditions in starched shirts and black pants, Freeman improvised one on the spot about how hard it is to be in love with two girls at once. "I guess it's hard being a player!" he riffed before the panel, massaging his head as he sat on a black wooden block set up in the audition room. "Can't believe it—*me*, Freeman, sittin' here thinking how I'm going to get two girls? I can get ten girls at a time!"

"Is that an original composition?" the head instructor asked when it was finally over.

"Yes," Freeman said, taking a small bow. "It's my own."

Ngawang's audition was even stranger. Unlike Freeman, he went in with considerable performing experience, gained over the course of many cultural gatherings within the Tibetan community. At such affairs, generally held in ethnic banquet halls in the outer boroughs, Ngawang would entertain his fellow countrymen with pop songs from home, lip-synching to the likes of Kunga, a Tibetan Elvis look-alike who is perhaps best known for his breakout hit, "Lhasa Girl." Ngawang opted for a love ballad that his judges could understand for his audition at Stella Adler. In a true feat of ingenuity, he did a spoken-word performance of "Sorry Seems to Be the Hardest Word," as sung by Elton John and the English boy band Blue. While Ngawang's competitors spent the previous night perfecting their lines, he was perfecting his song's accompanying boy-band moves, as demonstrated by the group in a YouTube music video featuring the clean-shaven singers in black suits around a white grand piano played by Sir Elton John. Sans backup, Ngawang was forced to be the whole band and learn all their lyrics, which he had scrawled onto college-ruled notebook paper, now crumpled from so much handling. "What have I got to *do* to make you *love* me? What have I got to *do* to make you *care*?" he intoned, once in a while interrupting his strange box step to clutch at his heart or stretch his arms up to the heavens. "What do I do when lightning strikes me? And I wake to find that you're not there?" When the instructors were left speechless by the emotive, fist-clenching interpretation, Ngawang performed it again—in Tibetan.

Much to their own amazement, Freeman and Ngawang both got into the Stella Adler acting program. Fortuitous as their experience has been, it is not really a predictor of the obstacles that many students face once they leave the school. No one is more optimistic than Dariana about the charms of the senior class, or more concerned about the challenges that they are up against as new and, in some cases, undocumented immigrants in America. As she sees it, International students must work much harder to be considered equal to their American-born peers. They have to prepare longer, talk louder, and dress sharper. Every last detail counts. Throughout the day, kids walk in and out of Dariana's office to ransack a garbage bag of hand-me-down clothes that she has collected for students to wear on job interviews. When Mukta came in wearing a splashy low-cut blouse before an interview with The Posse Foundation, a scholarship program that links high-achieving students from disadvantaged urban backgrounds with partnering colleges, Dariana literally gave her the pin-striped suit jacket off her back, saying, "We can iron it!"

Yasmeen is further behind than most of her classmates because of her problems at home and her absences from school. Since meeting with her siblings' lawyer, she has been doing a scavenger hunt for family records around the city in preparation for court, a task that has left little time for homework, and no time to think about a career. But today Dariana is determined to find her an internship like everyone else. For Yasmeen, an internship isn't just a gateway to a profession; it is a chance to put her own interests first, for once, and visualize herself as a successful, working woman. At the very least, it will get her out of her apartment for a few extra hours a day. Taking one last bite of a pasta lunch, Dariana slides a pile of papers out of the way so that Yasmeen can join her at the computer.

"So, my darling, let's look at some stuff," Dariana says, patting the chair beside her. "Come sit here." She thumbs through a stack of index cards on her desk and pauses over Yasmeen's. In response to the question about which careers she is interested in exploring, Yasmeen wrote "kidney doctor."

"It's called a nephrologist," Yasmeen says, looking over Dariana's shoulder, "but I didn't know how to spell it."

"Well," Dariana says, "let's look it up! Google is our best friend, isn't it?"

"N-E-P-H-R-O-L-O-G-I-S-T," Dariana reads off the screen, before getting the name of the hospital where Yasmeen wants to intern. "Do you live around there?"

"Yeah, it's not far."

Wasting no time, Dariana makes a phone call to the volunteer office at the hospital, while Yasmeen picks at the hem of her black-and-white checkered skirt. Despite the blast of heat in the office, she is still bundled in her winter clothes. She wears a long black coat over a striped pink col-lared shirt, and her black gym sneakers, which stick out from under her skirt like two wads of tar. Aside from her hands, the only visible part of her is her face, a perfect oval peeking through a pinned brown head scarf, lending her the appearance of a giant Pez dispenser.

Nodding into the receiver, Dariana jots down what Yasmeen will need for her orientation at the hospital: two letters of recommendation, the results of her TB test, and her immunization record. Lately Dariana has been trying to persuade her to consider another internship, one that has nothing to do with hospitals, where she has already spent so much of her time. Yasmeen has expressed curiosity about other fields, including women's rights and education, fields that Dariana thinks might be more suitable to her actual interests than medicine. Yasmeen hasn't mentioned the fact that this hospital is where her father died, or that a nephrologist might have been able to help her mother, who suffered from kidney problems.

"Do you understand anything I wrote here? I'll email it to you, because it's in Dariana handwriting," Dariana says, handing Yasmeen a piece of scrap paper, covered in chicken scratch. "So, did she call?"

"She" is Yasmeen's aunt and future mother-in-law, and for the past few weeks, Dariana has been inquiring about her on almost a daily basis. As far as Dariana can tell, Yasmeen's aunt is helping to arrange the marriage on her son's side, and therefore she has some measure of control over Yasmeen's future. Traditionally, the father is supposed to handle such negotiations; however, in the absence of a father, an older brother or uncle negotiates the marriage contract, called the *ahked*, which typically includes a cash sum or "bride price," and any other stipulations that the families have agreed upon. (In the United States, the agreement is legally binding as a marriage, but in Yemen marriage isn't considered official until it has been consummated, which can take weeks or even months after the papers have been signed, so the *ahked* is considered to be an engagement rather than a marriage.) Because both of Yasmeen's parents died, however, little about her situation is typical, and from what Dariana can gather, Yasmeen is handling some of the negotiations herself. She is not permitted to talk to her future husband; everything must pass through his mother.

Dariana is an experienced negotiator. When a student expressed interest in working in the pharmaceutical industry, Dariana emailed the CEO of Pfizer with the girl's personal story about fleeing Tibet on foot through the Himalayas and basically told him that her future was in his hands. (The company didn't hire high school interns at the time, but made an exception in her case, Dariana says.) When it became impossible to use the campus auditorium because other schools always booked it first, she brought a group of her most charming students to the office of Marty Markowitz to ask the Brooklyn borough president for money to transform a classroom into a dance and cultural center. They got $200,000.

Anyone who has ever seen her in action knows that Dariana rarely encounters a person she can't convince or a problem she can't fix. And yet, she doesn't know how to help Yasmeen, even though her need is obvious. "She needs a mom," Dariana says. She doesn't speak Arabic, and even if she did, the chasm between their cultures is just too deep to cross. Dariana has come to terms with the fact that she can't do Yasmeen's negotiating for her or change tradition—but she can ask about it, and she often does in the subtlest ways. At times her lunches with Yasmeen are more like undercover investigations, disguised as girl talk or internship meetings. Chatty and disarming as she is, curled up behind her cluttered desk, Dariana might as well be a detective sitting in some fluorescent-lit back room of a police station, pulling out confessions without ever having to resort to violence. *Here's a Coke and a sandwich*, she'd say. *So, why did you stab her?* In Yasmeen's case, Dariana phones the cafeteria to have someone send up lunch. "No pork because she's Muslim—no ham," she instructs, before turning her full attention back to Yasmeen.

"So, what kind of preparations do you need to do for your wedding? How does it work?"

"Well, the bride needs to pick up her dress and her jewels. A few weeks before, you choose your bridesmaids' dresses."

"Oooh! Have you thought about who would be your bridesmaids?" Dariana squeals, as a cartoon lightbulb appears over her head. "Oh, my God—can Jessica be your bridesmaid?"

"I want Jessica to be my bridesmaid, of course," Yasmeen says. "But I haven't asked her yet. I want it to be a surprise."

"What color is your dress going to be?"

"White."

"Can you put makeup on?"

"Yeah, and you go to a salon to fix your hair."

"You don't wear a head scarf on your wedding day?" Dariana asks.

"No!" Yasmeen says, laughing at Dariana's ignorance. "Of course not!"

And so it goes. The story comes out bit by bit, like *One Thousand and One Arabian Nights*, told over the course of weekly lunch breaks. Eating her microwaved pasta, Dariana listens with rapt attention as Yasmeen tells her about Yemeni nuptial traditions, like an all-female engagement party that's similar to a bridal shower, where she plans to invite all of her school friends, and another custom in which the entire point is to show off her bridal jewelry, or as Yasmeen calls it, "all my golds."

Once in a while Dariana interrupts the wedding talk to inquire about "him," which is what they call her future husband. "Are you *sure* he's going to let you go to school?" she asks, getting half-hearted reassurances from Yasmeen in return. "You're going to be looking for work, while you're going to school, and he said it's fine?"

"*She* did," Yasmeen says, meaning her aunt, and without going into it, she and Dariana both know that neither one of them is convinced that the aunt will keep her word.

For the most part, Dariana keeps their talk light. She plays the part of the giddy girlfriend, hanging on to Yasmeen's every word as if her life weren't just a series of devastations, disappointments, and no-way-outs, but an exciting telenovela full of twists and turns, suspense and romance. "Can we google-image your fiancé? Do you think he's on Facebook?" she asks one morning, her hand already on the mouse.

"I don't think you'll find him," Yasmeen says, shaking her head. "I don't know how to spell his name."

Consciously or not, Yasmeen has made the choice to play the part of the blushing bride and eternal optimist, spinning out scenarios of domestic bliss. "I can help him get his GED and go to college," she says one day.

"Where do you move to?" Dariana asks another day.

"We are thinking of staying," Yasmeen says, meaning staying in her family's apartment. She is already considering repainting the drab walls a sky blue.

As long as the conversation lasts, so can the fantasy that Yasmeen will go to college and eventually become a kidney doctor while simultaneously raising her younger siblings and helping her doting husband get his GED. But lunch is only thirty-five minutes long. At 11:35, when the sneaker stampede once again returns to the halls and Yasmeen gathers her books to join the crush of teenagers heading to fourth period, the fantasy is over.

Not many people know about Yasmeen's plans. But shortly after she accepted the proposal, she broke the news to her advisor James Rice, as well as Jessica and Mukta. In the past, Yasmeen and Mukta have had their disagreements. For a self-portrait project during their junior year, Mukta turned in a photograph of herself wearing a white veil and blue jeans, over which she had scrawled, "I HATE MY RELIGION!!! RELIGION SUCKS!!! I NEED MY FREEDOM!!!" In the corner of the frame, she wrote the words "bourkha" and "scarf" above a trash can sketched in maroon marker. Yasmeen was furious. For the same project, she had turned in a portrait of herself, her face obscured under her head scarf, kneeling in prayer and holding a copy of the Koran, surrounded by pictures of her family. Two very different girls, two very different portraits, two very different expressions of how Islam has shaped both of their lives—and yet, for all of their differences, Yasmeen and Mukta share the same dream to go to college and someday become doctors.

Yasmeen told Mukta about her engagement during a field trip to see the off-Broadway play *Home*, which they've been studying in English class. (Fittingly, the play by Samm-Art Williams tells the story of a black farmer who loses his sense of identity when he migrates north from a small Southern town, the fictional Cross Roads, to a "very very large American city.") They were walking with their classmates to the subway, past the leaping water fountains in front of the Brooklyn Museum, when Yasmeen mentioned Saif's proposal. "He asked for my hand," she said. Mukta was shocked. She was also full of questions, the foremost in her mind being, "Is he handsome?" In the coming months, Yasmeen would observe how that always was the first thing people wanted to know. "I think so," she would say. "He's very tall."

It's all the questions that follow that leave her grasping for answers. Not long after she became engaged, Yasmeen wrote to Jessica in their diary, weighing the pros and cons of marrying her cousin, with whom she had played as a small child. "You tell me what you think, but before that pretend that you are me, meaning that the way I live with my family, obeying my family and the way I live in general," Yasmeen began. If she married Saif, in some ways she would have more freedom in her community—she could have her own place someday, and maybe she would even learn how to drive. Considering the events of the past year, she couldn't find any reason not to marry him. But recently, one of her older brothers had told her that her younger siblings might not be living with her after all. "I just want to be with my siblings and be able to go to college," Yasmeen wrote to Jessica, but even college was not a guarantee.

Sometimes she wished she had never come to this country and gotten to know the outside world. "I which that I can wake up tomorrow morning and see, smell and think like I use to. I couldn't wait to go back to school last year and this year I can't wait for the day to be over. If I didn't get the chance to go to college, I will write books or anything to express how I feel to the world," Yasmeen wrote. "The world that is so huge but very small towards me."

A House on the Moon

Mohamed wakes for school at 6:30 AM. It always takes a few seconds to remember where he is. When he first moved in with the bootleggers, he slept on a couch in the living room, but recently he has started sharing a bed with one of the guys. Every morning when Mohamed opens his eyes, still groggy under a plush tiger-stripe bedspread, it is to see someone else's reality. The posters of Tupac Shakur, Bob Marley, and Al Pacino as *Scarface* that decorate the wall are tributes to someone else's heroes. The hanging plastic shoe organizer holds someone else's sneakers: Adidas, Nikes, and Filas in bright gumball colors. Except for the dent in the sheets, the room bears almost no trace of Mohamed's existence. Despite all the gifts he received from the people of Farmington, he left Connecticut much the way he came: with little more than the clothes on his back. He has no photographs from Sierra Leone, not even a picture of his mother. He has no mail with his name on it, no passport, no birth certificate—no evidence of the boy he was before he arrived in the United States a little more than two years before at the age of fourteen.

Every day when Mohamed walks out the door for school, it is as if he never walked in. But he did. In November of 2006 on the same day he vanished from Macy's, Mohamed appeared at a pink-bricked building on a residential stretch of Bedford-Stuyvesant and spent the night in the apartment on the top floor. A Sierra Leonean landlord owns the building and has filled two of the three floors with Fula brethren: not actually brothers, but younger countrymen who come from the same neighborhood in Freetown and are related by culture, if not by blood. Over time, they have managed to create a makeshift African village smack in the middle of Brooklyn. Except for Mohamed, who calls everyone Uncle, all of the men call each other Brother. As a sign of respect, they refer to the landlord as the Eldest Brother, and he is, in essence, the chief-in-residence, the one whom the younger men consult on all important matters within the building, and beyond. Since coming from Sierra Leone, the Eldest Brother has helped to bring more than a dozen relatives and friends over to America, finding jobs for some and schools for others.

The Eldest Brother lives on the first floor with his own family, including his elderly mother, his wife, their children, and assorted friends and relatives. In the beginning, when Mohamed needed food, he sometimes came down and ate with the landlord or Abu and Binta, two kids around Mohamed's age who also lived in the apartment on the first floor. For the most part, though, he stayed on the third floor. The younger men told Mohamed not to venture outside in case the police were looking for him—he didn't want to get caught, did he? Mohamed spent the first few weeks in his new home watching TV shows like *Hannah Montana* and *The Suite Life of Zack & Cody*, which follows the escapades of the two shaggy-haired blond brothers who live in a posh hotel in Boston. Once in a while, if he was feeling brave, he went to the store.

Fall passed. Outside the window, the leaves shriveled on the trees like brown cocoons. Mohamed bought a calling card, and in short installments he told his parents as much as he could before an automated voice told him how many minutes were left. One day he explained the seasons. In Sierra Leone, there were only two seasons: dry and wet. But in America, there were four. "The trees lose their leaves, and they regrow them," Mohamed said, as he watched the last of the autumn leaves helicopter to the ground. "That means they die and then they wake again," his father had said.

Winter came, and with it snow. Mohamed saw it for the first time in December. Shortly before Christmas, the boy who lived downstairs came up to the top floor and knocked on the door. "It's snowing again," Abu said when Mohamed answered. "Have you ever seen snow?"

"No," Mohamed said. The white people in Connecticut had tried describing snow once, and in Africa, Mohamed had seen it in a James Bond movie—when Bond goes to Iceland in *Die Another Day*. But he had never seen snow in real life.

"Look out the window," Abu said, parting the rose-red drapes. Outside, fat snowflakes floated out of the sky like wads of cotton and coated the tops of trees and the hoods of parked cars. It was just as the people in Connecticut had said—everything was white. Before long Mohamed and Abu were playing in the street. Mohamed grabbed the snow with his bare hands. He discovered that if he squeezed the snow, he could make different shapes, like balls and bricks. He could mold it, throw it, kick it, and even eat it. But after a few days of playing in it, Mohamed came down with a fever. In this state, coughing and sneezing on the couch, he called his parents in Africa.

"It's beautiful over here!" Mohamed said, speaking in Fula. "It's so white when the snow falls."

"What is snow?" asked his mother.

"It's like ice," Mohamed said.

"What is ice?" asked his father.

Mohamed racked his brain for the word for "ice" in Fula, but he wasn't sure if there even was one. He hadn't seen ice until he moved to Freetown.

"It's water," he explained. "It falls out of the sky, except it's hard, and once it lands on the ground, it becomes water again."

Then his parents passed the phone to his little brothers, and Mohamed tried to explain snow all over again, before his calling card ran out.

Snow was white and beautiful, but it could also be yellow with dog piss or grimy with soot. It could seep into your clothes and into your bones. Mohamed didn't have much more than the hoodie on his back when he first arrived in Bed-Stuy, but over time his roommates gave him hand-me-downs: sneakers, sweatshirts, and dozens of jeans. Around Christmas-time, one of the men asked Mohamed if he was willing to help out with their business. In addition to CDs, they sold a ton of movies produced in Nollywood—Nigeria's Hollywood—to Brooklyn's West African commu-nity. The first movie Mohamed ever copied was an African comedy called *2 Rats*, starring two midgets as kids who are forced by their wicked uncle to work as slaves in their own home. Taking a break from TV, Mohamed watched his own "uncle" begin the process. First, he dropped the master disc into the top tray of the duplicator machine, and then he loaded up twelve blank DVDs into the other drives and pressed start. The rest hap-pened automatically. "Do you want to try?" he asked Mohamed. "You can do it if you feel like it, and if not you can stop."

From that day on, Mohamed burned and shrink-wrapped boxes of DVDs and CDs until he couldn't see straight. He says he worked from 7 PM to 4 AM, stopping to eat, go to the bathroom, and sleep. Sometimes he watched the movies he was copying just to stay awake. They had titles like *Xchange of Power* and *End of Discussion*, and they involved juicy storylines about traitors and impostors, glamour and fame. "Enemies will fall like a pack of cards!" promised a deep male voice on the trailer for *Yankee Girls*, over footage of screeching car chases and Afroed femme fatales. "Who is the most glamorous? Most talked about? And the most *wanted*? Deals, plots, and counterplots will be showcased!"

The routine rarely changed. Mohamed slept all day, woke, ate, worked all night, showered, prayed, went to bed, and started again. In the back of his mind, he felt that he owed it to the men. They gave him food and clothes, and in return they expected him to work.

The New Year arrived, and on TV Mohamed watched the ball drop over Times Square. When his brother called, Mohamed talked up the city, but he never mentioned that he was working. Before Mohamed left Africa, Abdulai had spoken to him about struggle and that it's necessary for success. Over the phone, Abdulai reminded his little brother that the men he lived with had no real obligation to him. As long as they provided food and shelter, he should do whatever they said because he wouldn't be there forever. "You're going to leave someday," Abdulai would always say. "You're going to leave them the same way that you met them, and continue with your life."

Besides some social coaching and the occasional pep talk, there wasn't much more that Abdulai could do. He was thousands of miles away. Mohamed's mother was even more helpless in the village, and she looked to him—the oldest of her five children—for assistance. Mohamed could predict her reaction, should he ever complain about working for his uncles. "Suffering in America? Impossible," she'd say, her voice deep and weary. "No, no, no. We are suffering *here*. We have no money; we have no food."

Mohamed's father had three other wives and more than twenty children to support. As the fourth wife, his mother barely had enough money to feed herself, much less raise her three younger sons and her daughter and still pay their school fees. To supplement her husband's income from the diamond mines, she had started traveling from village to village selling whatever she could at market: cookware, women's clothing, and cow's milk. At best, with her measly earnings, she could afford to buy cassava and chicory, but not meat.

When they spoke, Mohamed sometimes pictured his mother wearing her white-and-blue cotton housedress and head wrap, her round face so slack and her eyes so heavy-lidded that a stranger might mistake her exhausted expression for one of serenity. She would sit on the gnarled roots of the huge mango tree near the main house, where all of the wives lived together, and talk on the Nokia cell phone that Abdulai had bought for the family. The story was always the same. After talking about her day at market, she asked Mohamed for money. Money for food, money for transportation, money for his little brothers to go to school. She assumed that Mohamed was working and getting paid, and no matter how many times he explained that he didn't have a job, there was no end to her pleas. "You're in America—send me money," she would say, her anguish traveling across time zones to reach the ears of her oldest son. "Don't lie to me."

Mohamed's mother wanted him to work, but he wanted to go to school more than anything he had ever wanted. For weeks Mohamed had been watching his downstairs neighbors, Abu and his sister, Binta, trudge down the slushy sidewalk with their backpacks casually slung over their shoulders. Peeping out the window from behind the rose-red drapes, he had memorized their comings and goings. They left the building a little before eight o'clock, around the same time an old man with a metal cart started picking through the trash for bottles and cans. They returned around four, when the streets were filled with kids riding bikes and throwing footballs near parked cars. What happened between those hours was a mystery, until one day Mohamed opened the window just as Abu and Binta were coming home.

"How was school?" he yelled down.

"Fine," said Binta, a thin sigh of a girl with light skin and straight hair.

"How do you get to school?" Mohamed asked her the next day.

And the next day: "How many hours do you spend at school?"

And the next day: "How many subjects are there?"

And the next day: "What are the teachers like? Do they talk fast?"

Soon Abu and Binta expected the sight of Mohamed leaning out of the top-floor window, lobbing questions at them like snowballs.

Sometimes Abu would come upstairs, and they spoke about what he had learned that day. In Sierra Leone, Mohamed had been a top student, but the longer he spent in America without going to school, the more he worried about forgetting everything he had learned at Hope Day: multiplication tables, geography, English. Mohamed still wanted to be a doctor, and he asked to borrow Abu's biology textbook. Late at night he pored over the graphics of cells, organs, and body systems.

The snow melted. *The Beyoncé Experience: Live* came out on DVD, and one night when he was burning discs with his bedmate, Mohamed asked if he could go to school. "Start going to school? What do you mean?" his uncle chided. "You don't have your papers. The school system here, they are strict. Do you know if they catch you, they will deport you? I don't want you to get in trouble."

Mohamed let the matter drop that night, but he remembered a conversation that he had had with Abu about the school where his sister, Binta, was a sophomore: The International High School at Prospect Heights. "You can go to school here without papers," Abu had said. "Go talk to Binta."

The next morning Mohamed found Binta in the first-floor apartment. Was it true what his uncle had said—that if he showed up at school without papers, he could be deported? No, Binta said, that wasn't true. She said that a lot of the kids at her high school were undocumented. All Mohamed needed was his ID and his birth certificate, which his brother could send from Africa.

Mohamed realized he had been lied to. At a loss for what to do next, he worked up the nerve to speak with the Eldest Brother, a family man who, in addition to enrolling Binta and Abu in school, had rented the upstairs apartment to Mohamed's so-called uncles. Sure enough, the Eldest Brother assured Mohamed that he would speak to his roommates, and he kept his promise. After the talk, the men agreed to enroll Mohamed immediately.

A month passed. Nothing happened. Mohamed realized he had been fooled again. With a cool head, he evaluated the situation. His brother Abdulai had said to do whatever the men wanted, as long as they continued providing food and shelter. But there was no point staying in America just to work for no pay—and Mohamed couldn't go back to Africa. That wasn't a choice, not when his mother was still counting on him to take care of the family, even though he was just a kid and didn't have papers or a job. The people at the Hope Day School in Freetown had sent Mohamed to the United States to pursue his education. Now he just had to figure out a way to stay.

Mohamed eventually recruited Abdulai as a sort of middle man—albeit one still based in Sierra Leone—to put some heat on his uncles in Brooklyn. In the eternity that stretched between Abdulai's phone call and the next time Mohamed saw his uncles, he imagined the worst. These men weren't his family or even his friends. There was nothing to stop them from kicking him back onto the street, where they had found him, or keeping him and making his life even more miserable. But in the end they did neither. Twice at an impasse, Mohamed had gone to the two most powerful people he knew: the Eldest Brother in Bed-Stuy, and his own brother in Freetown.

In the end, Mohamed's perseverance paid off. Summer came, and with it piles of paperwork, which one of the roommates begrudgingly filled out to get Mohamed into the International High School at Prospect Heights. In September of 2007, almost a year after he arrived in the United States, Mohamed officially enrolled in the ninth grade.

During Mohamed's first year in America, the days unspooled so slowly that they seemed not to pass at all, but by the middle of his sophomore year, time is burning faster than a bootlegged DVD. It's as if someone has pressed a button and fast-forwarded to February 4. To the other students in Mohamed's sixth-period science class, it is just another Wednesday, filled with typical Wednesday obligations, like after-school club meetings for newspaper and yearbook. But to Mohamed, who came to school dressed more formally than usual in a white button-down shirt and gray jeans, it is a day fraught with expectation and anxiety. Today is the day he is supposed to move in with Cindy.

"How do we survive?" Mike Incze asks, his voice calling Mohamed back to Earth. Holding an orange Xerox of the periodic table in one hand, Mike uses the other to click on the mouse of a white Mac laptop, and an illustration of a fiery streak searing through the night sky appears on the projector screen at the front of the classroom.

"Well, we have this little bubble that protects us. If we don't have *atmosphere*, we don't have protection," he says. "This is a shooting star. It's a rock that hits our atmosphere, and our atmosphere protects us, so usually it turns to dust. But sometimes the rock is so big that our atmosphere doesn't protect us. It hits the earth, and it makes a crater like this . . ."

Click. Mike illuminates a photograph of the Arizona Meteor Crater, which ripped a hole through the earth about fifty thousand years ago.

"This is space," he says, moving on to a NASA shot of an astronaut wearing an American flag on his suit and floating around in the starry blackness. "Can you go out there in your bathing suit?"

"No," Mohamed says, sitting at one of the small blue tables at the front of the room.

"That's right," Mike says. "If you were on the moon, you would need a space suit. If you stepped outside without a space suit, you would become unconscious because there's no oxygen. Do you know what it's like when you boil water? Well, that's what would happen to your blood."

"You guys have an assignment this week," Mike continues, over the oohs and aahs of the class. "I want you to imagine that Barack Obama put you in charge of building a place on the moon that humans could live and survive in. How would you make it? What things would you need to include so that humans could live there?"

"How do you spell 'building'?" another African boy asks Mohamed.

"B-U-I-L-D-I . . ." he begins, and stops, knocking his temple with his fist. "I'm sorry," he says. "My head is not stabilized. I am discombobulated today."

Mohamed is supposed to meet Cindy after class. Yesterday he saw her house for the first time. It was snowing, and Cindy had to take a couple of her students, the Martinez sisters, to midtown Manhattan for a reception where they were being honored as the winners of an art contest. Mohamed had won the same contest the year before, when Cindy submitted a self-portrait that he had painted in her class. At the time, he had missed the reception, so she decided to bring him along, too, and make a quick stop at her house on the way. Walking along Eastern Parkway, Cindy, Mohamed, and the Martinez girls turned left at the traffic lights a few blocks down, and from there it was only about a minute to Cindy's building, a two-story brick walkup with a gate out front. A wreath left over from Christmas still hung on the red door, and inside the rooms were filled with art—mostly Cindy's oil paintings. Some were still lifes and studies, and others passing scenes: an abandoned subway trolley, a dreary horizon of storage signs and smokestacks, a fleet of houseboats in an Amsterdam canal. A portrait of a young guy sitting at a bar in the afternoon took up most of one wall in the dining room, and from the front windows sunlight poured in, illuminating the bright-orange drink in the man's glass. Unlike Mohamed's uncles' apartment where everything was black or red, Cindy's walls were a pale mint-green in the living room and yellow in the kitchen, and he didn't need to look to know that there was lots of food in her fridge. While the Martinez sisters sat in her living room, Cindy introduced Mohamed to her black-and-white cat, Kittalina, and then took him upstairs to show him his future bedroom. The last occupant, the Brazilian film student, was still packing up when they entered, and the room was upside down, but Mohamed saw enough to understand that he would have his own bed. Then the phone rang, and Cindy ran downstairs to answer it. On the other end of the line, a woman's voice informed her that she was returning Cindy's phone call regarding health care for her son. The woman had gotten it wrong—Cindy never called Mohamed her son when she inquired about getting him health care—but that afternoon, as he helped her Brazilian houseguest carry her suitcases downstairs, she felt it was significant that someone else had.

Less than twenty-four hours later, Cindy sits in the art room waiting for Mohamed. "So, I was thinking we need to get you a new cell phone," she says when he comes to see her after sixth period. "I want to add you to my plan."

"Okay, Miss Cindy," Mohamed says. He takes a seat at one of the tables, splattered with yellow, red, and blue paint.

"Cut the 'Miss,'" she says, eyeing his collared white shirt and gray jeans. "Where are your bags?"

"My uncles started questioning me—what did I tell you . . ."

"They wouldn't let you pack your things?"

Mohamed swats at his ear. "They wouldn't let me leave without talking to you."

"Well, I don't want to be questioned," Cindy says, her voice hardening. "Damn." She examines her leggings, where a rip the size of a pinhead is widening. This morning she put on a slinky chocolate-brown dress with black boots and a mink fur coat—not exactly the kind of outfit she would have picked out with a confrontation in mind, especially not a confrontation with four young men who have been exploiting a kid without any apparent remorse, especially not on their turf. "What do you have to pack? Just books and clothes? Can't you just leave your things behind?"

"Please do me this favor," Mohamed says, clenching his jaw. "I want to leave there peacefully. I don't want them to say I'm ungrateful. They aren't even my family. I'm living with these guys for two years, and I never heard them say, 'I want to take you to Immigration to fill out papers for a green card.'"

Cindy scoffs. "They want the free labor, that's why. It's all very Dickensian, isn't it?"

Outside in the halls, lockers slam closed and the echo of screams fills the stairwell. In a few minutes, Mohamed is supposed to go to science club to help decorate recycling bins to put into different classrooms, but he doesn't budge. Instead, he picks the paint off the table like dried scabs, revealing the ancient graffiti beneath.

"Please, please just do me this favor," Mohamed says again. "Don't tell them that you know I work for them. They're afraid they're getting arrested. They wouldn't let me go without talking to you, and they said they needed to sign something."

"Illegal immigrants don't *sign* legal documents," Cindy says. "That's what being 'illegal' means."

People often ask Cindy whether she ever gets scared letting strangers stay in her home. Isn't she afraid that they might hurt her, or take advantage of her in some way? Not really. "I'm a trusting person," she says with a shrug. So far her instincts haven't led her astray. On the contrary, she has had some great experiences with her couch-surfers, and she is approaching her arrangement with Mohamed in much the same way. Cindy is used to having drifters pass in and out of her life—he is just one more. She may not know everything there is to know about the boy, but she knows enough. She knows what he wants from her: a chance to get his papers and pursue his education. She also sees what he needs: basic care, starting with some ointment for what appears to be vitiligo creeping across his face. Plus, she can't help it—like everyone else, she finds the kid charming, and she thinks that charm is a form of intelligence, and she respects intelligence. In some ways, her idea of Mohamed hasn't really changed since Nedda first described him as "a good kid in a bad situation." Cindy has seen evidence of "the good kid" in countless little gestures, but until now she hadn't really planned on getting involved in the "bad situation" with Mohamed's so-called uncles. About these men, she knows almost nothing, and she prefers it that way. More important, she doesn't want them to know anything about her.

Shortly after Mohamed leaves the art room, Cindy sits in her chair, her body as motionless as one of the still lifes up on the wall. She doesn't like the idea of being summoned so far out of her comfort zone to go grapple with a bunch of African bootleggers, but Mohamed hasn't left her with much choice. She is just grateful that she wore her mink today—a coat that she always describes as "big-ass" or "bad-ass." Just in case the full-length coat isn't enough to make her look like someone to be reckoned with, at the last minute Cindy asks Dariana to accompany her. On the way out, Dariana grabs the dance teacher, Eric Segovia, and Mohamed recruits Mike after science club. Before they know it, they have marshaled a small army to make the trek to Mohamed's uncles' building.

"How do you feel now?" Mike asks, rolling his bicycle down the hall.

"Safe, now that you're here," Mohamed says. "It's like a battalion. Someday I'm going to look back and laugh at this."

"Well, maybe you'll chuckle in wonderment," Mike says. "How far is it?"

Mohamed laughs nervously. "Far, far away," he says, his voice coming out shrill. "The magical kingdom."

In fact, it is only about a fifteen-minute drive from school to the building in Bed-Stuy, barely long enough for Eric to scarf down his deli sandwich. Staring out the window, Mohamed is silent, watching the blur of trees and benches along Eastern Parkway disappear, replaced by Baptist churches, liquor stores, and the Bedford-Atlantic Armory, a redbrick Alcatraz that the city plans to use as an intake center for homeless men. When they piled into the car, the mood had been light, with Cindy making jokes to mask her nerves. "Party! Bring the chicken wings!" she cracked as they turned down Classon Avenue. But as bodegas and beauty salons give way to deserted residential streets, the conversation lulls, and the car is quiet except for the static coming from the driver's radio. From everything Mohamed has said about his "uncles," they sound like bad guys. Clearly, they are brazen enough to take a kid off the street and put him to work in an illegal business. What else are they brazen enough to do?

"That's Harold's building," Dariana says, when they turn onto Quincy Street. She points out a brick walkup with neat green trim. Further down is a small Dominican grocery store. Except for the old men drinking from brown paper bags out front and a mewling gray cat, the street is empty.

Not a lot of cabs pass down this block, and most people still haven't come home from work, but Mohamed's "uncles" have been expecting Cindy. A few minutes after the taxi pulls up, there is a flurry of movement at the top window, and a shadowed face peers out from behind the dark red drapes.

When Mohamed opens the front door for the group, they are instantly hit by the oily smell of frying fish. It's dark and drafty in the vestibule as they climb the stairs, and when they reach the third floor, one of Mohamed's roommates, the same man from the window, appears in the hallway. He has light skin and bleary eyes threaded with red. He wears baggy low-riding jeans, but he tells Mohamed to pull up his own jeans in front of their company.

"Please come in," the roommate says, cracking the door.

The TV is on, but the lights are off, and the man never flips the switch, not even after he excuses himself to go downstairs.

"We'll be right back," Mohamed says, following his roommate out of the apartment and leaving Cindy, Dariana, Mike, and Eric standing in the dark.

"Well," Cindy says when the door shuts closed, "This is surreal." Eric rubs his elbows, and Cindy wraps her mink coat closer around her shoulders. Despite the temperature outside, there is no heat. "It's freezing in here," Dariana says. Through the rose-red drapes, a thin slice of sunlight illuminates the shapes in the room. On the surface are the spoils of a new life in America. Mohamed's roommates have pimped their top-floor apartment into a sweet bachelor pad, complete with a giant plasma TV, a weight lifting machine, and pleather sofas that smell of incense smoke. But beneath the facade, tradition still applies. Behind the TV, there is an embroidered red-and-gray prayer rug. Like the rug, the refrigerator in the alcove kitchen looks like it hasn't been touched in weeks, but someone has been putting in time at the weight lifting machine near the window. "Definitely a guys' place," Cindy says.

After a few minutes the roommate comes back. "The Eldest Brother wants to see you," he says. Dariana and Cindy exchange a look. *Eldest Brother?* Until now, they only have heard about Mohamed's so-called uncles. Occasionally one of the roommates would sign a permission slip for school, but Mohamed never mentioned anything about an Eldest Brother to his teachers, and the term sounds slightly ridiculous to their ears, as if a tribal chief awaited them.

In fact, the Eldest Brother is the one who issued the decree to deliver Cindy to his doorstep, and he has been waiting for Mohamed and his teachers in his apartment on the first floor.

"Please sit," he says when they walk in.

Standing around six feet with a slight paunch and umber skin, the Eldest Brother wears a T-shirt that says "My President Is Black" on one side, and "The American Dream" on the other. He stands as Cindy and the rest of the teachers settle into his pleather sofas, and then he sits on the highest chair in the room, towering over his guests.

The layout of the landlord's apartment is almost identical to the one where Mohamed has been living with his "uncles," down to the couches positioned around a plasma TV. But unlike the bachelor pad upstairs, the downstairs space has a homey feel; it belongs to a family. On one wall, a young girl in a gold cap and gown smiles behind a picture frame. By the stove, a willowy teenager stops stirring her pot to glare at Mohamed, who leans against one of the couches and stares at whatever movie the family was watching before he showed up. A woman holding two small children in her lap clutches her chest. "Investigation?" she whispers, her face contorted in fear. Mohamed's roommate hushes her in Krio and takes a seat against the wall next to another man wearing a skullcap and a sneer—another one of Mohamed's so-called uncles.

"You didn't tell us about this," he seethes at Mohamed.

Grabbing the remote, the Eldest Brother turns off the volume on the TV and picks up a hot-pink plastic clothes hanger. "I am the Eldest Brother," he says in a deep baritone that seems to rise from his gut. "This is *my* house." He points the pink hanger to the men sitting against the wall. "Those are *my* little brothers upstairs. If Mohamed had a problem, he should have come to *me*." Each time he speaks, he slaps the hanger against his palm, as if to hammer in his points. "I brought eighteen kids to America." *Thwack.* "All of them are going to school." *Thwack, thwack.* "I am happy with the International school. I know the principal—the Chinese lady?"

"She's Ecuadorian," Dariana says from the couch.

"I've sent four kids there, and now Mohamed," the Eldest Brother continues, pointing the pink hanger at Mohamed. "I pushed for you to go to school. When I saw you walking around, I said, 'You need to go to school!'"

"Can I—" Mohamed begins.

"If you have a problem, come talk to *me*," the Eldest Brother plows on. "He's going to go live with strangers? How can he go sign himself over to other people?"

"Can I—" Mohamed begins again, raising his chin.

"I was just in Africa," the Eldest Brother says. "What did I tell you— that I was going to find your mother. But she wasn't in town, she was way out in the village. You're just a little kid. You shouldn't be making these decisions on your own."

"Please, let me say something," Mohamed rasps. "Ever since I've been here, these guys never mentioned, 'Okay, let's go to Immigration to get your papers and stuff.' Now that this opportunity has come, I don't want to lose it. I'm here, and I want a better education for myself, and a better future. I think this is my decision, and I want to take it."

"Anything Mohamed wants, he gets it," the bleary-eyed roommate sneers, rocking his chair against the wall. "I give him money for food, clothes—whatever he needs."

A little girl with tawny hair and big brown eyes squeezes between the Eldest Brother's knees, demanding to be held. He picks her up and lets her tumble softly out of his arms until she's hanging upside down, her shirt rising to show her belly.

"Trust me," the Eldest Brother says. "When his father died, Mohamed came down here crying. I was touched, too. I wanted to help him, too. He is very, very smart and ambitious—but he's just a little kid. He shouldn't be making these decisions. If something was going on upstairs, he should have come and told me. I always ask him, 'Mohamed, is everything okay?' Every time I asked, he said, 'Everything is okay.' Until last night. He came down, and he was so hyper he was trembling." He points the pink hanger at Mohamed, again. "I want to know—why didn't he tell me sooner?"

"Well, that's just it," Dariana says. "He's just a little kid. He was scared. He's only fifteen years old."

Mike leans forward on the sofa. "Um, actually he's almost seventeen."

Pitching slightly forward on his chair, the Eldest Brother points the pink hanger back at the two roommates. "This is your boy," he says in Krio. "He has been living here for a long time, and you guys have been taking care of him. Do you want to let him go, or do you want to say something to these people?"

"They're American," he adds loudly in English. "They don't understand our traditions."

As the Eldest Brother taps the hanger against his knee, the two uncles exchange a few words in Krio. Finally, the man in the skullcap nods in Cindy's direction.

"We'll get back to you," he says.

Cindy shoots a look at Dariana as if to say, *Time to go.* She didn't want these men to know her name, let alone her phone number or address. Get back to her how? She hasn't come this far to leave Mohamed behind. If his "uncles" were angry last night, before Mohamed brought an army of teachers into their living room, what would happen after they were gone?

"I'm sorry," Dariana says, reading Cindy's thoughts. "You can't 'get back to us.' The decision has already been made. There's no affidavit of guardianship anywhere. We just want what's best for Mohamed, and this is what's best. He has a chance to get his papers, to go to college. This is about his future."

She never says, *It doesn't matter whether you approve or not. Your traditions are no match for the law, and if you fight, you will lose.* She doesn't have to.

"How can he live with strangers?" the Eldest Brother sighs, shaking his head.

He never says, *You don't know the whole story. How dare you invade my house and scare my family? You treat us like criminals, but we did what we could for one of our own.* That is understood, too. "If we had gone into their village in Africa and tried to take Mohamed, it would have been very different," Dariana says later. "But they're here, and they are powerless because they can't sign a paper. The Eldest Brother may be the leader in his village at home, but at the end of the day, there are things we can do that affect their village here."

As the evening wears on, more is said on both sides, but much more is left unsaid, and an uncomfortable silence settles in the room. On TV, two doctors stand side by side in white lab coats performing surgery on an infant patient. Rocking his chair against the wall, Mohamed's roommate with the bleary eyes watches the screen and occasionally glowers at Mohamed, as if he can't decide which activity is a better use of his time. Dinner is almost ready, and more people are starting to come out of the bedrooms in the back of the apartment. An old woman wearing a colorful print head wrap briefly wanders into the kitchen before turning back toward her room, confused by all the company. Once again, Cindy shoots Dariana a look. *It's time to go.*

"Mohamed," Cindy whispers.

Still leaning against the couch, Mohamed stares off into space. Only a few hours ago he was at school learning about the earth's atmosphere. Journals are due tomorrow, and he hasn't gotten very far with his blueprint for building a house on the moon. The structure could be a bubble shape, and he would pump it full of nitrogen and oxygen so that people could breathe inside, but breathing, alone, isn't enough to guarantee survival.

"Mohamed!" Cindy hisses again, and this time he turns, his eyes glazed and unblinking. "Have you packed yet?"

He shakes his head no.

Sunken into the mauve sofa, Cindy wedges herself forward just enough so that he can hear what she says next: three words that will set in motion the rest of his life.

"Mohamed," she says, shielding her mouth with her hand. "Go pack."

It takes a village to raise a child. The question is, which one? African or American? Old World or New? Poor or rich? A village of diamond miners and farmers? Or churchgoers and do-gooders? A village of bootleggers and undocumented immigrants—or a village of teachers? In his sixteen years, Mohamed has left a trail of villages in his path. There is

The Remote Village Where He Is From, where he witnessed his father being held at gunpoint by a boy who was around his own age, and where Mohamed's mother still lives in a mud-brick hut with no electricity and several children to feed. There is the affluent village of Farmington, Connecticut, with its famous church and trusting members, who live in pretty houses. Then there is the village inside of the pink-bricked building on Quincy Street on a residential block in Bed-Stuy, thousands of miles away from home. Each of these villages took care of Mohamed in its own way, and each he had left behind to deal with the aftermath.

The drive from Quincy Street to Cindy's house seems to take forever as Mohamed sits in the backseat of a cab filled with his stuff. He doesn't own a suitcase. After Cindy told Mohamed to pack, he went back to the upstairs apartment to grab his belongings and throw them into three garbage bags. One of his uncles cornered him before he left. "You betrayed us. You know what people will think?" he spat. "That you are ungrateful." *Ungrateful.* Even before it was uttered, Mohamed had feared that that word would travel among the Sierra Leonean community in Brooklyn all the way back to Freetown.

Outside, the Brooklyn Armory floats by as if the night were on rewind, but there is no going back, and so once again Mohamed moves forward. He helps Eric and Mike move his garbage bags out of the car when they get to Cindy's house. He laughs when she reads his heavy brow and says, "Just think of it as breaking up—it's not you, it's me." And, gradually, his mood lightens. When they walk into Cindy's living room, he lets Kittalina curl her body around his ankles and sniffs his nose at a strong mineral smell.

"You know how it smells in here?" Mohamed says when they walk past the door to the basement where she keeps her washer and dryer. "Like when I lived with the white people? It smells like that."

"Great—my house smells like white people. That's when you know you've made it," Cindy says, and Mohamed cracks up laughing.

Gradually, they fall into a familiar rhythm. After warning Mohamed not to go down to the basement—it is being rented out by a student from Japan who loves to do laundry but doesn't love visitors—Cindy teaches him how to work the alarm. There will be time to show him how to use the stove top and oven, the TV and computer. But it is late, and for now, the tour continues upstairs.

"This is the family room, even though I don't have a family," Cindy says matter-of-factly, when they pass a small den crammed with large canvases, including a half-finished self-portrait that rests on an easel. "And this," she says, opening the door to Mohamed's room, "is the Afro-Asian room."

The Brazilian film student only left yesterday, but already Mohamed's new room has been straightened up. Beneath a framed rice-paper rubbing from Thailand that hangs on one orange wall, there is a small glass table with wrought-iron legs where he can do his homework. There is a closet with empty hangers, and a stack of sheets, blue flannel with white hearts, which Cindy unfolds and uses to make his new bed.

"Do you want me to move this?" Cindy asks, picking up a tribal-looking musical instrument that appears to be a coconut covered in cowrie shells and rests on the dresser.

"No!" Mohamed shouts as he begins unpacking the first garbage bag, which is filled with dirty laundry. "Leave it here. It symbolizes me: Africa."

"Where do you want your head when you sleep?"

"By the window where it's more cooler."

"More 'cooler'?" Cindy snorts, tucking in a fitted sheet. "You can't use bad grammar in this house. It's 'cooler.'"

Mohamed shoves a pair of underwear under his knee. "Miss Cindy, what are your rules?"

"I'm not too picky," she says. "I have one major pet peeve. I had a boyfriend who used to live here, and he never flushed the toilet. *Always* flush the toilet. What time do you get up?"

"Six thirty," Mohamed says, folding a pair of True Religion jeans.

"Do you take long showers?"

"No," he says, pulling out another pair of jeans. "Boy showers."

"Boy showers. Okay."

In between talking, they unpack. In between unpacking, they observe each other closely. Sitting on the bed, Cindy watches Mohamed pull everything he owns out of the three garbage bags, and it is more than she expected. Item by item, she registers the inventory.

One used white Apple laptop, a gift from the assistant principal, Nedda de Castro. A pile of composition books and Regents prep guides for New York math A, world history, and algebra. One pair Air Jordans. One pair Nike Airs. One pair Adidas in blue, orange, and white.

"These are the first sneakers I ever bought in America," Mohamed says, holding up the Adidas.

Too many jeans to count: faded, ripped, and dark-washed, designer brand and no brand.

"Dude, I thought you were traveling light!" Cindy says, taking in the denim tornado that has wiped out any visible floor space. "If you pull out any more jeans, I'm sending you back!"

Mohamed laughs and takes out a pair of dress shoes to go with a pin-striped suit jacket, which he tries on over his shirt, spinning around with his arms out.

"It's a little short," Cindy says.

Among all the debris, Mohamed never pulls out a single picture of his family. But he does come across a few old journals and loose homework assignments that he saved from freshman year, including a crayon menu of priced African dishes that he made for math class and the speech that he wrote on a series of index cards when he ran for president of the African Club.

Still wearing his suit jacket, he rests the cards on the glass table for now and skims over his speech once more, lingering on the last line.

"This is the honorable Mohamed Bah speaking to you all," it reads in fading pencil.

Part III

ALMOST AMERICAN

Spring Forward, Fall Back

Spring came late to Prospect Heights. It slumbered through the tail end of March and showed up one morning in early April, slinking in like a delinquent student. There were times, especially during Regents testing and Portfolio presentations, when it seemed like it would never come, but once it did, it was hard to ignore. Outside in the groves of Prospect Park, red oak, sweet gum, and silver linden unfurled their leaves, and in the Botanic Garden new buds sprouted on the branches of cherry blossom trees, which would frill with pink flowers soon enough. Inside the school, jackets unzipped and shoes slid off in the middle of class. No sooner had the first thaw loosened the ice on the ground than the girls traded in their parkas and skinny jeans for backless halters and teeny camisoles, showing off satiny bra straps and glimpses of thongs in a kaleidoscope of colors. Spring was a total flirt. Despite PA announcements reminding students about dress code, one pale, thin Chinese girl showed up wearing a miniskirt the size of a postage stamp and a cheetah-print bikini under a T-shirt that read: "Slippery When Wet."

Even Chit Su started showing up in short skirts and pigtails, to the torment of a stocky, spiky-haired boy who called her cell phone daily to talk, despite the fact that they didn't understand each other. "Sometimes

I hate him," she groaned one day after school. "I say, 'I don't understand! You speak that crazy Spanish language!' He say, 'Nothing, nothing, nothing.'"

Spring made it hard to concentrate, and not just for students who suffered from senioritis. By mid March, all of the teachers were counting down the weeks to spring break. As the weather warmed, classes thinned. Schedules changed to accommodate internships, and the seniors began to leave after lunch to go to their various jobs around the city. Every Monday and Wednesday afternoon Freeman grabbed his walkie-talkie to make the rounds at the Prospect Park Zoo, where he was in charge of feeding the goats. Jessica started volunteering at the Museum of Chinese in America, which was a short walk from her rented room in Chinatown, and Yasmeen headed to work at the hospital, despite all the sad memories there.

On the days they stayed through sixth period, many of the seniors were easily distracted. During Ann Parry's English class, Kalsang's bathroom breaks became longer and more frequent. Others skipped class entirely, preferring to spend the sixty-five minutes across the street in Dr. Ronald McNair Park, where they could bum a patch of sunlight and maybe a smoke. After a long winter, the stoners reclaimed their benches, where they compared tattoos and hatched plans to do nothing. "Let's go somewhere, man," a Tunisian boy with a "Brooklyn" tattoo suggested one blue-skied day, in between drags of his cigarette.

"What time is it?" asked a skinny French junior whose wrist bore the Roman numerals "XIII" in honor of the arrondissement in Paris where he was raised.

A lanky blond Dane inked with the word "Imagine" unzipped his backpack to find that someone had stashed a classroom clock inside. "Why do I have this watch, man?" he asked, red-eyed and confused.

"I don't know, man," the Tunisian said. "Hang it on a tree. Then it'll always be there."

Time played tricks on the seniors, too. Spring meant that summer was near, but for the students who would be graduating in just a few months, sometimes it felt more like light years away. As the sap coursed through the trees, the double Dutchers reappeared in front of the Brooklyn Museum, the street painters lay thick stripes of yellow on fresh gravel, the old man who danced in the tunnels of Prospect Park dug out his tap shoes once again, the vendors wheeled out their carts of rainbow ice, and the seniors continued to wait and wait and wait for news from college admissions offices with the overwhelming sense that, any day now, life would begin.

And then, one day, it does. The kids who applied to community colleges are the first to hear back. On a Saturday, Yasmeen received a letter in the mail from Borough of Manhattan Community College. She recognized the seal on the envelope immediately and couldn't open it fast enough. When she read that she had been accepted, she screamed, though her excitement dimmed when she thought of the negotiations ahead. What if her future husband doesn't want her to go?

The students who applied to state universities are next. Mukta got into a number of schools including the University of Vermont and Bard, but convincing her strict Muslim father to let her live outside the city would be a challenge, and if she went to college out of state, she would be far from her boyfriend, Islam.

Each day as new acceptance letters trickle in, the college counselor Joanna Yip makes copies to post on a bulletin board in the halls of the fourth floor. A large number of the letterheads are from CUNY and SUNY schools; only a few bear the emblems of out-of-state universities or colleges.

For the most part, the results are as Joanna expected. She just wishes that she had managed the expectations of her students a little more vigilantly. Though Harold had been called back for a follow-up interview at Columbia, he doesn't get in. Jessica gets disappointing news, too. After weeks of checking her email for an acceptance letter from Tufts University, she finally receives a rejection letter. The rejections are disheartening for the students, but for Joanna, they are a reality check.

"Part of me feels like I shouldn't have kids apply to these schools. Relative to the pool of applicants, our kids are far, far behind," she says one day in her office, surrounded by felt pennants and T-shirts for universities like Rochester Institute of Technology and Syracuse University. "I feel like by saying, 'Go ahead and apply,' it's like saying they have a chance, but they don't, really."

February was the month of maybes, but March brings definitive answers, highs and lows, and heart-stopping variations on "Congratulations" and "It is with regret . . ." It delivers tears of elation and deep disappointment, and for some it delivers both. After getting rejected from Tufts, Jessica finds out that she got into the business and engineering program at Drexel University in Philadelphia, a move that she is considering, despite the fact that it would mean being separated from Harold. Over another weekend, Harold and Ngawang learn that they have been accepted by Syracuse. For Ngawang, Syracuse is a reach school that he never thought he could reach. He is ecstatic, until it dawns on him that he can't afford to pay the tuition.

In the minutes before class on the following Monday morning, the third floor is literally buzzing. At first glance, the scene looks like the aftermath of a tragedy. Marie Feline Guerrier, a tall, regal Haitian girl who is never less than perfectly composed, runs down the hall panting, her eyes red and raw, and one knee-high black Rocawear boot still unbuckled from passing through security. "Where's Harold?" she asks Mukta, who points to the row of red lockers. Hiding behind a striped hoodie and a sheepish smile, he stands a few feet away from Jessica, her face slack and her body limp, despite the many hugs that have propped it up for brief intervals this morning.

"What happened?" Ngawang asks, watching a clump of seniors gather outside Joanna's office. He is about to walk into the room when Freeman comes bounding out.

"I GOT IT! FOUR YEARS!" he screams, stopping to pump Harold's hand. "Congratulations!"

"Congratulations," Harold says.

Five of Ngawang's classmates just got some news that will change the rest of their lives. A couple months ago, Joanna had Ngawang and some of the other seniors apply to the Seinfeld Scholarship Program, an organization established by Jerry Seinfeld and his family. Every year, around ten to fifteen New York City public high school students are chosen to receive four-year scholarships to the college or university of their choice. Over the weekend, Joanna received the call that this year's Seinfeld scholars include five of her students: Freeman, Harold, Jessica, Mukta, and Marie.

The announcement marks a huge coup for the school. The five winners from International make up one third of this year's scholars, who were culled from public schools around Brooklyn and Staten Island. But it's also a major victory for Joanna. "I must have done something right this year!" she wrote hours after getting the news, updating her Facebook status. "Congrats to my 5 students, who just got a full-ride to the college of their choice, courtesy of Jerry Seinfeld!"

"Who's that?" asks one African girl after overhearing the buzz in the halls.

"He writes books," says a wiry Haitian boy.

Most of the students, including the newly christened Seinfeld scholars, don't know who Jerry Seinfeld is, but overnight the Lucky Five have become celebrities in their own right. Marie was the first of the students to get the call from the director of the Seinfeld Family Foundation. As soon as Marie heard her voice, she started yelling. When the director said, "Congratulations," Marie had to put the phone down so she could start jumping. Minutes later, her parents were calling everyone they knew and telling their friends that Marie had won "a scholarship." But it wasn't until they translated the word into Creole that their friends really understood. *"Bous."* That one word said it all. It said that Marie was a good student, but also that she was a good daughter, which meant that her parents were good parents, that they had made a good decision coming to the United States, and that all of their struggles until this point had been *worth* it. It also said she came from a good country that turned out good people. Within hours of getting the news herself, the word spread across the Haitian community. On the streets, strangers congratulated her. On Radyo Pa Nou, a Haitian radio station based in Brooklyn, the deejay trumpeted her name, prompting listeners to call in for Marie's phone number. They wondered if she would talk to their kids. *"Bous,"* Marie said later. "Once you translate it, they get a deeper meaning, especially Haitian parents. They know you must be a hard worker. They understand it better than you."

Bous in Creole. *Jiǎng xué jīn* in Mandarin. *Beca* in Spanish. *Britti* in Bengali. Over the weekend, the word had spread in as many different languages as the winners spoke. It passed over crackling phone lines from Bed-Stuy to Santo Domingo, where Harold's relatives live, and from Chinatown to China, where Jessica's mother couldn't believe the news. "That can't be true. Why would someone give you money to go to college?" her mother asked. "You're too lucky."

At lunch, the five winners will sit together at their own table, reminiscing about how they found out and fielding questions from underclassmen. "Yo, how can I get that?" "What did you do?" "Nooooo!" Mohamed groans when he hears the news, slapping his forehead in regret. Even though he is only a sophomore, he thought that the five winners had edged out his chances of getting the scholarship himself, and he chastises himself for not applying. "No, baby, that's not how it works," Cindy corrects him when they are alone. "Don't worry. When you're a senior, you'll get your turn."

Throughout the day, it's obvious who the winners are just by the way they carry themselves. In the halls, they float in a giddy haze, wearing semidemented smiles, like dental patients who suddenly have been discharged into the outside world before the novocaine has worn off. Everyone handles the attention a bit differently. Mukta can't stop grinning and clapping. "This proves that International High School students can do anything!" she squawks in the stairwell.

Jessica drifts through the halls as if sleepwalking. She is still in a state of shock when she wanders into Dariana's office. "I got Seinfeld scholarship," she whispers, as if afraid to jinx it, and then explains, "I don't want to brag."

Freeman has no such qualms. "Ngawang, you better find another scholarship!" he shouts out in first period, moments before making a farting sound when Hasanatu gets up to grab the bathroom pass.

"Freeman, you shouldn't have come to school today!" Yasmeen says, whipping around in her seat, her face a jigsaw of irritation and amusement. "You should go to Manhattan and party. Go to the top of the Empire State Building and scream, or something. You're going to get kicked out of class today, I guarantee it. You should go home."

An hour later, in Room 337, Ann is already at the whiteboard when the students trickle in for second period. "Congratulations Freeman + Harold," she writes in black marker just as Ngawang walks in and dumps his backpack on one of the light-blue trapezoid tables. As an afterthought, she picks up a red marker and adds:

+ Ngawang

A few minutes later, Genesis appears in the doorway, her breasts spilling out of her tank top and last night's unfinished homework spilling out of her notebook. Wearing her brown winter coat over her *hijab* and carrying a worn copy of *To Kill a Mockingbird*, Yasmeen is close behind. Ann picks up the red marker again.

+ Everyone

By late March the sense that one season has ended and another begun is palpable. In Room 337 the shift is subtle, but it is there. It is in the way that Rocio Cisnernos glares at Freeman when he barely notices her, an undocumented girl with deep watchful eyes and dark brown hair cut bluntly at her shoulders. "Okay, you got it, good for you," she mutters when he's out of earshot. "You don't need to be screaming."

A similar hardness has settled over Ngawang's features, and his teachers have begun to notice a heaviness of spirit that didn't exist there before, when Syracuse was still within his reach. "Ngawang's face has changed after not getting the scholarship," Dariana says. "He's breaking my heart."

Six years ago, Ngawang squeezed inside that suitcase traveling from Tibet to Nepal and experienced the most excruciating twenty-four hours of his life. But in some ways, the twenty-four hours that followed his realization that he couldn't afford to go to Syracuse have been just as hard to bear. Within that span of time, Ngawang touched his dream and had it taken away.

Overnight, the Class of 2009 has been divided into two camps. On one side, there are the five scholarship winners. On the other side, there is everyone else. Most of the kids are going to college, just not on a full ride. Some have been wait-listed at prestigious schools. Others have been wait-listed for life because they are undocumented. The sudden cleave is noticeable, and in the hours after the scholarships are announced, the victory rankles some of the students who aren't sure if they'll be staying in the country, let alone attending college. A few have begun wondering why they bother coming to school at all when they feel destined to work in corner bodegas, nail salons, and restaurants, like their parents.

More than five years after illegally crossing the Mexican border into Laredo, Texas, Rocio Cisnernos applied to college like everyone else. However, recently her grades have slipped because instead of studying she has been working, stuffing burritos at Chipotle from 4 PM to 11:30 PM every day after school. "The teachers, they're always giving us a lot of support saying we don't have to give up our dream. But it's not really easy," Rocio says one day before work, sitting with Jovita in the park across the street.

"If you want to find a work, you get paid the minimum," Jovita adds. "Even if you work harder than other people, it doesn't matter. If they have papers, they get paid more."

"Before, we don't really care about it," Rocio says. "But when you become a senior and you want to apply for financial aid, it's really sad to see you cannot do it. You can't go to college. They say you can, but you have to pay more. Like me, I work, and I say, 'Maybe I will . . . ' But for me to pay for college and books and everything, I know that will not be realistic. Sometimes you really wish you could do it."

Of the kids who are headed to college, with or without a scholarship, the staff worries that a good number won't survive the first year. By May, the twelfth-grade teachers spend most of their team meetings venting fears about their students' futures and most of their classes venting frustration at the students themselves for loosening their grips on fundamental lessons that they should have learned long ago. In math class, Alex Harty has begun repeating himself so frequently that Freeman spends the class period drawing cartoons of him. "I am tired of explaining this over and over again!" a frustrated Mr. Harty says in one sketch, a speech bubble floating over his head as he stands at the whiteboard. "Oh!! Lord.

The seniors don't know how to Round," the cartoon teacher says in another drawing. "What I am going to be proud of when I let them go?"

In English class, Ann has to interrupt Rocio in the middle of reading a book passage aloud after she fails to stop at periods or pause at commas, lulling everyone to sleep. "A sentence is like a song!" Ann says, graphing out sentence structure on the whiteboard. James Rice isn't so patient. When a student uses the word "childs" for the millionth time, he blinks once, calmly walks over to the door, and proceeds to bang his head against it eleven times until finally the class screams for him to stop and James can be sure that, once and for all, they have learned that the right word is "children."

In his social studies classes, James Rice has been stressing the importance of keeping up with college-level reading by skimming texts and using shortcuts like a table of contents. "See," he says one morning, picking up a thick book and pinching together the pages of one chapter, about a centimeter thick, to make his point. "It could take you *two days* to read all this."

"Two days?" scoffs Milagros, the Dominican girl who wrote her college essay about working as a supermarket cashier. "More like a semester!"

James laughs along with the rest of the class. Second semester is supposed to be about building new habits, but he spends most of his time breaking old ones. "Stab me, just *stab* me," he groans when a student turns in a written assignment without using a single capital letter.

Walking around the room, James takes attendance while the seniors plug their flash drives into the Mac laptops signed out from the computer room. For the past couple of weeks, the students have been brainstorming topic ideas for the research papers that will count for a large part of their final grade in social studies. As long as they follow the steps that James has laid out for conducting research and submit their papers in accordance with the guidelines of the *MLA Handbook*, they can write about whatever topic they choose, which is why the assignment is called "I-Search." The hope is that the kids will be more motivated to research a subject if it's one that they are already interested in, whether it's the history of jazz or the role of women in Islam. A few days ago, James asked the seniors to dig into their own experiences in order to answer the first prompt: "What I Know." Last night's homework was to come up with a list of questions in answer to the second prompt: "What I Want to Find Out."

"Here is where you put down one or two paragraphs' worth of questions about your topic—questions that you want badly, even desperately, to have answered," James says as he circles the room. At every table, the seniors sit in groups of two, reading each other's questions on computer screens.

"These questions are the passionate, fiery fuel that will guide you through the *morass* of library work," James continues. He pretends to bushwhack his way through the jungle, pushing aside a tangle of branches and peering through a skein of leaves. Halfway to Yasmeen's table, he gets stuck in an invisible pit of quicksand, flailing his arms, and she laughs in recognition without ever having to open the dictionary.

Over the next few weeks, he explains, the class will be taking trips to the Brooklyn Library to begin their research, ultimately answering the third and final prompt: "What I Learned." But first James wants every-one to have a game plan. In between listening in to conversations and glancing at computer screens, he offers advice to those who appear to be struggling. He already knows that Yasmeen is writing about pancreatic cancer, the disease that took her father's life. Sitting across from her, Kal-sang reads aloud her questions about anorexia, and Harold raises some pressing questions about the history of anime. In the final minutes of the period, the room hums with voices. "Some things I want to know are, What are ghosts? What is the relationship between ghosts and humans? Can ghosts harm human beings?" Freeman asks, drowning out Bing Xin He, a soft-spoken Chinese girl, who has an identical sister and is writing about twins.

"Uh, what's your name . . . ?" James asks, momentarily blanking when he stops in front of Ngawang. He taps his head and remembers. "Nga-wang. What's your topic?"

"Tibetan monks," Ngawang mumbles.

"Okaaay, but what *about* Tibetan monks? You have to be more specific than that," James says, leaving Ngawang to ponder their daily rituals and

Buddhist monasteries. "Why they give up so much in their life?" Nga-wang will write in his final paper. "What do they believe? How do they keep up with their monk hoot? What happens if they give up?"

"What's your topic?" James asks Jovita.

She exchanges a look with Rocio. Jovita chose deportation as her subject, but she doesn't say why. Both she and her mother are undocumented, but Jovita has a younger sister who was born here, making her a citizen.

"The deportation of immigrants from Central America," Jovita tells James, and a nervous giggle escapes her.

"Okay, so you might want the viewpoint of the people being deported," James suggests. "Maybe the children of those people. Maybe the opinion of the Obama administration. Maybe some of the people who live or work along the border of the United States and don't like immigrants."

A few feet away, Hasanatu and Genesis sit in total silence. Wearing no makeup and a million bobby pins in her obsidian hair, Genesis is in a battle of wills with her own head, which keeps nodding closer and closer to her desk. Beside her, Hasanatu is sprawled out across the table in a bright yellow top, like a runny egg moments before it's scraped off the bottom of the pan.

"What part of 'read aloud' do you not understand?" James asks, folding his arms.

Hasanatu bites her lip coquettishly and squirms in her seat. "Mr. Riiiiiice, I don't want to read it," she whines, but James remains unmoved.

"Hasanatu, we don't have all day. READ."

Hasanatu picks up her head and squints at the words on the screen, where she has the beginnings of a story about the day she first witnessed a female circumcision ceremony. She was seven years old and playing outside her family's compound when four girls in white T-shirts, sarongs, and matching head wraps slinked by like lizards. "Why are they dressed like that and why is that girl crying?" Hasanatu asked her older sister, who just laughed and said, "When your turn comes, then you will know, okay? Just play."

"I remember the first time I saw a female cirva . . . ," Hasanatu begins.

"Okay, stop," James says, splaying his hand. "Sir-come-sih-jun," he says.

Hasanatu tries again, the syllables rolling around in her mouth like glass marbles. "Circuncizon."

James points to his lips and says it more slowly. "Sir-come, like 'come here,'" he says, gesturing as if for someone to join them, "sih-jun."

Smiling shyly, Hasanatu tries again. "Circumcision."

"Good," James says. "Now, what do you want to find out?"

"Why all the Muslim people does not do female cirva . . . circumcision?"

"Okay," James says. "So, you might ask, 'Why only African Muslims?'"

James checks the clock. He has time for one more. Scrunching his nose, he stands behind Genesis and peers at her computer screen.

> *Since I was in Ecuador I heard about the Bermuda triangle. Since I heard about it I start thinking about it and I start thinking about some questions like where is located the Bermuda triangle. If in the Bermuda triangle there are people with life?*

The Bermuda Triangle. For some reason, whenever students have trouble choosing a subject, they almost always end up with the Bermuda Triangle. Like the legend itself, their interest in the brackish waters where countless ships and aircrafts have mysteriously disappeared is a phenomenon that simply cannot be explained.

"I don't have enough information," Genesis says, sinking her chin into a net of fingers.

"You don't have any information, sugar," James says. "Are you passionate about this?"

Genesis shrugs. "No."

"Yeah, I sensed that," James says. "You have to change topics immediately. Is there a subject you're passionate about?"

"She's a great dancer. Write about that," Hasanatu says, but Genesis seems not to hear her.

"Write something you know about," Hasanatu says, waking up Genesis's computer screen. "What do you know?"

Gnawing on the straw in her pink Glaceau Vitamin Water, Genesis shakes her head. "I was thinking about abortion," she says.

*   *   *

It didn't take long for the scholarship winners to form an exclusive club. Unlike at other after-school clubs like drama club or horticulture club, not everyone could be a member. Shortly after they got the good news, the scholars were invited to brunch with Jerry Seinfeld himself. Suddenly they found themselves sitting at white-clothed tables at Tavern on the Green, eating eggs and croissants and waiting for their famous host to arrive. In preparation for the event, Freeman had watched a bloopers reel of old *Seinfeld* episodes on YouTube, and he calmed his nerves by insisting loudly to anyone who would listen that "having breakfast with Jerry" was really no big deal. "You're a human, I'm a human," he said.

Sure enough, when Freeman finally did meet Seinfeld, he introduced himself as "the next Jerry Seinfeld." That in and of itself would have set Freeman apart from the other scholars, who each had to say their name, the college they would be attending, and what they planned to major in. But Freeman was the only student who answered, "acting and zoology."

Back at school, Freeman made sure that everyone knew he was going places—places with dripping crystal chandeliers and celebrity hosts. He brought pictures of himself posing alongside Seinfeld as proof. "Me and Jerry," he bragged to Genesis during first period, moving on to the next person when she failed to seem interested. Normally, Genesis would have at least taken a peek at the pictures, but a few weeks before the Lucky Five found out they had won scholarships to any college or university of their choice, there was another surprise announcement. It, too, was met with whispers and stares in the halls, and yet there was little fanfare. During a meeting of Ann's advisory, Genesis told the class that she was pregnant. No one screamed congratulations. No plans were made to celebrate over brunch at a restaurant with white tablecloths and chandeliers. In fact, not much of a plan has been made at all. Genesis has a boyfriend, a former student at the school, but he doesn't have a job. Her father, a parking valet, and her mother, who is in and out of work, are supportive, but they are already strapped. Soon, in the crowded apartment that she shares with her older sister and parents, they will have to accommodate two more. Genesis is having twins.

She isn't showing yet. She still dresses for boys, not babies, wearing skin-tight jeans and low-cut tops, her hair in a swooshy ponytail. But in a few weeks, even as the other girls break out their crop tops, Genesis will opt for baggy sweatshirts, and she will spend lunch alternately napping and showing off some pictures of her own—sonograms of the twins on her cell phone. Already Ann has noticed a change in her mood. Her grades are slipping, she is missing class more than usual, and she still needs to pass four Regents exams to graduate. "It's almost like she's in shock, like a bomb dropped next to her apartment," Ann says. "She's catatonic. I don't think she fully comprehends what two children will do to her life."

Ann doesn't have time to think about that right now. She is late for the senior team meeting. From the fourth floor, she jogs down the stairwell and through the halls. Beating James Rice by a few seconds, she opens the door to Room 340 and takes a seat at one of the light-blue trapezoid tables.

Twice a week the twelfth-grade teachers meet in this room for a team meeting. Now and then the knob turns again and another teacher comes in late. A few minutes after Alex Harty walks in wearing his Blue Jays cap and carrying a giant plastic Dunkin' Donuts cup filled with water, Hasanatu appears in the doorway with an armful of Regents prep books, unsure whether she should leave or come in. "I'll find you later, Hasanatu," Alex says.

Despite the occasional interruption, the senior team meetings are the most predictable part of the week. Ann is the team leader and usually the first to arrive in the classroom, carrying her daily planner along with warm stacks of whichever assignment she just photocopied.

"Hey, guys," Ann says, thumping her planner on the table.

Today they are doing curriculum shares, an interdisciplinary exercise that will continue over the next few weeks. Each teacher on the senior team is supposed to share a unit that they have taught in class, in the hopes of getting feedback from their colleagues and improving the curriculum for the following year. This afternoon's meeting is being devoted to I-Search reports. The students have turned in their first drafts, and both Ann and James have selected a handful to share with the other twelfth-grade teachers. "The rationale for me is, the more somebody is invested in something, the better they will do," James sums up.

That said, some of the students showed a little too much interest. Ann mentions the Russian boy who wrote his paper on breast cancer and got weirdly excited about the visual PowerPoint presentation that went along with it. Other kids showed too much progress in too little time, raising their teachers' suspicions. As James distributes copies of the first essay around the table, Ann shares a story about one Bangladeshi boy, who handed in a report about the harmful effects of smoking that turned out to be written by Mukta, his girlfriend and a top student in the senior class. James tells a story about another Bangladeshi boy who wrote his paper on the history of cricket, which would have been fine if he hadn't plagiarized it. James quickly deduced that the boy in question had cut and pasted the content from various sources off the Internet.

"He denied it in class, so I took him outside and started reading," James says. "Oh, let me see . . . 'Even though both cricket and baseball *derive* from the same category, they have huge differences.'"

James bugs his eyes at his colleagues. "I said, 'derive?' He said, 'definition.' I said, 'mitts?'"

"We know they don't know the word 'mitt,'" Ann cuts in. "But then, I wonder, what did you expect? He has trouble just writing a sentence."

In contrast, there is the essay written by a Haitian girl who is considered to be one of the best writers in the senior class. At the next curriculum-share meeting, Ann passes out her report, which is about voodoo in Haiti, and Vadim starts reading it aloud.

"Just reeeeaaaddd to yourself, please," Alex says.

"Fuck yoooouuuu," Vadim says.

"All right," Ann says, trying to get everyone back on track. "So, we'll make some observations. Someone can just spit it out."

"I see missing articles and capitalization, misspellings, plural and singular in the same sentence, wrong tenses," Alex says, not bothering to look up from the long, unbroken line that he has been tracing on his attendance folder. "I don't know what you call that situation."

"Conventions," Ann says. "Well, I noticed that her sentences are complete. You can understand what she's saying."

"Also, her sentences are complex," James cuts in, and reads an example of one out loud. " 'Throughout history,' *comma*, blah, blah, blah."

"But if she turned this in in college, they would be horrified," Ann says.

For the past few weeks, all of the twelfth-grade teachers have been working against a ticking clock to prepare the kids for life after high school, when they will be released into a world that is far less accommodating to new immigrants who are still in the beginning stages of learning English. Every once in a while they hear reports of former students whose experiences speak to the difficulties that lie ahead. For instance, there is the African girl who was at the top of her class at International and won a scholarship to an out-of-state university, only to have it cut off when she struggled to keep up her GPA. Joanna has begun collecting surveys from the inaugural class about their lives after high school, and she is working with the entire staff to better prepare the next class of seniors for college.

Still, with time running out until graduation in June, none of that can help the Class of 2009; and as the twelfth-grade teachers sink deeper into the pile of essays that Ann and James have brought for the curriculum share, it begins to feel like a futile exercise.

"Let's get one of the hard ones out of the way," Vadim says.

Ann passes out another essay, and instantly the name on the page sends up a red flag. The author is a quiet, bulky Mexican boy, who still struggles to form basic sentences in English. With this assignment, he didn't quite grasp that the purpose was to research and learn about a new topic. For his subject, he chose to write about his family. He titled the essay "Family Communication."

"Ugh," Ann says, and reads the first few lines aloud. "I have born in a Mexican family. My parents gave and they continue giving the life for us, and because that . . ." She looks up from the paper, a nervous cackle already climbing up her throat. "I'm grateful of them and I will always are."

"Oh, God," James says, fanning himself. "I have never in my life heard that: 'I will always are.'"

"This is too much," Ann says, and continues to read. Each paragraph is composed of bold starts and sudden stops that never fail to surprise the ear. Each sentence is like a bad act being booed off the stage.

"My family is all that I have and the most important for my."

"Ohhhh," sighs Rachel Huang, who teaches physics. "So wrong."

". . . and I hope to continue counting with them."

"Oh, Lord," Ann sighs. "You have to admit, he needs a grammar lesson."

Ann also points out that if the boy were writing the same paper in Spanish, it would be grammatically correct, almost word for word. That's the problem, she says. "He still thinks in Spanish. For example, the last sentence: 'And I hope to continue counting with my family.' In Spanish, it's *'Y espero continuar contando con mi familia.' Contando* means 'counting,' but it means counting *on* them, and instead of 'on' you say *'con,'* which means 'with.'"

James nods his head in agreement, but in the final minutes of the meeting, another line makes Ann pause, and no matter how hard she tries to crack it, she can't see any meaning other than the one that's right in front of her.

"I have learned many things," she reads aloud as the other teachers begin to pack up. "But not enough to live in this world at this time."

A couple of days later, the senior team meets again. This time the meeting is short and no one is laughing. Earlier in the day, Nedda de Castro, the assistant principal, gave the twelfth-grade teachers a list of all of the students in the Class of 2009. Some of the names had been highlighted, the different colors indicating who was passing, who was failing, and who was on the edge. There shouldn't be any surprises on the list—the senior advisors have been monitoring their advisees' progress all year—but Nedda printed out a copy, anyway, and instructed Ann to review it with the other teachers, as a group.

"Just read the ones who are passing," Alex says flatly. "It'll go faster that way."

As the list goes around the table, Alex explains the color-coding system. Purple means that they still need to pass Regents. Rachel drags her finger down the page: "Hasanatu Sowe." Blue means that they are failing a class. Almost everyone finds a name in blue. When the list reaches Ann, she skims down to Genesis's name, which is highlighted in fluorescent green.

"Green," Alex says, still doodling on his folder, "means they're royally screwed."

Makeup and Head Scarves

There is no highlighter color for the students who simply disappear. Their names remain on attendance sheets and manila file folders long after the students themselves have stopped showing up in class. If Jing Zheng had stuck around until the spring, her name might have been highlighted in green, too. Instead, all that remains is her photograph on the bulletin board in Room 407. In the picture, she is smiling beneath a spray of black bangs, her cheeks fringed by longer pieces of hair, bleached at the tips. Every Monday and Wednesday, when the students in James Rice's advisory meet during second period, they see Jing's face on the wall, but her seat is empty.

The day Jing came to say good-bye, another one of James's advisees was celebrating his twentieth birthday. The class was eating Cheetos and strawberry cake on paper plates when the door opened and Jing walked in, wearing a navy-blue hoodie and a nervous smile. For months she had been missing classes, and recently she had a fight with her mother and was thinking of moving out, maybe working at a Chinese restaurant in Washington, D.C. James had been emailing Jing for days about her decision to drop out, and finally he asked her to come in for advisory.

"We have some news," James said to the entire group when she sat down. "Lots of things have been happening real fast, and Jing is think-ing about leaving school and not graduating with us in June. She thinks it's too much. Classes are too hard." As he spoke, the heater banged on, and Jing stared at a smooth spot on the conference table and didn't say a word. Her fingers moved to play with a white power adapter that some-one had left out or to pick at the glittery polish on her nails. "She's wor-ried about her Regents," James continued, and a tear wobbled in her eye. "I asked her to come in today to say good-bye, because I'm not very excited about her decision."

Putting a hand on Jing's shoulder, James looked around the room. "Anybody else not in favor of her decision?"

"Jing, wait for me!" joked Rachelle Gaspard from Haiti.

"Don't give up!" someone else shouted.

"I have something to say," Yasmeen said, rising. "As everyone knows, my parents passed away in September and November, and I thought I wasn't going to survive." Abruptly, she stopped talking, and her eyes filled with tears.

"What she's trying to say is," Rachelle cut in, "even though you're having trouble at home—"

"No," Yasmeen said louder. "I'm trying to tell you that I know what you're going through. Life took from me my parents. But I'm going to take from life as much as I can. You've already overcome so many ob-stacles—learning English, coming to the U.S. There's only a few steps left. Just get the diploma, and then do whatever you want."

"Exactly," echoed Berely Garcia, a Mexican girl with indigo eyeliner and long black hair. "Just get the diploma."

"A few more months," Joe said, passing Jing a piece of strawberry cake with white frosting. "A few more months."

Despite her classmates' encouragement, Jing dropped out the next day.

Several months later Yasmeen sits at the same conference table with her advisory and an announcement of her own. Over the weekend she got married. She hasn't told anyone yet. But on her finger there is a new gold ring. As her classmates take their seats, she hides it under her other hand

and stares ahead as if her life didn't just turn upside down since she sat at this table last Wednesday. It is Monday; that is all.

"So, what did everybody do this weekend?" James asks, passing out juice and animal crackers. "I went to a party," Joe says. "Chinese party."

"Work," says Maria, who works at a factory and a fruit stand, six days a week in all, when she isn't at home with her son or at school.

"I went to the Botanic Garden to see the blooming magnolia trees," Berely says.

"Me, too," mumbles a ponytailed Mexican boy who sometimes caresses Berely's palm under the table.

Yasmeen is next. Clasping her hands, she opens her mouth as if to speak and then closes it. "*Well?*" James asks, his orange eyebrows bunching like fuzzy caterpillars. "Did you stay home? Did you play basketball?"

Everyone laughs, including Yasmeen, who simply says, "I stayed home."

She did stay home; that is true. She was at home when the flight carrying her cousin and aunt arrived from California. She was also at home when her brother and uncle accompanied her cousin and his uncle to the mosque to sign the marriage papers on Yasmeen's behalf. Yasmeen was at home when the phone rang and the imam asked her if she accepted Saif as her husband. As her aunt sat on the sofa, Yasmeen answered shakily: "I do." Earlier that morning she had cleaned the apartment and picked out a long, black dress in anticipation of her aunt's visit. After the marriage was made final, Saif was supposed to go back to a relative's apartment where he would be staying until the engagement party, but at the last minute he decided to pay Yasmeen a surprise visit. She was fixing her hair in the bathroom when he came to the door, prompting the various female relatives, friends, and neighbors who had gathered in her apartment to start shrieking. "He's outside!" "What are you doing?" "He's waiting!" "Come on, hurry up!" In a panic, Yasmeen rushed from the bathroom to her bedroom. While he sat on the couch in the living room, she tried to compose herself, chewing gum and drinking water. But chewing gum didn't stop her hands from shaking, and all the water in the world couldn't keep her face from turning red. Thank God for makeup and head scarves. As he waited, she primped, putting on a cute black-and-white polka-dot scarf.

The younger women used liquid liner to trace her eyes from tip to tear duct, and were about to apply shadow when the older women put a stop to it. "It's his first time seeing his wife," they argued, "so let her be natural."

Yasmeen was at home when she laid eyes on her husband for the first time. Saif wore a black suit, white shirt, red tie, trimmed beard. He gave her a gold Seiko watch and a ring that was too small, and for the entire length of the visit, even as Arabic wedding music played in the background and their relatives snapped pictures and took video and a tear fattened in Yasmeen's eye, the newlyweds exchanged only one word. "Smile," he told her.

That was Saturday, two days ago. Yesterday was a chaperoned trip to shop for running sneakers for him and a new ring for her, and a date at McDonald's, where they ate while Saif's mother waited in the car. This morning first period was a blur, and by the end of second period, as Yasmeen lingers behind in Room 407, the events of the past couple of days seem unreal, almost as unreal as the ring on her finger, a filigreed cuff of yellow gold laced with silver that she wriggles on her hand after class for James to see.

"What is that?" James asks. He stops riffling through a pile of internship time sheets and stares up at her open-mouthed.

"He came to see me on Saturday," Yasmeen says. "He gave this to me after signing the marriage papers."

"The marriage papers?" James barks. "I thought you weren't getting married until next year! I thought this was just your engagement party!"

Twisting the ring, Yasmeen explains how her cousin went to the mosque with her brother and uncle who acted as her representatives in an all-male ceremony, later celebrating together in a restaurant.

"You mean you weren't even *there*?" James says, tapping his forehead. "You weren't even *present*?"

"Well, they called for my permission," she says quickly. "It's okay. I got to talk to him. Thanks God, he's an American guy. He thinks like me. He likes to run. He's interested in reading about the way the brain works. He's curious about the world."

James smiles a tightlipped smile and makes his eyes bulge like a couple of rubber eyeballs in a novelty bin at a Halloween store. It's a look that Yasmeen has seen before, a look that appears in class whenever his students come up with a bogus excuse as to why they can't turn in their assignments on time. The same look usually precedes the punishment, which he utters with equal parts rage and glee: "Big fat zero." Maybe it's the sight of her face—the twitch of her cheek, the wince of her smile— that causes James to rearrange his own.

"So, the men's ceremony was this weekend?" he asks. "I'm kind of upset, because I feel like I missed it. Can you at least bring pictures from the women's ceremony?"

"Not to the males. Sorry."

James rolls his eyes. "I'm just gonna stand outside and wait, like this," he says, making a Chaplinesque sad face and slumping down against the wall. "Maybe I can sneak in if I pretend to deliver flowers."

"I still have to pick music and set up the hall," Yasmeen says.

"*And* do your homework," James adds. "I can't believe I can't go! You must, *must* bring him in to meet me. I am not joking." He sighs. "It's like giving your child away. I haven't even met this person!"

Standing up, James opens his arms to give her a hug, before thinking better of it, and giving her an awkward high five instead. "Congratulations, darling."

James watches Yasmeen walk out the door. There was a time when he thought anything possible for her, but as he pushes her chair back into place at the table, he can't shake the feeling that she has set in motion a life for herself that she can't stop. The feeling only sinks in deeper following an after-school meeting with some of his colleagues. Just about every teacher at International knows of at least one Muslim girl who got pregnant immediately after her wedding ceremony.

The possibility of Yasmeen having sex hadn't even crossed James's mind on Monday morning, but by Monday evening, three days before her engagement party, he thinks about the fact that, over the weekend, Yasmeen had become a wife and daughter-in-law. How much longer before she would become a mother? On the one hand, he could imagine a scenario where Yasmeen persuaded her husband to get his GED while she went to college. On the other hand, she isn't above being persuaded herself, and the idea of her capitulating to the expectations of her husband and mother-in-law fills James with dread. "This is a slippery slope," he later remembered thinking. "First of all, she got *married*. He's going to move in, and she's going to get pregnant. It's over. She thinks she's going to college. She's not. *'Who's going to be your advocate?'* No one—not if she's in a situation where there are two people and a culture against her."

Two days later, James paces the halls of the fourth floor, his nostrils flaring and an iPhone clenched to his ear. "Get your butt in here!" he shouts. Just outside the boys' bathroom, a boy with dark matted hair and a whiff of nicotine on his clothes cowers briefly before realizing that the directive is aimed at someone else. "We're all waiting for *you*," James yells into the phone. "I don't care what you're doing. No—nuh, uh-uh. Get. Here. Now."

It is just before lunchtime on Wednesday, one day before spring break, and Room 407 is set for a party. On the table is a spread of bagels, cream cheese, and orange juice that James picked up from Bergen Bagels on his way to school this morning for his advisory. The guests are in attendance. "Congratulations" is written on the board. Everything is in place but for one small detail: the guest of honor is missing.

The door opens, and James comes back into the classroom. "Yasmeen's on her way," he says, thumping a bagel the size of a baseball mitt onto his plate. Reaching over each other for cups and plates, the students who did bother to show up this morning can see that James is in a mood, but they don't know why. Nor do they know the reason for the party.

Shortly before Yasmeen left on Monday, James told her that he wanted to celebrate her announcement at the next advisory meeting. Unsure as he is about her shotgun marriage and the events of the past few days, he is sure that he doesn't want her to go through the next few days alone. In hindsight, James wishes that his advisory would have been more supportive after Yasmeen's parents died in the fall. "She didn't share much publicly until afterward. During it, the advisory knew, but she wasn't here a lot, and I think she went through that mostly alone," James says. As for her engagement, "I wanted this to be a situation *not* like that—where the kids could actually participate. This is a big deal. I wanted to give my other advisees the chance to share that with her, and for her to share it with us."

As much as she has revealed to her closest friends, Yasmeen has concealed even more, and her sudden absence is troubling. In the halls on Monday, Yasmeen showed Jessica her new gold ring and told her about Saif's visit over the weekend, but she neglected to mention that they had gotten married. Nor has she been entirely clear about the fact that Saif is also her first cousin. Yasmeen spent many lunch breaks in Dariana's office talking about whom she planned to invite to her party. In addition to her closest friends, the list includes all of the girls in her advisory and a few female teachers, including Ann Parry. But no one received a written invitation, and by first period this morning, she still hadn't shown.

When Yasmeen finally does show up half an hour after James's phone call, the bagels are eaten and the juice is gone. "Sorry I'm late," she says, taking a seat.

"What's going on?" Rachelle asks.

"Just tell them," Yasmeen says, shooting James a look.

"So, it's the last day before vacation. But we're also celebrating something else," James begins.

"She's pregnant?" gasps Maria.

"She's getting married!" Joe says. "I saw the ring!"

Rachelle is incredulous. "*You* have a *boyfriend*?"

"No," Yasmeen says. "He's my cousin. He's twenty-one years old."

"You're marrying your cousin?!" Rachelle squawks.

"Yes," Yasmeen says, lifting her chin ever so slightly, "It's okay to marry your cousin in my culture. It's very common."

The clock hands move to 10:55, but no one is thinking of going to internships now. As the halls fill with students, Yasmeen is bombarded with questions. "Where will you live?" "Will you and your husband have a place of your own, or stay with your brothers and sisters?" "You're still going to college, right? RIGHT?"

"Yes, my plan is the same," Yasmeen says. "He is moving to New York, but that will be later—after the wedding next year. Tomorrow is the engagement party."

"Are we invited?" Joe interrupts. "I'm going!"

"Just females," Yasmeen says, smiling at James. "Sorry."

"What will your last name be?"

"It will stay the same."

"Wait, what was it before?"

Everyone laughs.

"Was it your family who arranged it?" Rachelle asks. "Are you mad?"

Before Yasmeen can answer, James cuts in. "Whose culture has the tradition of arranged marriage? Raise your hand."

Lobsang props up his elbow with his other hand. As usual, his eyelids are at half-mast.

"Why don't you explain it, Yasmeen," James says.

"Well, his mom picked me to marry him," Yasmeen begins, staring at her hands. "But I wouldn't marry him if I didn't like him. Thanks God . . . he picked me, too."

Sitting at the end of the table, a quiet Ecuadorian girl named Jenny Zea hasn't said a word all period. But as the blood rushes to Yasmeen's cheeks, Jenny can't help but read the expression on her face, which no makeup or head scarf could conceal.

"You like him!" Jenny blurts out, jumping up from her seat. "You *like* him!"

Long before Yasmeen told her advisory about her engagement party, her family was busy making plans. They chose to celebrate on the first Thursday of spring break. A hall was rented and a ball gown bought, and heaps of yellow-gold jewelry were set aside. Plans were made to take Yasmeen to a Pakistani beauty salon in Coney Island to get her hair curled, and various young women offered to help with her makeup, while the older women said they would provide bread and tea for her guests. As the date neared, the details of the procession emerged. In the absence of their parents, Yasmeen's older sister would escort her into the women's hall. Male and female parties are always separate, but before the end of the night, Yasmeen's brothers would walk Saif into the all-female ceremony to dance with his wife and help cut the cake.

For months Yasmeen has known that someday she would be walking down the aisle at her own engagement party, but the notion that she is a married woman—at least by American standards—seems to flit through her thoughts like some half-remembered dream, hazy and unreal. On the one hand, she has spent countless hours divulging the details of her party dress and beauty regimen to Dariana and asked both Jessica and Mukta to be bridesmaids. On the other hand, when Yasmeen told her advisory that the actual wedding would happen next year, she neglected to mention that she is already a wife.

"I do." Over the weekend, those two words changed her life, but she doesn't have time to think about that. After all, there is still a party to plan and a banquet hall to decorate with streamers and balloons. Somehow, announcing the details out loud in advisory has set the next twenty-four hours in tilting motion—and when Yasmeen barges into the student-government office after lunch, trailed by a couple of excited senior girls, she seems stunned that tomorrow is finally here.

"Have you seen Jessica and Mukta?" Yasmeen gasps, her black polyester *hijab* slightly askew. "Where are my bridesmaids?"

"Calm down, dear," Dariana says. "Did they say they would meet you here?"

Only a couple of hours have passed since Yasmeen calmly told her classmates about her plans, but in that time her cool demeanor has been hijacked by pure panic. Her cheeks are damp and flushed from running down the halls. In her hand, she clutches a scrap of paper scrawled with pencil—directions to her party. At the last minute Yasmeen decided to invite what seemed like practically half of the school's female staff, including a couple of science teachers, an assistant principal, a social worker, the college counselor, and Ann Parry, just to name a new. She spent lunch tearing pages out of her notebook and jotting down all the details. Before second period ended, she also extended an invitation to all of the girls in her advisory, and ever since it came out that she would be spending tomorrow morning in the salon, a few of the girls have been following her around like mini Perez Hiltons, trying to get the scoop. "Oh my God! We're going to see your hair?!" "Does Mr. Rice know? He's gonna be so mad!" "Can we take pictures?" "What should I wear?"

"Wear whatever you're comfortable with," Yasmeen says, just as Mukta and Jessica walk in. "Oh, thanks God you're here!"

As the other girls flutter around the room, Yasmeen consults her bridesmaids about the plan for tomorrow. Even though the party doesn't start until 4 PM, she is planning to start her beauty regimen at 9 AM sharp with a trip to the salon.

"While she's at the salon, I'll bring my straightening iron and do your hair!" Mukta tells Jessica.

"But her hair's already straight," says Berely Garcia, the Mexican girl from Yasmeen's advisory. She holds up Jessica's limp locks to prove her point.

"Actually, she's coming with me to the salon," Yasmeen says, grabbing Jessica's arm. "I want my hair curved."

A thin cloud of disappointment passes over Mukta's face, but before she can protest, Yasmeen insists that both girls meet at her apartment first thing in the morning. As an extra precaution, she sits down at a computer against the wall and pulls up MapQuest. "Be there by nine," she says, ripping another sheet out of her notebook to write down the directions to her building. "Otherwise, you guys are fired!"

"Oh my God! I'm so excited! I'm so nervous!" Mukta babbles on her way out the door. As the rest of the girls clear out of the room, Dariana gestures through the window for Yasmeen to come into her office. Dariana is leaving for a trip to Florida tomorrow and can't go to the party. There's a small part of her that doesn't want to stick around to witness one of her favorite students getting married off so young. But, like everyone else, she doesn't want to miss Yasmeen's Cinderella moment, and she wishes she could be there to help. Over the past few days, Dariana has offered to lend Yasmeen various flower vases and centerpiece decorations left over from last year's prom, to no avail. As usual, Yasmeen just insists that she can handle everything herself.

"So, how are you feeling?" Dariana asks when Yasmeen sits down.

"Okay. But I'm tired, my throat hurts, and I'm worried about my eyebrows because they do this funny thing when I'm really tired," Yasmeen says, smoothing a few unruly hairs before digging through her purse. This morning, as she ran out the door, she grabbed some of the jewelry that Saif had given to her as a gift. After a few seconds, she pulls out a pair of yellow-gold chandelier earrings, followed by a small crystal box padded with velvet. "This is the first ring that he gave to me," Yasmeen says, opening the lid to reveal a diamond ring sized for a child's finger. "I'm lucky. He's much better than the other suitors."

"'The other suitors.' I love it," Dariana says, cradling the crystal box in her hand. In between examining the ring, she steals glances at Yasmeen's face, its color deepening into a painful, mottled crimson. They lock eyes for a moment, and Yasmeen quickly looks away, packing her bag to leave. "I have to clean the house and decorate the hall," she explains, looking out the window. It is still snowing.

"You're cleaning, too?" Dariana asks. "You can't do it all by yourself, Yasmeen. You're in over your head. You need help."

"I'm fine," Yasmeen says, her voice hoarse. "I can handle it."

Dariana watches Yasmeen head out the door a little before noon. Outside, the streets are coated with brown slush, and rain is falling in hard rhythmic slats against the window. A few hours from now, Dariana will be packing up her bikini, and Yasmeen will begin decorating the hall for her party, hanging gold and white balloons with pieces of tape. Tomorrow is one of the most important days of her life, and she still has snacks to prepare, tables to set, music to select, and an entire apartment to clean before her guests arrive, and Dariana can't help but feel a little guilty. Before she leaves the office, she calls Yasmeen at home in a last-ditch effort to urge her to recruit some more friends to help out.

"You're in over your head," she says again. "I know you're used to doing things by yourself, but you have a million things to do, and you want to look pretty! Tomorrow's your day."

On the other end, Yasmeen politely insists that she has everything under control, but when Dariana hangs up the phone, she isn't convinced. "Yasmeen is nervous about her eyebrows," she says and rolls her eyes. "It doesn't matter what your culture is. Every woman has the same feelings. It's *her* day. She has butterflies in her stomach."

Right before hanging up the phone, Yasmeen had told her, "I just want to look beautiful."

*   *   *

In the early 1970s, a blighted section of Crown Heights got its first new apartment complex in several decades: Crown Gardens, a 239-unit co-op with a fifteen-story tower and a garden court enclosed by town houses on three sides. At the time, the development was heralded as an innovative step in urban design for a crowded and poverty-stricken community. Today the hulking compound attracts a broad mix of tenants in a neighborhood claimed by Caribbean blacks, Jews, and Arabs. The dissonance plays out on the streets, where wig shops and West Indian dives like Cock's Bajan Restaurant and Bakery share turf with a mural featuring famous African Americans such as Jesse Jackson and Stevie Wonder, and a halal warehouse whose blue and yellow facade is spray-painted in curdled-blood red: LIVE CHICKEN MARKET. Nearby, Crown Gardens takes up most of a residential block lined with trees and curbside trash.

For the most part, the streets are quiet and clear in the daytime, but at night, in the courtyard lobby, a security guard keeps watch in case anything out of the ordinary should happen. One dark and rainy afternoon in April, it does. A little after 4:30 PM, several dozen figures cloaked in black descend onto the complex like a flock of crows. In the courtyard outside the banquet room on the ground floor, they tiptoe across the wet grass as imperceptible as shadows. It is only when they are safely inside that the cloaks come off, and Yasmeen's Yemeni friends and relatives are unveiled.

"Dude, you look like a ninja!" one of Yasmeen's cousins says to her friend, who is halfway through the sliding-glass door when she begins to take off her *hijab* and coat, showcasing a belt of shimmering belly-dancing coins. A few minutes later two women wearing matching black face veils enter the room, taking in the mirrored walls, gold balloons, and garlands of white roses through one-inch slits.

"Your eyes look hot!" one girl says, admiring another's sparkly eye shadow through her flap.

One by one, more figures slip through the door—a steady stream of dark veils, long dresses, and coats blotting out faces, ages, and attitudes like spilled ink. From a distance, it is impossible to tell who is young and who is old, who is beautiful and who is hiding a mustache or a few extra pounds. With the exception of a few who show up in full-body veils, most of the women wear black scarves, their faces luminous and round or pale and waning like so many phases of the moon.

Whatever isn't covered is decorated, down to the last centimeter of skin, anything they can get away with. Eyelids are painted electric pink and chrome yellow, and glittered with heavy-metal shades of silver and rust—a little Lady Gaga under the veil. Lips are glossed in sports-car colors, like Maserati red. Wrists are bangled. Nails are polished. Hands, hennaed down to the fingertips that type text messages into hot-pink Sidekicks. Even the old women have stenciled intricate designs under their sleeves. And that's just what the outside world is allowed to see.

Gradually, all of the veils come off to expose the women beneath. They are fat, thin, curvaceous, and pregnant, wrinkled, lightly mustached, and heavily made up. Many carry children in tow. Everyone is dressed for a night out. Among the group there is a gold sequined cap, one fuchsia headdress, and a sheer black top revealing a satin bra and substantial décolletage. The transformation is instant and overwhelming.

"Oh my God! I love your hair!" a girl screams when her friend takes off her *hijab* and shakes out a head full of ringlets. "Let's party!" another woman says, raising the roof with her hands.

Sitting at a long table set with white and gold doilies, Ann Parry and the girls from Yasmeen's advisory gawk at a cluster of women who have gathered in front of one of the mirrored walls, brandishing curling irons and eye-shadow palettes, blush brushes and powder compacts. "Oh, wow," says Berely Garcia, watching an attractive girl with long blown-out hair and a big butt examine her reflection.

"They're so pretty," Bilguissa Diallo, from Guinea, says with a sigh. "I'm surprised."

"I feel a little underdressed," Ann says, hiding her jeaned legs under the table. An hour before, she was the first guest to arrive. Yasmeen's little brother was still taping a few last balloons onto the wall when Ann sat down and a middle-aged Yemeni woman walked into the room, took one look at her blond hair and blue jeans, walked out, and came back in again, asking, "Am I in the wrong place?"

Shortly after, Berely showed up wearing a red-chiffon scarf that she had borrowed from Mukta, followed by Bilguissa in an African head wrap and several other girls in a motley mix of jeans, black pants, and peasant blouses. "It's like *we're* the weird ones," Berely says, casting a nervous glance around the room. "Everybody's looking at *us*."

In fact, there might as well be two separate parties. On one side of the room sit Yasmeen's friends from International: a bunch of girls from Mexico, Ecuador, Guatemala, and Guinea. The other side of the room belongs to Yasmeen's Arabic friends and relatives, who can be counted on to show up at engagement parties like this one throughout the year, and who can be broken down into four categories: the shrewd old ladies of Old Sana'a, the middle-aged matrons, and the Real Yemeni Housewives of New York City, a group of twenty-something, stay-at-home moms who relish the chance to sit around and unload about their husbands and mothers-in-law. "I'm so pissed off at men right now," one woman complained at a similar party a couple of months later, while bouncing two children on her lap.

"You're not just marrying him—you're marrying his mother," hissed another.

Despite being the smallest in number, the fourth group is the most conspicuous: the unmarrieds. They catch everyone's eye, but especially the attention of the older women, several of whom are matchmakers hoping to make connections for their sons and nephews. Reputation is everything, and parties provide the perfect opportunity to fact-gather about a prospective bride. *What have you heard about so-and-so? Is she a good girl? Religious?* Some matchmakers set up local girls with men back home known as "boaters"—a derogatory term used to describe Yemeni bachelors who want to marry Yemeni-American women for their papers. "That's why everyone goes all out," one girl explained. "You never know who's watching."

And so: the glimmery gold eyes demurely cast down, the curve-skimming dresses outlining childbearing hips, and the extra-conservative face veils. Every once in a while one of the younger women who is still cloaked comes over to the other side of the room to offer clove tea and Entenmann's cake to Ann and the girls from Yasmeen's advisory. "I'm smiling at you right now," a girl with hazel eyes says to the table, her mouth hidden behind a curtain of black. "Are you having fun?"

In fact, the girls are so enthralled that they haven't noticed the time, until now. More than an hour has passed since they first arrived, and there is still no sign of Yasmeen. Both Bilguissa and Maria have left their babies with sitters in order to be here, and as the Yemeni housewives continue to primp in front of the mirrored walls and their children play and pop balloons underfoot, they crane their necks toward the door.

"I have to go," Maria says finally.

Sensing their restlessness, an old woman with dark circles under her eyes comes over to the table and pours some more tea.

"It smell good," Bilguissa says, bathing her face in the steam. A few minutes later another relative brings over a selection of clay-oven breads and more frosted cake.

"Thank you, but we don't want to eat," Berely says. "We just came to see Yasmeen's hair."

Not long ago Yasmeen asked Allah for a favor. "God, if you think this is a good husband for me, who will make me happy, help encourage me or send a sign for me to say yes," she prayed. "Make me confident." She had gotten through the most daunting part—saying yes—but when she woke up this morning, the day of her engagement party, her confidence was in low supply, and her voice was almost gone from staying up late with a sore throat. To make matters worse, the woman who was supposed to drive her to the hair salon in Coney Island didn't show up on time, throwing the whole day off schedule and sending Yasmeen into a queasy panic. At the last minute, even as Mukta and Jessica arrived to help her get ready for the ceremony, Yasmeen cracked and told her older sister that she couldn't do it—she couldn't go. "You have to go," her sister said in Arabic. "It's your engagement party."

For the first hour and a half, the bride is a no-show. Five thirty comes and goes, and finally so does Maria Mendez.

"Where is she?" Ann asks aloud, checking the time on her cell phone. At the front of the room, a pair of white wicker chairs that have been set up for the bride and groom remain conspicuously empty. The gold and white balloons that Yasmeen herself taped to the walls have begun to fall to the ground, where they are immediately popped by screaming children. The tea has cooled, and the cake is almost gone. Soon the sun will set, which means that everyone will have to stop what they are doing to kneel for the sundown prayer.

A little before six o'clock, Ann is about to leave when a tall old woman with a craggy face stands up near the entrance of the banquet hall, wraps herself in a tie-dyed brown-and-white scarf, and screams: "U-LU-LU-LU-LU-LU!" Moments later another shriek lances the air, and soon the entire room is whooping and wailing, "OOOO-LOOO-LOOO-LOOO-LOOO-LOOO! LI-LI-LI-LI-LI! AY-AY-AY-AY-AY!" Lips that were sipping tea only moments before part to reveal teeth and tongues, thrashing against the insides of cheeks like trapped lizards. In the frenzy, plastic utensils and cell phones clatter to the ground and a flat-nosed woman does a two-fingered taxi whistle. At every table, women grab the coats and robes that have been resting on the backs of their chairs since they arrived and rush to cover. Hoods and veils whoosh over heads, hiding ringlets and smiles. Breasts and hips vanish as if under a magician's curtain, and in a matter of seconds the room goes black. "Hurry up!" someone yells, signaling the approach of the men. "They're coming!"

Wearing a lavender dress and a single purple flower in her hair, Yasmeen's little sister is the first to enter the hall, scattering metallic rainbow confetti as she walks down the aisle. Behind her, Yasmeen's remaining siblings stand close by, waiting for a cue.

"Where's Yasmeen?" Berely asks, turning around in her seat.

Throughout the room, chairs screech and robes rustle as various friends and relatives strain to get a better look, and then they see her.

"Oh, my God!" Berely gasps.

Standing in the doorway, Yasmeen is barely recognizable in a butterscotch-colored ball gown with a tight, sequined bodice and voluminous satin skirt. Except for a bouquet of white lilies and baby's breath that she carries in her hands, she is a vision of gold, from the glitter on her eyelids to the flowers in her hair. Her hair is dark brown, woolly in texture, and longer than anyone imagined, all the way down to her butt. Tonight it is pulled into a long ponytail of cascading ringlets with blown-out bangs.

For four years Yasmeen's classmates haven't seen so much as a loose strand of hair slip out of her veil, and suddenly the sight of her bare neck and arms is almost too much. As she walks by, it's as if a gust of wind has blown into the room with her, spraying confetti in all directions and pricking everyone's eyes.

"She looks so different—I can't believe it's her," Bilguissa says, wiping away tears with a napkin. "She's beautiful."

"She looks like a model," says Mukta, who had slipped into the room moments before the big entrance. Sitting next to her in a short gun-metal-gray dress, Jessica just stares transfixed. The sight of Yasmeen is so overwhelming that it takes a minute for everyone to notice the young man by her side: her husband, the second big reveal of the night. Tall and slim with close-cropped black hair and a neat goatee, Saif wears a dark suit, a red-and-black tie, and a stiff expression as he leads Yasmeen to the wicker sweetheart chairs at the front of the room, past the peeping eyes and ululating tongues.

"He's *cute!*" Ann says. "I can see why she chose him."

"I can tell he's nervous. I put my hand on his back, and he was shaking," a young Yemeni woman tells the girls at Ann's table. "Look at how he doesn't smile—that's because he's scared. He's not allowed to look at anyone."

Anyone but his wife. Stealing glances at her as they settle into their chairs, it seems as if he is trying to memorize her face while he still has the chance. Her expression is serene, but her smile is hieroglyphic. Earlier, Yasmeen told Jessica that she was worried about looking too happy or else tongues would wag; after all, her parents only recently died. At the same time, Yasmeen was worried about looking too sad; she needed to show Saif that she was proud to be his wife. "I want him to be happy," she said, "that he chose me." After the party, Saif is scheduled to return to California, where he will stay until their wedding next year—an extravagant affair that will mark the beginning of their life together under the same roof. In the meantime, his mother will continue to help work out their living arrangements, since Saif and Yasmeen are not allowed to talk themselves. All they will have to remember each other are the few moments that they've shared so far: having tea in her living room, shopping for sneakers, and eating at McDonald's.

Tonight is technically only their third date, and the pressure is on to make it a memorable one—enough to carry them through the year. Every moment is a photo op, another memory to savor until they see each other next. During their first dance, Yasmeen is shy and hesitant, surrounded by friends and relatives armed with camcorders and cell-phone cameras documenting her every move. As the night goes on, she becomes bolder. When Saif cuts a piece of three-tiered yellow cake to feed her, she cups his elbow and guides his hand toward her mouth. When Yasmeen returns the favor, interlacing her arm with his, Bilguissa can't contain herself and screams, "Give him a bigger slice!"

Before the ceremony, Yasmeen told her bridesmaids about some of the Yemeni traditions, including one in which the groom dresses the bride in gold jewelry, but seeing it play out in person is more exciting than they anticipated. Yasmeen has never been seen uncovered by a man outside her immediate family before, let alone been touched by one, and the sexual tension between the two newlyweds is thick enough to cut with the cake knife. With trembling hands, Saif inserts the first of two yellow-gold chandelier earrings into Yasmeen's pierced lobe, and the room explodes in whoops and screams. Next, he fastens a matching choker around her throat, briefly fumbling with the clasp. Each time he touches her, carefully navigating his way around the delicate cartography of her collarbone, her shoulders, and the nape of her neck, he exhales a deep sigh of relief, and she leans a little bit closer, even as her expression remains unreadable.

"Oh my God—that's so romantic!" Jessica sighs, just as a flash goes off.

She turns around to see Yasmeen's little sister, Amani, peering through the camera's viewfinder. Earlier, at Yasmeen's request, Jessica lent her digital camera to Amani to capture the night in Kodak moments: Yasmeen and Saif cutting the cake, Yasmeen and Saif dancing, Yasmeen and Saif posing and smiling in front of their sweetheart chairs. Amani has spent the past couple of hours running around the room snapping pictures, and her memory card is full of images of women with their veils off and their hands up. Jessica had been planning on transferring the photos to Yasmeen's flash drive when she got home, but before she leaves, Yasmeen stops her at the door.

"Don't show these to anyone," Yasmeen says.

The rest of her instructions are drowned out by the din of Arabic music and shouting women, but Jessica nods to show that she understands.

Sure enough, an hour later when she walks into her room in Chinatown, Jessica transfers every last picture onto a flash drive for Yasmeen's eyes only, just as she said she would. Then, also as she said she would, she hits the delete button, and wipes the camera's memory clean, as if the night never happened.

Soup or Salad?

In Room 443, Chit Su sits at a small blue table watching her English teacher, a petite Puerto Rican brunette named Minerva Moya, pretend to stir an invisible pot of soup. It is just past noon, and the freshmen and sophomores who make up Minerva's fourth-period class are still giddy from lunch. Next to Chit Su, a gangly Tibetan boy with spiky hair laughs at Minerva's exaggerated motions, and she abruptly stops stirring her pot to clap her hands in three staccato beats. "Students, *focus!*" She wears a red leather headband and black tights under a metallic-gray dress, and around her neck, dangling from a purple cord, is a ring of keys that jingle as she bounds across the classroom like a cheerleader trying to rouse a tough crowd.

"This is important. I need you to pay attention," she says, stopping in front of Chit Su, who is fumbling through the contents of her slim leather purse. The heavy Mead backpack that she wore back in the fall is long gone in favor of a cooler look. Today Chit Su is dressed in a gray hoodie over a tight white camisole with a short jean skirt, leggings, black Converse All Stars, and ankle socks stitched with tiny American flags.

"Do you remember what 'assimilation' means?" Minerva asks, putting her fists on her hips.

Pinching her lower lip, Chit Su breaks into an embarrassed laugh.

"Ooh, I know, I know!" shouts a Muslim girl in a burgundy head scarf. "It's like mixing."

"*Bingo!*" Minerva shouts. "So, in other words, "I've got this pot, and I'm cooking." Still stirring her pot with one hand, she turns on the projector and shows the class a photograph of a stockpot bubbling on a stove, under the label MELTING POT.

"Now, I'm going to throw some Tibetans in there! Then I'm going to throw some Mexicans in there, and maybe a few Dominicans." She points to a sprout-sized girl from Puebla with straight black hair who erupts into giggles. "This is the idea of assimilation," Minerva continues, "all these different cultures blending together. And this"—she taps the image of the stockpot—"this is America."

Chit Su studies the stockpot with a pencil eraser between her teeth. As the rest of the students slowly absorb the idea that America is soup, Minerva flips to the next photograph of a tossed salad that is supposed to illustrate how America is made up of different immigrant groups that don't necessarily blend into the whole completely, but rather mix together while still retaining their original cultures and characteristics.

"What happens when you mix this up?" Minerva asks the class. "Are you still going to be able to tell where the cucumber is? Are you still going to be able to pick out your tomato?"

A few heads nod, as their owners readjust to the idea that maybe America is actually salad.

"Say the tomatoes are the Tibetans," Minerva explains. "The carrots are the Chinese. The Mexicans are the lettuce—you live in this country now, but you still retain your green color. The Tibetan tomatoes still maintain their seeds. The Chinese carrots are still orange. You don't have to sacrifice changing any of your qualities. You are who you are."

At International, everyone adapts at a different pace. Depending on the student, it may take a week, a month, one year, or several to feel comfortable enough in this country to call it home. There are kids like Jovita, who has lived in America for almost four years and is still hesitant to speak English outside of school for fear that no one will understand her accent, and there are kids like Freeman, who will talk to anyone in any language. There are the Bangladeshi girls who wear traditional clothes and head scarves that will be traded in for jeans and layered haircuts by junior year. And there is the case of Mukta Mukta, whose entry into American life collided with the undoing of her religious faith, when, in a tenth-grade English class, she started reading Greek mythology that challenged everything she had been taught by her imam. "There's no such thing as god," Mukta wrote in an essay during her junior year. "That's what I discovered coming to the United States."

More than six months since she came to the United States, Chit Su still hasn't fully unpacked. No one would know from the way she comes to school dressed in perfectly assembled outfits day after day, but in a cramped basement apartment in Sheepshead Bay, Brooklyn, shoved against one wall of the room she shares with her fourteen-year-old sister, there are piles of plastic sacks subbing as suitcases and filled with clothes. There is no bed, not even a mattress. The girls sleep beside each other on a dirty rug covered with a light-green sheet and random debris— a stray sewing needle, used Q-tips and cotton balls, and the occasional cockroach.

Her little sister is the messy one. Chit Su is more organized. Every night before she goes to bed, she picks out a few items from the sacks and lays out her outfit for school the next morning. She has done her best to clean and warm up the place. In the corner of the room is a makeshift wastebasket made from a Top Choice Assorted Biscuits tin box, lined with an orange plastic bag. Tweety Bird gift-wrapping paper and Santa Claus stickers decorate the wall near Chit Su's pillow, above which hangs a postcard of Burma's famous Shwedagon Pagoda, its golden peak shining like a night-light.

On a desk near a computer are several photo albums. A few months ago, Chit Su was afraid to say much more than "hello," but today, in her ever-improving English, she tells a small part of her story through pictures and short sentences.

"My home in Burma," she says, pointing to the light-blue house where she lived in Mogok, a city in a region known for its ruby mines; hence the ring on her finger, a silver flower with a sanguine center. "This is me." She pauses over a snapshot of a little girl with rouged cheeks and painted red lips who appears to have been dolled up for a party.

A few pages later, Chit Su flips to a photo of a faceless crowd: women, children, and saffron-robed monks waiting in line for ice cream on an endless expanse of sun-scorched grass. "This is Thailand," she says. In fact, the scene is at the Nu Po refugee camp in Tak Province on the Thailand-Burma border, where tens of thousands of people have sought temporary asylum since fleeing the Burmese army, which has committed some of the worst human rights violations in recent history. Along with her mother, grandmother, older brother, and younger sister, Chit Su lived at Nu Po for three years in a bamboo hut with a thatched roof, bed sheets for walls, and access to a simple pit latrine. (The day that they served ice cream, it must have been a special treat. A typical food basket is filled with rice, beans, soybean oil, fish paste, salt, chili, and fortified flour. When ice cream is sold, it is sometimes a local variety that may be scooped onto sticky rice or served between bread, more of an "ice-cream dog.")

Somehow, through all of her traveling, Chit Su has managed to hold on to photos documenting her life at the camp. One stands out. On her desk, in a tiny picture frame that says "Cutie Pie," is a snapshot of a teenage boy with dark hair and a pale narrow face winking against the bright-blue backdrop of the sky.

"My brother," Chit Su says. "He died." He was seventeen, the same age she is now, when he was killed in a freak accident after taking a day trip about two hours outside of the camp. He had gone to pick some pomelos, similar to grapefruit, and a tree fell, crushing the back of his head. "Like this," Chit Su says, lowering her own head and chopping at the nape of her neck. "Lots of blood." She was the one who found her brother's body, which was buried at Nu Po. Chit Su has a photo of the white casket, wreathed in pink and yellow flowers, moments before it was dropped into the ground at the funeral. Soon after, the family left for the United States, one fewer member. "I miss my brother every day," Chit Su says, picking up the Cutie Pie frame and laying her thumb over her brother's face. "That's why I look here."

The amount of space differs little between the bamboo hut that Chit Su shared with her family in Nu Po and the basement apartment that she now shares with her sister, grandmother, aunt, uncle, and two cousins in Brooklyn. A few weeks ago, Chit Su's mother moved to Texas, which has a sizable Burmese population, to find work. Even in her absence every inch of floor, wall, ceiling, and surface is covered with the wreckage of lives interrupted. The living room and kitchen area is so cluttered that it is hard to make out the shapes of specific objects. There are mounds of soiled laundry and a canopy of children's clothes drying from pipes overhead. Electrical wires shoot out like vines and creepers from random places, and bits of stale, fallen rice crunch underfoot. "I don't live here—very dirty," Chit Su says, crinkling her nose at the untamable mess that begins just beyond her door. "I live in my room."

Despite the transient nature of her living situation, Chit Su has managed to make a home for herself at International. In the past few months, she has gone through boyfriends and best friends almost as fast as new outfits and hairstyles. When she's ready to take the subway home after school, she doesn't say, "Let's go." One of her many best friends, a tiny Mexican girl from Puebla, taught Chit Su how to say "*Vámonos*" instead. She still talks on the phone regularly with the chubby Spanish-speaking boy who has been courting her since fall and recently started asking her for kisses in the halls. Pizza, once so mystifying on her first day in the cafeteria, has become commonplace, as have burgers and fries, which she now dips in ketchup mixed with mayonnaise and shares with one of her other boyfriends, a pimply Uzbek with an affinity for westernwear.

Chit Su has come a long way since her first day of school—such a distance, in fact, that she is able to look back on it now and explain in English what she couldn't say at the time. A few weeks into spring, Chit Su turned in her part of a publishing project that Minerva had assigned to her fourth-period class. Working in groups of four and five, each staff of students had to create and design their own newspaper on the subjects of education and assimilation. "You can talk about bilingual education. You can do an advice column, such as 'Dear So-and-So, I am the only Nepalese student in my school,' and your group mate can write back, 'Dear Sad and Lonely Child . . . , '" Minerva explained. "But you all need to explore a real newspaper. What is a letter to the editor? What does a book review look like? What is an op-ed?" As long as they stayed on theme, the students could contribute whatever kind of feature they wanted, whether that was a news article or a crossword puzzle. After discussing some options with her group, Chit Su had chosen to draw a comic strip about her first day of school. She titled it "Chit Su's First Day of School," and drew herself in a miniskirt and knee socks—not the fluorescent-green T-shirt and jeans that she actually wore that day.

"Hi," says a speech bubble coming from the cartoon girl. "My name is Chit Su. I'm imigrant student. I came from Thailand."

"Hi," says the cartoon Ms. Moya. "My name is Moya. I am English teacher."

In twelve panels, Chit Su went on to illustrate the highlights and low points of her first day: getting lost on the way to the principal's office, meeting her advisor Ms. Suzannah, having to use the toilet but not knowing where to find it, and getting lost on her way out of the school building. Clearly she loves to draw, and she took pains to depict the various students who rescued her throughout the day, giving the girls cute outfits and the boys spiky anime hair. Still, when Minerva reviews the assignment, it isn't the drawings that make the strongest impression on her, but the accompanying words—which Chit Su had strung into sentences and crafted into a story.

"I have one problem," the cartoon Chit Su says in the second panel. "My one problem is I can't speak English language. I don't know how to speak class, office, lunchroom, exit, bathroom, read, write, I don't know how to work in my group."

More than six months since she arrived at International, Chit Su has made a breakthrough. Yet just a few days before, she had had to make a tough announcement. Every week since September, Minerva has been asking the students to answer the prompts: "One good thing that happened this week was . . ." and "One bad thing that happened this week was . . ." Shortly before she turned in her comic strip, Chit Su volunteered to share her journal reflection with her English class. One good thing that happened, Chit Su said, was that she brought her uncle to the social security office and was able to translate on his behalf.

"One bad thing was yesterday and today I am very sad," she said, "because my mom call my phone she say me, next month you need to come to Texas state, so yesterday I am cry because I miss my mother, and then next month I change Texas state."

It took a moment for the class to understand what Chit Su had just said. She had been so excited to read aloud that she was still smiling by the time she had finished. It was as if she hadn't even absorbed her own news. But Minerva had understood. Chit Su's mother was taking her out of school in one month because she had found a job in Texas, where they could be part of a settled Burmese community.

It didn't take long for Chit Su's news to reach the ears of her advisor and global studies teacher, Suzannah Taylor, who was disappointed but not surprised. Every year students leave as suddenly as they arrive. They stay long enough to figure out what not to wear and which table to sit at during lunch, and then they are pulled out midyear for reasons that someone has deemed more important than going to school. Chit Su had made great strides since the beginning of the year, but now she was moving because her mother needed her to work. There was no father in the picture, just a woman who had been separated from her oldest daughter for too long, after traveling thousands of miles away from home, and who wanted to put her family back together again, at least what was left of it. Suzannah understood the mother's motivation, but she also witnessed Chit Su's reaction firsthand. "I don't want to go," she said several times over the next few days, talking to friends and teachers at school. "Miss, I don't want to go to Texas state."

Suzannah resolved to call the mother and ask her to consider letting Chit Su stay, at least until the end of the school year. Part of Suzannah's job as an advisor is to make sure that her students' voices are heard by their own parents. Chit Su is seventeen, soon to be eighteen. Suzannah isn't sure about Texas, but in New York, students "age out" of the public school system at twenty-one. If Chit Su wanted to continue going to school and learning English, she would have to stay on track, or else she might not get the chance. Staying for just a few months longer in order to finish the ninth grade could mean the difference between Chit Su graduating high school someday or dropping out and cutting herself off from the same opportunities that her classmates will get.

"It's a scary feeling that she's leaving. I have no doubt that if she were here at our school for another three or four years, she would achieve proficiency in English," Suzannah says one day after class, surrounded by picture books and laminated maps. "She just needs time. Time to raise her hand, time to do her homework, time to figure stuff out."

A little more than half a year since Chit Su walked into her classroom, Suzannah still knows almost nothing about her. And yet, she is certain about one fact: Chit Su is split. She wants to be with her mother in Texas, but she isn't ready to go. She said so herself.

Every day, when students leave the International High School, many go home to buildings that are filled with entire communities that have relocated together, like separate and distinct ingredients in Ms. Moya's tossed salad. Ngawang lives in a three-bedroom apartment with his father and brother, as well as several Tibetan bachelors from their village and the surrounding area. Hasanatu calls the low-income high-rise where she resides Building Pita, nicknamed in honor of all the refugees from Pita, Guinea, who have moved there in recent years.

A similar pattern plays out at school. International doesn't have the traditional cliques of popular girls, mean girls, jocks, and geeks. But left to their own devices, the student body generally separates along ethnic lines, with many kids gravitating toward other speakers of their own language. Still, one thing that almost all of the students share in common is the desire to become American, and nowhere is that transformation more obvious, or more confusing, than on Facebook. From the time they get out of school to the time they go to bed, students write on each other's Walls and post results from social surveys about everything from the pointlessness of homework to what sex position suits them best.

Take Dinice Liu, for example. According to the Facebook quiz, "What Alcoholic Drink Are You?" Dinice would be a margarita. If she were a fashion label, she would be Juicy Couture, and if she were a type of shoe, she would be stripper heels; at least that's the result she got after taking the quiz, "What Type of Shoe Are You?" Her perfect celebrity match for a boyfriend is Colin Farrell. There's just one problem: Dinice has no idea who Colin Farrell is.

Eight years since she emigrated from the Fujian province of China, Dinice's grasp of American pop culture is still tenuous, but there are certain references that almost every student at International knows. For instance, if Dinice were a character in the movie *Mean Girls*, she would be Regina, the queen bitch—that's according to the Facebook quiz, "What 'Mean Girl' Are You?" Then again, in the photos that Dinice posts of herself online, she plays the part of the moony naïf. Shot after shot, she poses with pouty lips, puffed cheeks, and wide eyes the size of satellites. She is the picture of innocence, which is ironic consider- ing her answers to a slew of Facebook surveys like "Another Have You Ever." Dinice marked "X" next to questions such as *Have you ever: Had Sex? Dyed your Hair? Skipped school? Been in a fistfight? Been called a bitch, slut, or ho?*

For someone like Dinice, who changes her name almost as frequently as she changes the color of her contact lenses, Facebook is the perfect place to try on different identities until she finds one that sticks. Even Kalsang, who is too cool for school, is addicted to taking online quizzes and surveys, like one where she listed twenty-five random things about herself. No. 2: "I like the sound the rice cooker makes when you first open it and all the steam rushes out." No. 11: "I listen to a lot of urban underground hip-hop music." Never mind that Kalsang is Tibetan and lists Dharamsala, India, as her hometown. Over time, she has become a fan of entire pages created in honor of expressions like: "Nigga, Please," "Bitches Be Trippin'," and "I Love Being Black."

Online, everyone is soup. There are no foreign accents on Facebook, and the only type of status that kids talk about is the kind that comes delivered via their daily status updates, hourly when school is not in ses- sion. February and spring breaks are always Facebook fests, with students chronicling their long stretches of boredom with the occasional blast about a cheating boyfriend or a broken heart. Freeman whittled away Christmas vacation by posting endless YouTube videos of people farting to the tune of "Jingle Bells" and farting in the gym. (The videos were titled "Jingle Farts" and "Farting in Gym," respectively.)

Conversations that had started as passed notes in class or insults hurled in the halls escalated on friends' pages online. After Freeman took the quiz, "How Many People Wanna Fuck You?" and got a score of six, Livenski immediately commented: "Who are they? lolz . . . can't wait to meet them . . . hahaha."

Mostly, though, kids work on their own profiles, crafting their About Me sections and filling in their favorite activities, music, movies, TV shows, and quotations with more careful attention than has ever been paid to homework or even college essays. Kalsang became a fan of "Dear Homework, You're Not Attractive and I'm Not Doing You," but for all of her space-outs and bathroom breaks during English class, she is moved enough by reading *The Diary of a Young Girl* to post the words of Anne Frank as a status update.

Another day Ngawang simply asked, "Who am I?????"

It is the question that everyone is trying to answer. Some kids, like Freeman, just have a clearer idea, or at least it seems that way, according to his bio: "Hey Yall This is freeman Aka Pollofrito. Togolese born and well-bred. I Speak 4 languages but want to speak more. Friendly and like jokin a lot. Hit me up."

Never mind that Freeman doesn't fit into any one group at school; on Facebook, he is the popular guy with hundreds of friends, and no one outside of International would know that many of those same friends roll their eyes whenever he walks toward their tables at lunch.

Never mind that Hasanatu was made anatomically different from other girls when she was still a child in Africa; on Facebook she is the class flirt, posting pictures of herself posing in tight blouses while out with friends.

Ngawang can put up the head shots he took to jump-start his acting career, and no one would know if he never got an audition. Jovita can list soccer and rock music as her personal interests, and no one would know that she is still reluctant to speak English outside of school. Mukta can describe her religious views as atheist, Yasmeen can avoid the relationship status prompt altogether, and Jessica can list her hometown as Brooklyn, NY, even though in real life her home is much harder to define.

Wherever they have come from and wherever they are headed, on Facebook the students at International can craft themselves into whoever they want to be.

A few weeks before Mohamed moved in with Cindy, his student IDs fell out of his pocket, and Mesbah picked them up. Mohamed still carries around his freshman and sophomore IDs, and before handing them back, Mesbah compared the boys in both photographs. "This is you as you really are," Mesbah said, referring to the younger Mohamed, a skinny freshman with prominent ears. He then examined the newer picture, in which Mohamed appears bigger, broader, and slightly more at ease. "This one is more American," Mesbah said. "This is who you *wish* you were."

Just as Geppetto's Pinocchio wanted more than anything to be a real boy, by spring, Mohamed wants to become a real American boy, at least in the legal sense. Until he gets his papers, if they ever come, in some ways he will continue to be the boy in the freshman ID. But on Facebook, he is "Jadon," an alias that he chose to hide his identity online. Jadon seems to be the closest that Mohamed has come to being the boy he wants to be.

In fact, Mohamed and Jadon share a lot in common, to judge by the information on Jadon's Facebook page. They are both seventeen, both Sunni Muslim, and single. Both enjoy watching *The Boondocks* and the History Channel, and their favorite books are *A Long Way Gone* and *Things Fall Apart*. But while Mohamed's hometown is a small village in Sierra Leone, Jadon's is Brooklyn, and nowhere does he mention that he is African. In real life, Mohamed is awkward around girls, but Jadon has a natural swagger. "I am a cool guy," he says in his About Me section. "I love hanging out with the hot girls." Mohamed belongs to a school-based R&B group called The Intellectuals, but Jadon likes to listen to 50 Cent, Lil Wayne, and Jay-Z, to whom he tips his hat in the section for his favorite quotes: *Before me, there was many. After me there were none.*

Compared to African Mohamed, American Jadon is a smooth operator. But every once in a while, in his attempt to be like everyone else, Jadon hits some odd notes that can only be attributed to the real-life

Mohamed and chalked up to a full-blown identity crisis. In April, Jadon became a fan of Taco Bell and Will Smith. Fine. But he also became a fan of Portland, Oregon, Guantánamo Bay, and hemorrhoids.

Implicit in all of these shared personal stats and pictures is the biggest difference of all: Jadon lives a public life. Unlike Mohamed, who is still undocumented, Jadon has documented every last detail of his day-to-day existence since moving in with Cindy in February. Mohamed's legal status is not budging anytime soon. Since Mohamed moved in, he and Cindy have spent hours in the fluorescent-lit lounges of Family Court waiting to give testimony in front of a judge, only to be rescheduled for the next month. It's just as well, because they are still missing important documents that they need for court. Mohamed's Sierra Leone passport is most likely languishing in a drawer somewhere in Farmington, Connecticut. He received a copy of his birth certificate from his brother, who keeps the family records in Freetown, but the affidavit for guardianship has yet to be delivered to Mohamed's mother in The Remote Village Where He Is From.

By April, Jadon's Facebook page is like a montage in a Hollywood movie, starring Cindy and himself in picture after picture, page after page. There they are standing side by side in an art gallery considering a wall of abstract canvases. Along with broadening his art horizons, Cindy has been schooling Mohamed in everything from English grammar and elocution to Harrison Ford movies to British rock. Watching a television series featuring the Beatles, Mohamed thought that every white guy with a shaggy haircut was either John, Paul, Ringo, or George. "Is that the Beatles?" he asked when the Kinks came onto the screen. "Is that the Beatles?" he asked upon seeing Mick Jagger. "No, baby," Cindy said. "That's the Rolling Stones." "Oh," Mohamed said. "Do you know them?"

In another picture that Jadon posted online, he and Cindy stand by the steps of the Capitol Building in Washington, D.C., where they traveled to meet her family over spring break. Over the span of a few days, they visited the National Gallery of Art, the National Air and Space Museum, the National Zoo, and the White House. They stayed at Cindy's parents' house, where Mohamed celebrated his first Easter dinner and had his first taste of Cindy's homemade apple pie. Mohamed liked pie so much that when they got back to New York, Cindy hosted a pie-eating party, and they spent an evening sampling homemade tarts of every flavor. "So, there are many different kinds of pie, and we are exploring them," Mohamed explained to their guests. "There is peach pie, apple pie, key-lime pie, which I'm about to eat, sweet-potato pie . . ."

For Mohamed, the months since he moved in with Cindy have been filled with firsts. About two weeks after he settled into his new room, he had his first birthday party. It was held at the home of Nedda de Castro, who baked his first birthday cake: yellow with chocolate frosting. Nedda was also the benefactor behind his first housewarming gifts: a navy-blue Perry Ellis bathrobe so that he could "shower in style," and a value-sized package of assorted candy bars. "Don't tell Cindy," Nedda warned Mohamed with a conspirational wink before shoving the candy under his bed. "She doesn't like to have junk food in the house, so just hide it, okay?"

Mike Incze, Mohamed's advisor, gave him his first bike, a beat-up BMX. And in quick succession, once Cindy signed Mohamed up for health insurance and a primary-care physician, he went on his first trips to the dentist (first cavity and first brush with happy gas), the ophthalmologist (first pair of glasses), and the dermatologist, where Cindy explained that, in order to determine what was causing the pink spots around his mouth, the doctor might have to perform some tests on him. Mohamed's reaction has since become part of Cindy's growing collection of Funny Stuff That Mohamed Says. "You mean," he said, his eyes widening, "they test on humans?"

At a certain point, Cindy began collecting these anecdotes—little Mohamedisms—like baby photographs in a wallet, an amusing catalog of growth. When Cindy asked whether Mohamed wanted to go to the circus with Nedda and her teenage daughter, he replied, "What's the circus?"

Cindy hated the circus—hated making her way past the PETA protestors outside Madison Square Garden, hated the bleachers that, she said, "smelled like piss, and I don't mean from the animals"—but they went anyway and sat in nosebleed seats. Cindy tried not to breathe in too deeply as Mohamed stared, transfixed, at the pirouetting acrobats, hoop-jumping poodles, and human cannonballs. His favorite act was the kick line of elephants that stepped onto tiny metal stools and placed their paws on one another's bristly backs, graceful as girls in a chorus line. A few times he was tempted to run up to the fence to get a better look. But he didn't leave his seat once, not by himself.

"You're not allowed to go to the bathroom. We don't want to 'lose' you," Nedda had told Mohamed earlier, only half joking. "I know you haven't told me the whole story yet, and that's okay. But maybe someday you will. The important thing is that you're here, no matter how you got here."

For now, at least, he is content to stay put. As for Cindy, Mohamed's arrival in her life has seemed, at times, auspicious. A little more than a month after he moved in, she had to put her cat to sleep. As usual, Cindy handled the situation with a light and cheeky touch, inviting friends over for an impromptu memorial service for Kittalina, but she also mourned losing a pet that had been her most loyal companion for eight years. After Kittalina died, Cindy cried all morning before going to work, but she found some solace in knowing that she wouldn't have to come home to an empty house. Mohamed would be there.

Over the past few months, Cindy has insisted to anyone who asks that having Mohamed in her house is really no big deal. "He's like a couch-surfer," she says, "only he stays longer."

Nedda doesn't buy it. "You don't take your couch-surfer to the doctor," she says. "I remember, he went out on his bicycle one day, and he didn't tell Cindy where he was. I get a frantic call—'Nedda, where is Mohamed?' You don't do that with your couch-surfer." For the first time in a long time, someone actually cared if Mohamed came home.

Cindy has had a few firsts of her own, too. One Sunday morning in May, she woke up to find a necklace and a musical Mother's Day card in a pink envelope resting on her computer keyboard. "So much of the person I am is because of the mom you are," it read on the cover, amid twining rose branches. Accompanied by guitar, a woman's voice sang to her from a tiny sound chip when she opened the card.

Dear Cindy,

I am really, really happy to write you this thank you not. It is to express my feelings for you. I love you very very much, words can't even express the way I feel about you. You are a mother to me. You take care of me very well, anything I ask for you make sure that I get it. You take care of me more than my own mother would. You gave me shelter when I needed it the most. You took me out of the dark and showed me light. Ever since I entired to your house, I felt like I have been reborned again, but this time in heaven, which is your home. I am much confortable and safe living with you. With you by my side, my future now seem to be clear. Thank you very much "mother." I know that I cannot pay you all this back, but my plan is to show you that I understand.

You are the BEST MOM EVER.

I wish you the best in life, and hope next mothers day met us in good conditions.

Love you.

Mohamed had signed the card from himself and Kittalina, and Cindy had to smile. An ex-boyfriend used to send her a Mother's Day card signed with her cat's name every year, even after they had broken up, as a recurring joke. But this was the first time that she had gotten a real Mother's Day card, and something about Mohamed's effusive expression of love and gratitude almost scared her. She didn't know why.

Dress Rehearsals

Like most enduring traditions at International, prom was initiated by members of the inaugural class. Make that one member: a queenly Senegalese senior by the name of Hawa Kebe. The majority of the 411 students who were enrolled in the school during its first year had never heard of "prom." There is no translation for it among the more than twenty-eight languages spoken regularly in the hallways, including French, Hawa's native tongue. One of sixteen children, Hawa had heard about prom through her older sister, who immigrated to the United States first and taught her everything she had learned about high school in America. Without Hawa's knowledge, traditions like Spirit Day and Twins Day—even the senior yearbook—might not exist today at International. But of all Hawa's legacies, nothing compares to prom, a night she had been anticipating ever since she had arrived in Brooklyn in the eighth grade.

In the late fall of her senior year, with Dariana Castro's help, Hawa set up an ad-hoc prom committee, comprised of about half a dozen of her closest girlfriends. Each Wednesday after school, over animal crackers and apple juice, they met in the student-government office to discuss everything from hairdos to venues. Once they settled on the location, a swanky banquet hall in Williamsburg, they had to consider the buffet menu. Many of the kids had never eaten out at a restaurant before, let alone one that served Italian cuisine, and had no idea what to make of offerings like fried calamari and linguini, until they looked them up in a Google image search. In addition to new foods, they began to familiarize themselves with prom customs—everything from electing a prom king and queen to losing one's virginity on prom night—by watching teen movies like *Mean Girls* and *She's All That*.

Despite all the committee's research and planning, the prom almost fell through. Instead of being excited for the biggest party of the year, many of the students were totally apathetic or nervous wrecks. The boys worried that they wouldn't be able to find dates, and the girls fretted over what to wear, just like any high schoolers. But other questions were unique to International students: *How do you spell prom? Is it a graduation requirement?* One Chinese girl said she would bypass her senior prom, preferring to go to her college prom instead.

To many students, prom was just another school dance, a lame one with teachers, and no alcohol. But to Hawa, prom symbolizes much, much more. It is a rite of passage, not just for high school, but also into American life. "We live here now," Hawa says. "Maybe some of us will never go back to our country. If you just be like, 'Oh, I'm sticking to my culture, I'm sticking to my people, I'm sticking to what I know,' how would you be able to survive here? Prom is almost like the beginning."

One year after the inaugural class put on the International High's first-ever prom, the event has become part of the school's lore, so much so that Cindy decided to write a play about it. On the surface, *The Prom* is a comedy about a group of clueless International students struggling to find dates and dresses for the biggest night of the year. There are several stock characters: the hottest girl whom every guy wants to ask out, the nerdy girl who is afraid of being rejected, and the bully who falls for her, to name a few. The same nerdy girl later transforms into the belle of the ball after a full makeover—and it's hard not to think of the Tibetan yak herder who went through a similar metamorphosis last year, after Dariana Castro hooked her up with a hair-and-makeup discount at her sister's salon.

Other roles are one of a kind. Writing for an audience of teenagers whose English proficiency levels run the gamut, Cindy made sure to stuff the scenes full of gags and inside jokes. James Rice, known to be unable to turn down a free meal, makes a cameo in the final prom scene, as indicated in the stage directions: *"Mr. Rice, playing himself, comes onto the stage, gets a plate of food, and sits down upstage and eats."* Mohamed plays an overly earnest senior named Ernest, and Ngawang plays a student who is the only person in the entire school who speaks his language: pig latin. "Iway an'tcay aitway orfay ethay ompray!" he shouts about a third of the way in, prompting another student to inquire: "How is it you've been in this school for four years and you still don't speak a word of English?"

Cindy wrote the play as sheer entertainment for herself, her students, and her colleagues. But on another level, it also functions as an instructional guide, with familiar characters asking many of the same questions that the seniors asked Hawa and Dariana last year, when they were attempting to mount their first prom. The result of Cindy's labor reads a lot like a play that a Peace Corps volunteer might put on to educate villagers about how to prevent malaria, or how to have safe sex—only the not-so-hidden message is about how to do prom. "What's a prom?" one character asks. "It's a big party to celebrate our graduation," another student explains. When a boy runs to "Ms. Kariana's" office complaining that he can't find a date to the prom, her response is: "You've only known about it for an hour. Give yourself some time."

For many of the underclassmen, the play is packed with essential information: Prom 101. But for the seniors, most of it is already old news. Thanks to the experiences of the Class of 2008, the Class of 2009 has a head start. Earlier in the year Dariana took a select group of seniors to sample the Italian buffet at Giando on the Water, the Williamsburg banquet hall where last year's prom was held. When they got back to school, the new committee spread the word about everything from Giando's chafing-dish offerings to its breathtaking views of the East River at sunset. Dariana reserved a date in June, and all of the twelfth-grade teachers started talking to their advisories about bringing in checks or cash for the $75 ticket. The girls have been dying to see Alex Harty wear something other than cargo shorts, a T-shirt, and his Blue Jays baseball cap, and the question of who he is taking as his date to prom has been a topic of constant speculation, since he is rumored to be dating multiple teachers at once. Hasanatu, in particular, had a good time torturing Alex on a bus ride to Six Flags Great Adventure, where the seniors went on their class trip. "Mr. Haaaarty!" she screamed from the front seat. "Let me close my eyes, and see you in a suit."

"Ask Mr. Harty who he's bringing to prom!" Yasmeen joined in.

"Yeah," Mukta said. "What size he wants?"

"What *size?*" Vadim asked, confused.

The actual prom committee is as disorganized as ever; already, tasks like designing flyers to put up in the halls and figuring out the flower arrangements are falling on Dariana's shoulders. But some of the girls have begun bringing back issues of *Teen Prom* magazine to class, where they fawn over photos of tulle and taffeta ball gowns with designer names like Fire & Ice and Bella Prom by Venus. The boys have started whittling down their Top Five lists of hottest girls. Everybody wants to take Elaine Vasquez from the Dominican Republic, but it is widely known that she is going out with King Capo, the Peruvian mastermind of the rap group 718 La Familia. Owen Zhu, whose Rubik's Cube–twisting skills had failed to impress the girls earlier in the year, asked her anyway. "Be serious," Elaine said, unsure of what to say next when Owen was still loitering by her side a few minutes later.

"You still haven't given me answer," he said.

Lately Elaine has been considering avoiding the date question altogether and going to prom with a group of girlfriends instead. "That's, like, the last time we'll all be together," she says one afternoon, hanging out with Dinice and Kalsang in the park across the street from school. "Yeah," Dinice says. "We're not going to bring our boyfriends. Otherwise, we cannot chill with each other."

At least they have a plan. One day in May, Freeman spent the entire lunch period wandering around the cafeteria, asking random girls to be his prom date—or his wife—and getting eye rolls in response. Freeman has tried passing on some seduction techniques to Ngawang, whose luck hasn't been much better.

Because Jessica is part of an established couple, everyone knows that she is going to prom with Harold; everyone but Jessica, that is.

"Who you going to ask to prom?" she asked Freeman one day at lunch in between reading chapters of *The Joy Luck Club*.

"You! Didn't you know that? Break up with Harold!" he replied.

"What?" Jessica gulped, blushing all the way down to the collar of her sequined yellow Garfield T-shirt.

Unknowingly, Freeman had struck a nerve. After some waffling about whether or not she wanted to stay in the city, Jessica has chosen to go away to college at Drexel University in Philadelphia, while Harold plans to start college at Syracuse in the fall. Since deciding that they would be attending different colleges, their late-night phone conversations have taken a dramatic turn, and all they talk about is their future together. He thinks that they have one; she isn't so sure. "His opinion is 'no relationship, no friendship,' but I feel like that's too absolute," Jessica says. "Does he even know about love at this age?" They are only about a year apart, but the difference in maturity is starting to be a problem. Lately Harold has been paying more attention to his video games than to Jessica, and after he failed to romance her on Valentine's Day, she trotted out the old let's-just-be-friends line, only to let Harold talk her out of breaking up. "I can't continue much longer," she says.

While some matters are simply a question of time, trial, and error, there are still plenty of tried-and-true lessons to be gleaned from the Class of 2008, who, along with the legacy of prom itself, have left behind an unspoken list of do's and don'ts. For instance, *don't* ask out more than one girl. That ended badly for a shy Haitian boy who approached four different girls last year, two of whom said yes, one of whom made a death threat against him, and none of whom ended up going as his date. But *do* ask one girl more than once, if necessary. Perseverance paid off for a handsome Mexican boy who asked out his Tibetan crush (the one-time yak herder) twelve times. On his thirteenth attempt, the day before prom, she said yes.

Finally, *don't* tell your parents more than they need to know. Desperate to dance the night away alongside her classmates, one Bangladeshi girl was crafty enough to tell her traditional Muslim father that prom was a graduation requirement. He bought it and later took pride in draping his daughter with the finest dyed silks and gold jewelry that a fruit vendor's small fortune could buy.

Jessica Tan does not own any copies of *Teen Prom*. Unlike some of her classmates who have been watching YouTube videos on how to master the perfect messy updo or the art of the smoky eye, she has no clue what to do when it comes to hair and makeup. Even if her mother, once the enforcer of bowl cuts and turtlenecks, didn't remind Jessica on a regular basis to spend her time studying instead of worrying about her appearance, she is too far away to help. Prom is in just a few weeks, and Jessica still doesn't have a dress, or even a clear idea of what a prom dress should be. All she knows is that she wants something, anything, pink. With that in mind, Jessica shows up at school one Saturday in May for the second annual prom-dress drive, which is being held in Alex Harty's math classroom on the third floor.

A few weeks ago, some friends of Dariana's who belong to a women's social networking group offered to round up used gowns and dresses to donate to girls who couldn't afford to buy their own. The volunteers have been working all morning to transform Room 338 into a makeshift boutique. By 10 AM full-length mirrors lean against the same walls shared by huge graph-paper projects on projectile motion, acceleration, and free fall. Since the students sat in their groups yesterday afternoon, several light-blue tables have been draped with orange cloth, brightening displays of free cosmetics, shoes, and accessories. Every inch of floor space has been covered with racks and racks of dresses—recycled bridesmaid dresses, slinky cocktail dresses, Cinderella ball gowns and flirty halters in lime green, midnight blue, buttery yellow, and sparkly silver—but not one, as far as Jessica can tell, that is pink.

"Are there any pink dresses?" she finally asks a preteen girl who is helping out.

"There are pink gloves," the girl says.

"Really?"

Following the girl's lead, Jessica walks past a station where volunteers are showing some of her classmates how to style their hair into French twists. Then, on a table piled high with beaded clutches, gauzy shawls, and pearl chokers, she sees them: two shocking-pink opera gloves, arranged in such a poised and artful way that it looks as though, at any moment, they might walk off the table by their own free will.

"Ohhhh," Jessica sighs, stretching the tight satin over her fingers, past her wrists, and all the way up to her elbows. "What do you think?"

Before the volunteer can answer, a petite Haitian girl wearing an emerald-green gown and eating a chicken drumstick knocks her aside. "You're the one who take my gloves! I'm looking for this!" she screams, ripping the gloves off Jessica's arms. "*Thank* you very much!"

"I'm done," Jessica mutters, watching the girl run out of the room and down the hall.

Jessica wouldn't know, but the girl in the green dress, whose name is Mitou Belizaire, has been involved in her fair share of prom drama. Last year, Mitou was one of the four girls who were asked out by the same boy, a revelation that came to light when Dariana helped host a similar dress drive for the Class of 2008.

This year Mitou is better prepared. For the past hour, she and several friends have been dashing back and forth between two rooms in various states of undress. Down the hall from Room 338, another classroom has been turned into a makeshift dressing room, crammed with more than a dozen half-naked bodies in teeny thongs and lacy bras. Minutes after swiping the gloves from Jessica, Mitou was squirming out of her green gown and into a sequined fuchsia frock, a few feet away from where Dinice Liu was stepping into what appeared to be a French maid costume. "Oh, my goodness!" Yasmeen says, slapping her hand to her mouth when she walks in seconds later with Jessica.

"YAZ!" Hasanatu screams, squeezing her large bust into a shiny maraschino-red gown. "Are you coming to prom?"

"No," Yasmeen mumbles. "I'm gonna have my own party at home."

Yasmeen is not allowed to go to prom. She has come to browse the selection and help Jessica. After a few false starts, they finally find a dress that Jessica likes enough to slip over her tank top and jeans: a short black frock with a giant green, blue, and pink bow attached to the bust that makes her look like a wrapped present with two limp arms poking out the sides.

"Oh, my God—you look so cute!" Yasmeen clucks, circling her and pinching the fabric where it is too loose around Jessica's hips. "Maybe you can take it in."

Nearby, still bursting out of the red satin dress, Hasanatu twirls around with her arms out and her eyes shut tight.

"What size shoe are you?" Dariana asks.

"Eight, nine, ten . . . ," Hasanatu guesses.

Dariana doesn't blink. She walks over to the shoe table and grabs a pair of red sling-back heels to go with Hasanatu's gown.

"Here," Dariana says, handing the shoes over, "just so you can see what it looks like."

"I can't walk with that," Hasanatu says with a wince.

"Let's see if you can," Dariana says, shoving the heels her way.

"No, I can't!"

"Yes, you can!"

Wearing a black-and-white head scarf and an Obama sweatshirt, Bilguissa comes over to weigh in. She and Hasanatu belong to the same after-school club for African girls. For the past few months, they have been asking their supervisor to teach them basic etiquette, everything from how to hold a fork and knife to how to dress for a formal party—and prom is putting all that they have learned to the test. After exchanging a few words in Fula with Hasanatu, Bilguissa turns back to Dariana.

"In African Club, we was learning how to walk in heels," she explains coolly.

"That's what you guys do in African Club?" Dariana asks.

"Ach, let me just put heels on, okay?" Hasanatu groans, snatching the shoes out of Dariana's hands.

One by one, compacts and costume jewelry disappear off the tables, and gowns vanish from the hangers. A little before noon, Genesis shows up in a low-cut tank top under a baggy sweatshirt to comb the racks for a garment that will fit over her ever-expanding belly. She leaves with a size 12 black Banana Republic dress.

Normally, Bilguissa would opt for a practical style, too. But in between talking to a couple of female security guards about brands of baby food, a strapless maroon gown with a white satin belt and a rhinestone buckle catches her eye. "This one so pretty," Bilguissa says, cutting the conversation short to take the dress into the next room.

Heading to an empty corner, Bilguissa takes off her Obama sweatshirt, shimmies the gown over her head, and peers at her reflection in the mirror. She hasn't told many people yet, but her life is about to change dramatically. After graduation, Bilguissa is sending her daughter, Mariama, back to Africa, where her family still lives. Her mother will raise the baby, so that Bilguissa can go to college and work part-time. Soon, Bilguissa will pack Mariama's pink knapsack for the last time, before seeing her off on an airplane headed to the other side of the world. But that day is still several weeks away. Today Bilguissa is just another girl getting ready for her senior prom—and she needs shoes to go with her dress. Spotting the red sling-backs that Hasanatu left discarded in a corner, Bilguissa slides the heels on when no one is looking. Then she takes the first of many wobbly steps, one foot after the other across an endless expanse of bluish-gray linoleum, until she is no longer shaking.

A few weeks after the dress drive in Room 338, the drama club finally puts on their production of *The Prom*. One day during second period, teachers and students file into the auditorium and take their seats as Cindy corrals the cast backstage. After months of rehearsing, Mohamed misses his cue in the final act, but he comes to after a few tense seconds of dead air and some prompting by Cindy in the wings. Ngawang gets the biggest laughs of the night for his squeaky-voiced portrayal of the only pig latin speaker at school, and the audience howls when James Rice storms onto the set during the last scene at prom, heading straight to a small table set with real fried chicken, which he loads onto a plate and eats onstage.

The entire cast gets a standing ovation, but Freeman steals the show. Earlier, Cindy had asked if he would work the curtains backstage, where he stays until the end of the play, but as soon as the music comes on, he runs onstage and begins breakdancing and moonwalking, all the while loosening his tie and unbuttoning his shirt to reveal washboard abs. The crowd goes wild and bum-rushes the stage, jumping up and down and screaming his name: "Pollo Frrriiiittttoooo!"

After the show, Freeman stretches his fifteen minutes of fame all the way to lunch, where he proposes marriage to several Bangladeshi girls and whisks the prettiest one out of her chair, twirling her in circles, as the cricket team claps out a beat.

Today, Freeman really is the Popular Guy. But when lunch is over, with only a week and a half left until prom night, he still hasn't found a date.

Party in the U.S.A.

Dinice Liu looks nothing like Keira Knightley. But that hasn't stopped her from asking a hairdresser in Queens to give her Keira's slightly rumpled chignon, which she spotted in a book of celebrity hairstyles titled *INSPIRE*. The problem is, after sitting in rollers and eating hair spray for the past hour, Dinice doesn't even look like herself. Her normally straight black hair has been curled into rigid coils and fusilli-shaped spirals and sprayed into a dull shellac mold, like some pasta art project gone awry. Despite the tears rolling down Dinice's cheeks, the Hispanic hairstylist doesn't seem to know that there is a problem—and there wouldn't be if Dinice were a Dominican girl getting ready for her quinceañera, like many of the clients who frequent Fausto & Jackie's Salon in Jackson Heights. Unfortunately, she is a petite and pale-skinned Chinese girl getting ready for her prom, and so far the day has been a total disaster. Cupping her mouth to keep the hair spray out and the screams in, Dinice punches a number into her cell phone. Two seconds later, another phone rings just a few chairs down, where Kalsang is getting her hair teased by a man named Armando.

"Oh my God!" Kalsang screams into her BlackBerry, over the whirring of hair dryers. "I'm so stressed *out*!"

"I hate my cuh-huurls," Dinice whimpers. "I look like a crazy lady!"

"It's better than mine," Kalsang says. "I *want* your curls."

"Now you're making me feel better."

Looking at her own reflection in the mirror, Kalsang sighs. She had hoped for big diva waves to go with her gown, but her hair is still as limp as ever.

"Let's just go," she tells Dinice.

"Okay, bye."

"Bye."

"FUCK MY HAIR! SHIIIIIITTT!" Kalsang screams once they are out on the street.

Oblivious to the oncoming traffic on Roosevelt Avenue, she bends over and shakes out her long black mane until it is back to its original waveless state. "Give me some volume!" she yells, and an elderly woman in a brightly colored sari stops in her tracks with a stunned look on her face, as if to say, *Who, me?* Drying her eyes on the sleeve of her gray baby-doll dress, Dinice trails behind, suffering under her crown of curls as if it were a crown of thorns. "Everybody's looking at me and laughing," she says as they pass an Afghan kebab house and a metal cart selling roasted nuts on the way to Kalsang's apartment.

Kalsang lives in Elmhurst, Queens, a short subway ride away from the salon where she and Dinice got their hair done in Jackson Heights, a neighborhood with large Hispanic and South Asian populations. They ended up at Jackie's at the last minute, but the original plan had been to go to Brooklyn, where Carmen Alfonso, one of the Dominican girls at school, had offered up the services at her mom's salon. Everything was set until Dinice decided that she didn't trust Dominicans to style Asian hair. The African girls went to an African salon; they came to class yesterday with crisp origami curls and buns shaped like breakfast danishes. Likewise, the Haitian girls went to a Haitian salon and showed up at school wearing scarves to protect their artful bobs. At the eleventh hour, Kalsang had planned to find an Asian salon in her neighborhood, but by the time Dinice finally got to her apartment, they were already running late, and they went to the first place they could get an appointment.

Despite getting off to a rocky start, the rest of their plan is still intact. Carmen may have her mother's salon, but Kalsang's father is a limo driver, and he has offered to chauffeur her and Dinice to prom in his Lincoln Navigator SUV, one reason why they decided to get ready at Kalsang's place. A little past seven, they walk through the front door, passing a huge picture of the Dalai Lama and a shrine of seven silver bowls, eight gold Buddhas, three lit tea candles, a Tibetan flag, and one very bewildered looking father on the way to Kalsang's room where, on a rose-colored bedspread, she already has laid out her gown: a brilliant scallion-green halter dress featuring a single spangled band of silver beads and blue rhinestones.

"Do you like it?" Kalsang asks tentatively. "My dad was like, 'Your dress is too open.' I'm like, 'Uh, yeah, that's the point.'"

Resting her purse on Kalsang's bed, Dinice inspects the gown, which Kalsang found at a vintage store, and which, in addition to being backless, is also somewhat frontless with a plunging neckline and stomach-baring slits.

"I want to see you in it, because when you see my dress, it doesn't look that pretty, either," Dinice says, smoothing over the slight insult with some friendly assurance. "You have to see it on."

Dinice is already spreading out her slinky midnight-blue gown from Topshop when Kalsang comes back fully changed.

"Oooh, you look so Bollywood," Dinice coos.

As Kalsang completes the look with gold chandelier earrings and matching sequined shoes, Dinice sets out her pewter stilettos and a small gold clutch. Somehow she remembered to pack her lucky crystals (pink for love and green for money), but she forgot to bring her wallet and her favorite eyebrow pen, and after her hair debacle it is almost enough to derail her night completely.

"Everything is turning out wrong!" she moans when one of the Dominican girls calls to check up on her. "Elaine, my hair is fucked up. I'm not even kidding. How's your hair?"

"She likes her hair," Dinice tells Kalsang after hanging up. "Elaine is the fakest person I've ever met."

"She's not fake," Kalsang says.

"She is fake."

"You know it's eight already, right?" Kalsang asks, changing the subject.

In between gossiping about girls, they gossip about boys. "I like Rafael. I think he's really hot," Kalsang says, referring to a strapping Dominican baseball player with dark skin and huge shoulders.

"But he gotta small head!" Dinice objects. In between talking about boys, they work like surgeons performing triage, trying to repair the damage done at the salon. Makeup bags are brandished like first aid kits, and their contents spilled onto the hard wooden floor—hairbrushes, blush brushes, foundation, mascara, and a palette of Victoria's Secret eye shadow in brown, gold, and pink.

"Moisturizer, primer—go, baby, go!" Dinice says, dropping on her knees in front of the mirror to put in her gray contacts.

"My skin's really bad today!" Kalsang cries, examining a zit on her forehead in the mirror.

"Did you pop that other one?" Dinice asks, referring to a budding welt on her back. "Your dress is low, so you have to pop it."

Kalsang is squeezing the pimple when her father knocks at the door. "We'll be out in fifteen minutes!" she yelps.

"Where's my earring? Do you remember where I put my earring?" Dinice panics, "I haven't done my pedicure yet!"

"Do it in the car!" Kalsang huffs and gives her hair one last flip, her face reddening under a thin veneer of sweat and sparkle as they head out the door.

Prom has already started by the time they jump into the Lincoln Navigator with Kalsang's father at the wheel, and as he pulls out onto the street, the girls apply some finishing touches in the backseat.

"Oh my God," Kalsang moans, twisting to see the angry red spot near her shoulder. "Can I borrow your powder?"

"One minute," Dinice says, examining her T-zone in a Neutrogena compact.

"Why are you so shiny?"

"It's so hot in here! My nose is sweating like hell!"

In the front seat, Kalsang's father plays the part of the unconcerned driver, staring ahead and occasionally checking the directions. But even he can't prevent the occasional bump in the road, traveling on the Brooklyn Queens Expressway. "Sorry," he says, when they hit a pothole that sends Dinice soaring and spread-eagled against the side door.

"Sorry about the panty!" Dinice says, pulling her dress back down.

A few minutes later, she whips out a bottle of glittery nail polish. With shaky hands, she paints each toenail silver until her foot looks like a school of minnows, and toxic fumes fill the car. "Sorry if you hate the smell," she apologizes again. "I have to do my nail!"

Taking the exit to Williamsburg, Kalsang's father smiles calmly at both girls in the rearview mirror. But on the dashboard, a small gold Buddha rattles ever so slightly as he steps on the gas.

Last year, the same Bangladeshi father who paid for his daughter to drape herself in silk and gold for her prom also hosted a pre-prom party for her friends, an Ecuadorian girl and two Tibetan sisters. A fruit vendor who wasn't working at the time, he didn't have much to offer, but what he did have he laid out on the kitchen table: a spread of whole apples, bananas, and oranges. As the girls nibbled on fruit, in between painting their nails to the beat of Bengali pop music, other students started the night off much closer in spirit to the American tradition: they began hatching their plans to get wasted.

This year, Marco is keeping the tradition alive. The plan was to drink a few beers early on, and then sneak some tequila into the prom for later. Shortly after Kalsang and Dinice step out of their SUV in the parking lot outside Giando on the Water, Marco turns up noticeably buzzed and posturing like Tijuana's answer to Al Capone in an oversized suit with a blood-red shirt and matching felt fedora. "You look like the Mexican mafia, man!" a Yemeni senior says, slapping his palm. Marco's date for the night is another Mexican boy, who wears a soft gray fedora over his silky long black hair, and it is clear that they both have been drinking from the way that they leer at girls, with lusty eyes that are only partly obscured by the angle of their hats.

Over the course of the night, the guests arrive by car, train, bus, bike, and skateboard. Around the same time that the Haitians pull into the parking lot in a white stretch limo that they have rented until 5:30 AM, Bilguissa's husband, the taxi driver, drops her off with Hasanatu, both girls fresh from the salon. Shortly after, Alex Harty rolls up on his long board in cargo shorts and a Catasauqua baseball T-shirt—a far cry from the tailored look that Hasanatu had been hoping for. Ngawang surprises everyone who didn't know he had gotten his learner's permit when he drives up in a car that is on loan from his father, who promised to try to make himself invisible in the passenger seat.

More than an hour earlier, Harold and Jessica were among the first to arrive, with her father at the wheel. They met at Mr. Tan's apartment building. Harold was waiting on the street when Jessica came out wearing her black satin dress with the multicolored bow, a beaded purse, gold sandals, and her silver star earring dangling from one lobe. As she walked to the car, she covered herself up with a powder-pink coat and told Harold that she didn't like the way she looked, but he thought she looked beautiful; in fact, the word that leapt to mind was "stunning." He would have told her so if her father hadn't been standing right there. Instead, after shaking Mr. Tan's hand, Harold just told Jessica that she looked "nice." "Thanks," Jessica said, eyeing Harold's navy-blue suit, and the peach shirt and paisley tie that his mother had helped him pick out at Macy's. Taking in the whole outfit, the word that leapt to her mind was "professional."

Most of the students come with friends or dates, but a handful come solo, bravely climbing the stairs alone to the third floor, where they are greeted by their own reflections in a full-length mirror and a table set with small place cards bearing their names. It is only a few feet from the stairwell to the banquet room where the party is being held, but after weeks of anticipation, it is a tough threshold to cross. Wearing a short black cocktail dress that shows off her muscular calves, Jovita freezes halfway down the hall, as if she wanted to retrace her path back down the stairs and out onto the street, until her friends push her forward, yelling "*Ya basta!*" Enough already! "Can we hold hands?" Dinice asks Kalsang when it is their turn. They stop to fix their hair in the mirror and link arms walking in.

Inside, students sit at round tables covered with white cloth and decorated with glass fishbowls stuffed with pink and yellow roses. Crystal chandeliers sparkle overhead and cast their reflections in the panoramic window, where a bunch of Chinese girls have gathered to point out the Williamsburg Bridge and the East River turning a dusky gold. A few of the boys are already at the buffet serving themselves Caesar salad and penne pasta as tuxedoed waiters look on with bored expressions, but most of the students still sit at their tables, picking at bread rolls and eyeing the door.

"Freeman!" Hasanatu screams when he walks in wearing a shiny dark-blue suit, black alligator-skin shoes, strong German cologne, and a curvaceous Latina girl on his arm whom no one recognizes. Having struggled to find a date, he asked out a girl from his acting workshop at the last minute, only to find himself suddenly in demand. "After I told the girls in my school that I will pay for whoever will be my date, they were all over me," Freeman later claimed. He never got the memo about the American tradition of buying a corsage, but, as it happened, Freeman had bought his date a necklace, bracelet, and earrings, all featuring rhinestones set in lime-green elastic to match her dress. He is in the midst of clasping her necklace when Hasanatu slinks by in her skin-tight red satin gown. "Wooooooo!" he says, eyeing her substantial butt like one of the maraschino cherries garnishing the glass of his fruity virgin mocktail. "Boom BOOM!"

One by one, the latecomers roll in, striking poses and pumping their hands in the air as if to say that now the party can begin. As girls begin to slip off their shoes to dance, a bunch of guys from Panama and the Dominican Republic stand outside in the hallway, discussing the best way to make their entrance and show off their dark shades, fresh cornrows, and '70s-style leisure suits. A few weeks before prom, they went to Rags-a-GoGo, a vintage shop in Greenwich Village, to buy their outfits: a dizzying spectrum of styles ranging from a black-and-blue smoking jacket with a floral brocade to a brown-and-white seersucker blazer and matching polyester pants. Moments before they walk in, Eduardo Pimentel, a ropy Dominican with thin lips and slick curls, pulls his boys aside to choreograph their red-carpet moment: a staggered line of poses straight out of *Saturday Night Fever*. "Stand behind me, and when I open the door, one, two, three—everybody raise their hands," he says, lowering his dark sunglasses. "I'll go first."

The Dominican boys are followed by the Dominican girls, whom everyone has been waiting to see. Wearing dangerously high heels and butt-hugging satin dresses in gold and aubergine, they pose cheek to cheek with smoldering stares and parted lips. "Oh my *God*," Marco says, doing a slow clap when Elaine walks by, smiling coyly over her shoulder.

Appreciated as she is, Elaine is forgotten as soon as the door opens and Mitou Belizaire walks in wearing the pièce de résistance: a raspberry-colored gown with a silver-embroidered bodice and a skirt big enough to hide the entire population of Port-au-Prince. "What *is* that?" Ann Parry asks, watching Mitou's tulle train spread through the crowd like an over-turned bowl of Hawaiian punch. A few steps behind, a boy in a black satin suit runs after her and gathers her voluminous hem so that she can walk more easily. For the rest of the night, he carries her skirt as she swans from table to table, air kissing friends and loading her plate with roast beef—the pink gloves that she took from Jessica nowhere in sight. (Mitou had later decided that they clashed with her new dress.) "Thank God Mitou can't booty dance in that gown," Dariana says, observing the spectacle.

Luckily, Mitou brought a backup: a black minidress that she changes into, once her food is cold and the dance floor heats up. At the front of the room, a deejay spins an eclectic mix of techno, bachata, and compas, and as the music gets louder, bodies grind closer.

"Ah, my ears!" Jessica yelps at her table when a reggaeton song comes on. "It's weird!"

"Huh, your ears are weird?" Harold shouts over the pumping beat. "Oh, you're not used to loud music!"

She nods, and they stare out at the dance floor, where Mitou is thrust-ing her butt into the crotch of the boy behind her so fast and hard that he has to hold on just to keep from falling. Nearby, Kalsang is getting hot and heavy with the Dominican baseball player she likes, her green gown sweeping the floor as she bends down low, and he looks on approvingly behind dark shades.

"No touching!" James Rice shouts, motioning for the Mexican boy in the gray fedora to unglue his pelvis from the satiny yellow backside of a girl who is not his girlfriend. The girl who is his girlfriend is busy glaring at him from the edge of the dance floor. Oblivious to her evil eye, a couple of songs later the same boy tires of the girl in the yellow gown and goes after her friend, a pouty bobbed-haired Dominican girl in a clinging purple dress.

"Aye, this party is so boring, and this music wack," she moans. "I need something to dance to."

"What color is your dress?" he slurs, staring at her cleavage.

"*Es morado*," she says, rolling her eyes. "Purple."

"Oh, I thought it was brown."

"No," she purrs, stepping closer so that he can get a better look. "*Es morrrrrado.*"

As the night goes on and the music changes, Harold and Jessica take to the dance floor. When Beyoncé's "Single Ladies (Put a Ring on It)" comes on, she rests her hand on his shoulder, and they do the box step at an accelerated pace. Around them, kids pop and lock, moonwalk, booty dance and contra dance, but Harold and Jessica continue stepping to the beat of their own private waltz. "I'm so 3008! You're so 2008-and-LATE!" Freeman sings along to "Boom Boom Pow" by the Black Eyed Peas, a couple feet away from where Marco dances with Bilguissa, who is wearing his burgundy fedora with her burgundy dress. Nearby Odanis strikes a disco pose in his seersucker jacket, and does the Batusi with Ann Parry, making V-shaped glasses with his index and middle fingers, like John Travolta in *Pulp Fiction* and peering at her as he swivels his hips. Owen Zhu takes over for the next slow song, and when he unabashedly rests his sweaty hands on her waist, Ann bugs her eyes at Alex Harty, who laughs from a safe distance near the bar in between keeping an eye on Marco, whose drunkenness is getting more noticeable by the minute.

Shortly before midnight "Thriller" comes on, and James Rice makes a scene, chasing after Nedda de Castro with zombie claws, just as Milagros walks through the door.

"You made it!" James says, rushing to give her a hug.

Milagros smiles, hiking up the bust of a tight red dress upon which the tops of her massive breasts float like buoys. Until a couple of hours ago, she hadn't planned on going to prom. She was working the cash register when, just by coincidence, James rode his bike by her store in Bed-Stuy and invited her to come out. She didn't want to go at first, but after some prodding, he convinced her. At the last minute she went home, showered, gelled her hair, and put on her dress.

Milagros never found her name card on the table in the hallway because she hadn't bought a prom ticket. But one of her best friends had: Genesis. Several months pregnant with twins, Genesis had had a hard time finding a dress that fit her the way she wanted it to, and when the last song had played, her folded name card was still perched on the table, the only one that hadn't been claimed.

Prom ended in the parking lot. After the last mocktail had been sipped and the last dance danced, everybody spilled out onto the asphalt behind Giando on the Water to figure out what to do next. Along with the girl he liked, Ngawang left with some of the Chinese kids who were going to a house party. Jessica hitched a ride with the college counselor and Harold, who spent the drive home holding a vase of roses for his mother. The Haitians had their limo, where they planned on having a "second prom," dancing to compas and driving around the city, and as they climbed into the backseat, neon lit and lined with leather, outside a bunch of Spanish-speaking boys huddled together to go over their options.

"We can go to Times Square and see all the girls," Freeman suggested, long after his date had been picked up by her mom.

"Everybody got money?" asked a junior from Panama with bling the size of ice cubes in his ears. "Rent a hotel. Or a motel—it's cheaper."

The Dominicans and Panamanians eventually decided to stick together, and Freeman was left alone. He had been hoping to join the Haitians, but earlier he had gotten yelled at for taking pictures of himself posing outside their limo. Freeman had given his digital camera to Owen Zhu for the task, and as Owen clicked away, he leaned against the hood and pretended to gaze longingly at the horizon, in between shouting orders: "Get my profile! My *profile*! I'm gonna put it on my Facebook page!" When one of the Haitian girls saw what he had been up to, she shooed Freeman away, saying that the car was for Haitians only. But right before leaving, a spot opened up in the back. "Freeman!" the girl yelled out the window. "There's one more seat—let's go!"

Slowly but surely, the students cleared out of the lot. Meanwhile, Dariana tried helping the kids who didn't have rides find a way home. Everybody was worried about Marco, who kept weaving into the street and was determined to walk home alone, a bad idea considering that he was wasted and dressed like a cartoon gangster in the middle of industrial Williamsburg past midnight. Finally Alex Harty had seen enough and pulled Marco aside.

"You gotta be careful," he said as Marco swayed in the breeze. "I'm telling you man-to-man. You're drunk. You don't feel it?"

"Nah, man," Marco said, his bloodshot eyes matching the color of his fedora.

"Well, it's very visible. Maybe you should get a glass of water."

"That will make it more vizzzzzible!" Marco said, tipping his hat as he stumbled into the street.

"Marco!" Alex yelled, breaking into a sprint. "You're not walking home alone!"

Alex eventually dragged Marco back to the parking lot. But in the span of about five minutes, he took off on foot several more times. Each time, Alex was there to redirect Marco back to the parking lot, where he played coy until his next attempt. Meanwhile, at the edge of the lot, a number of Marco's friends had gathered in a growing mass, the girls' gold and purple gowns forming a pool of sparkly iridescence, like spilled gasoline, inching slowly toward the street.

In the end, Marco didn't walk off alone. He was joined by about a dozen of his classmates, including Jovita and a tall, brooding Eastern European boy whose name no one could pronounce even when sober. They had no destination, and they were following the lead of a drunk classmate temporarily possessed by an urge to run head-on into traffic, but no one seemed to care. The air was balmy, almost tropical. The sky was the color of a new hickey, purplish and dark except for a thin sliver of moon, dangling over the Williamsburg Bridge in the distance, as tiny and perfect as two charms on a bracelet. The night was still young, and at least for the first few blocks of sprawling industrial emptiness, it belonged entirely to them.

Walking

Just a couple weeks after prom, the seniors find themselves walking together again, at graduation. This time, they know exactly where they are going: the shortest route from the wide double doors of the Prospect Heights campus auditorium down to the stage, where the first two rows of seats have been reserved with light-blue signs bearing the school logo and the one word that says it all: GRADUATE.

A little after three o'clock, when the ceremony was supposed to start, the auditorium is still mostly empty, and it seems as though the sixty graduating seniors will outnumber the parents, friends, and relatives who have come to see them. But every few minutes the doors open, and the students begin to see familiar faces: African matriarchs in a colorful array of waxy print robes and matching head wraps, like a rainbow of melted crayons, and African patriarchs still wearing their Bluetooth headsets; Bangladeshi women in gem-colored scarves and tunics and Haitian grannies wearing netted bonnets and their Sunday best; Dominican bombshells with flame-colored hair and fading beauty and young Chinese guys with fresh tattoos and fresher haircuts. Some of the guests carry flowers and teddy bears for the graduates. Some are reading the programs that were passed out at the door and have no idea that on the back page, where the names of the graduates are printed in alphabetical order, a few members of the Class of 2009 have been left off the list. Names like Genesis Carolina Matamoros Pozo, who stayed home today, and one Bangledeshi boy, who is being held back but came in to support Mukta. Sitting in one of the middle rows, he waits for her, every once in a while touching the gift that he bought her, a small pillow picturing a puppy wearing a mortarboard and tassel, as if to make sure it is still there.

Gradually, the thrum of voices speaking in Fula, French, Arabic, Bengali, Spanish, Mandarin, and Mina begins to fill the auditorium, and standing just outside the double doors, Dariana takes the loudening din as her cue to rally the students as they finish adjusting their caps and gowns. "Get off the phone!" she hisses at Odanis. "Do you need help?" she asks Hasanatu, sending a teacher to fix the detachable collar on her white robe before she can answer. Near Hasanatu, a group of Haitian girls are just starting to close their gowns over the satiny minidresses that they wear underneath. "It's time!" Dariana yells. "GO, GO, GO!"

Over the speakers, a string version of "Pomp and Circumstance" crackles to life, and Owen Zhu is the first to walk in, unable to suppress the metallic smile on his face as he leads his classmates in the footwork that they have been rehearsing for days: left, right, together; right, left, together. He is followed by Mukta, whose enormous strides cause her tassel to keep hitting her in the face, and a chubby Haitian girl in high heels who comes jiggling and jerking down the aisle in her vain attempt to step to the rhythm of Sir Edward Elgar's march. Marco is close behind, with a wolflike grin on his face and a slight limp as he makes his way to the stage.

The distance from the double doors to the front-row seats is short, and the entire walk takes only a few minutes, but the seniors have spent the past several weeks preparing for it. Formations have been choreographed and walks practiced in corridors. And yet, in another sense, the graduates of the Class of 2009 have been walking toward this moment for their entire lives. Some students, like Harold and Freeman, know exactly where they are headed after high school. Some students, like Genesis and Islam, have come to terms with the fact that they are staying behind. Others, like Jovita and Rocio, are still in limbo. They stand side by side with their classmates. They wear the same glowing white caps and gowns specially fitted to their size. They will get the same diploma signed by Chancellor Joel Klein and affixed with the same gold seal. They, too, will wear their tassels on the right side, before receiving their diploma cases, and turning them to the left. They, too, will wait for their principal to utter the words "By the power vested in me . . ." at which point they will throw their caps in the air, just like in the movies. But as soon as they walk out of the building, many of the students, especially those who are undocumented, will be on their own, and when Alexandra Anormaliza takes the stage to welcome the crowd with some opening words, those are the students to whom she is talking today. "Some of you intended to attend college in the fall but are not able to do so because of lack of funding. Hang in there. Your life has been interrupted, not ended," she tells them, her jaw squared and slightly trembling. "Once there was a little girl who came to this country as an undocumented immigrant. She was lucky; immigration reform right around the time of her senior year allowed her to go to college and become a teacher. Today, she is a school principal."

As Alexandra finishes her speech, more family members sneak through the doors and look for empty seats to watch the rest of the ceremony. Taking the podium and sharing the stage with several of her teachers who sit on metal folding chairs, a Mexican girl from Yasmeen's advisory gives the first student address, getting big laughs for her windy introduction—"Good afternoon, *buenos tardes, ni hao ma*. My name is Berely Garcia Gonzales, and I am from a place called Totomochapa, Municipio de Tlapa de Comonfort, Guerrero, Mexico"—and bigger laughs for her initial impression of her advisor, James Rice, during freshman year. "My first teacher was crazy, bald, and had a funny red beard," she says. Later in the program, a Haitian girl sings a pitchy version of "I Believe" by the gospel singer Yolanda Adams, followed by the handing out of senior awards.

Certain kids are shoo-ins. Harold predictably gets the award for Academic Achievement in All Subject Areas, and no one is surprised when Freeman accepts the award for International Spirit, a gold and purple trophy that he lifts in the air as if it were the Stanley Cup. Other kids are hard to peg. Earlier in the semester during a team meeting, the twelfth-grade teachers jokingly nominated students for made-up awards. Ann suggested a Haitian boy for the Bite Me Award, since he once told a teacher to do just that. Alex nominated the Bing sisters, identical Chinese twins, for Cutest Anime Characters in the entire senior class. "Seriously, man, their expressions are like, Laaa! Yaaay!" he said as the table cracked up. But once the laughter subsided, everyone struggled to come up with an award that would capture everything that Bilguissa Diallo has accomplished as a top student and aspiring nurse who has managed to balance her high school career with her duties as a mother and wife. "Can't we just give her the Having Your Shit Together Award?" Alex suggested.

Only a few people know about Bilguissa's decision to send her daughter, Mariama, to live with relatives in Guinea so that she can continue her education here. Once, she had thought she would be able to manage both raising a child and going to school, and for a while she did, but it would be near impossible for her to continue studying without the kind of support that she has gotten at International. After her name is called, Bilguissa receives a handshake and the award for overall Academic Improvement, an honor that still fails to capture the breadth of her journey but that she accepts graciously after walking across the stage in her strappy metallic heels. Settling into her seat, she glances back a few rows and beams at her family. Soon, she will have to say good-bye to Mariama. It won't be long before she is walking, too.

"Jovita Victoriano," Ann Parry calls out over the microphone, and Jovita rises with a giggle. The twelfth-grade teachers voted to give Jovita an award for Athletic Achievement, and as she walks down the stage it is with an extra kick in her step normally reserved for the soccer field. Once they finish with the awards and begin announcing the names of graduates, Ann calls Jovita to come onstage again to accept her diploma case, a navy-blue leather holder embossed with the Internationals Network for Public Schools logo. The seniors still have to come back to school one more time to pick up their actual diplomas signed by Chancellor Klein and affixed with the golden seal.

Only a few years ago, Jovita walked across the desert knowing that America would be waiting for her on the other side. Today, with her mother in the audience, she crosses the stage and becomes the first person in her family to graduate from high school. After graduation, they will celebrate at the taqueria where her mom works as a waitress. But even with her diploma case in hand, Jovita still doesn't know what awaits her on the other side of International. She worries about her mother being deported and separated from Jovita's little sister, who was born here. As of this moment, Jovita has no plans to go to college. Nor does her best friend Rocio, who turned up today wearing a satiny aqua dress under her white gown; several weeks pregnant, she is just beginning to show.

Taking the podium, the physics teacher Rachel Huang reads the names of her advisees. "Hasanatu Sowe." At the last parent-teacher conference, Rachel informed Mrs. Sowe that Hasanatu wouldn't graduate unless she passed two Regents exams, in English and in math. But that was just the short-term goal; if Hasanatu wanted to make it past high school, Rachel said, she needed to build her confidence. "She always comes to me and says, 'I can't do this, I'm stupid,'" Rachel told Mrs. Sowe, who simply nodded and said, "She needs to say, 'I'm good.'" Then she told Rachel that Hasanatu works hard. Very hard. "Sometimes she gets up at five in the morning and do her homework," Mrs. Sowe said that day. "She wants to *learn*. I tell her, 'If you want to, God will help you.'"

Today she, too, watches her daughter become the first member of their family to graduate high school. After weeks of studying when no one was watching, and at the eleventh hour, Hasanatu passed her Regents exams. Adjusting her white cap and walking across the stage, Hasanatu exchanges a glance with her math teacher, Alex Harty, who sits on a folding chair onstage, and is more dressed up than usual in a black shirt, a red tie, and khakis. Alex never did grant Hasanatu her wish to see him in a suit, but a few days ago, in a display of rare emotion, he signed her yearbook. Four years since Hasanatu started International barely knowing how to read or write, it took her a while to finish Alex's inscription, which took up nearly half the page. But midway through, a small smile crept onto her lips. "Hasanatu," the message began, "You are by far the most amazing student in the entire senior class. Knowing where you started from & how far you have come in the past four is incredible. I am so proud of you & you should be proud of yourself. You are a smart, beautiful & funny young woman, and I can't wait to hear about all the great things you are going to do. You have my undying respect for all you have achieved. Congratulations & Good Luck. Love, Alex Harty."

One by one, all of the senior advisors step up to the podium and read off the names of their advisees. Vadim calls Freeman, who stops showing off his trophy for just long enough to show off his diploma case. Rachel calls Jessica Tan, who is honored with the award for Highest Achievement in English Language Arts, having come so far since arriving in the United States during her junior year. On the program, Jessica is listed as "Yuan Tan," and only a few people in the crowd know that that is her real name. Among those people is Jessica's father, Mr. Tan. Jessica didn't see her father walk in, and he didn't make an attempt to get her attention. But today, she has his. Mr. Tan sits in one of the middle rows, just close enough to be spotted if she happens to turn and look into the crowd on her walk to the other side of the stage, and far enough away to be out of her view completely, if she doesn't.

Mr. Tan left his wife and sons behind to watch his daughter accept an honor that symbolizes everything he has given her, including a ticket to the United States and the means to pursue her education and future, as well as everything he has denied her: a home and a father. There is no way he can undo the painful events of the past year, but soon Mr. Tan's new family is going back to China, where they will stay for the summer. While they are gone, he has asked Jessica to move back in so that they can spend time together before she leaves for college in September.

After shaking hands with Rachel at the podium and accepting her diploma case, Jessica returns to her seat. She didn't look into the crowd for her father, but he is waiting for her.

Some parents couldn't make it to watch their child graduate, parents who couldn't get off of work, or who, like Jessica's mother, are on the other side of the world expecting a phone call at some twilight hour. Parents who said good-bye to their children a long time ago or just recently.

"Yasmeen Salahi," James Rice reads, standing behind the podium, and from the crowd comes a familiar taxi whistle and the sound of shrill, joyful whoops. In addition to The Boy and The Girl, several of Yasmeen's Yemeni girlfriends have come to watch her graduate, and as she rises from her seat, they shout and shake the bouquets of roses and sunflowers that they have brought to shower her with once the ceremony ends. Despite the huge female turnout, Yasmeen's older brothers have not shown up to support her, and neither has her husband, who is back in California. Yasmeen wishes her mother could have been here, and, in a way, she is. "I'm pretending my mom is after me everywhere I go. That way people will say, 'She was raised by her mother,'" Yasmeen says. "She is expecting me to graduate."

Not long ago, Yasmeen had thought she wouldn't make it this far. But almost six months since she posed for her yearbook portrait, she wears her cap and gown for real, and this time they are not just borrowed props, nor is her diploma. On her way to the small table where her diploma case rests with all the others amid vases of white and yellow roses, she passes James and he says, "You did it!" curbing his impulse to give her a hug.

"I know, I can't believe it," Yasmeen says, and awkwardly shakes his hand. She might not be walking on this stage if not for James, and he wouldn't be standing here for as long as he has if not for her. Along with her classmates, Yasmeen voted for James to receive an award for teacher of the year, a role that requires he also deliver the commencement speech.

When James woke up this morning, just a few hours before he was supposed to take the podium, his notebook was empty, and he still had no idea what he was going to say. He felt like one of his students—at a total loss for words. And then it hit him. He would do what he always tells the kids to do when they are struggling to write an essay—he would start with a true story. A story about a boy who asked for a pencil. The request was mundane enough, but this was a boy who hadn't spoken a word of English all semester, who had been afraid to, and the entire class was in shock when James asked the boy to repeat himself, and he screamed at the top of his lungs, "PENCIL!" That day, after the period had ended, James had wondered what it took for the boy to speak up, and today, wearing an ironed white shirt and a narrow black tie and standing in front of the Class of 2009, James wonders again, just what it took.

"I mean, was it easy for him? Had he been tricking us into thinking he knew less than he did? Or . . . ," James says, his lips holding the shape of the word, the shape of a smoke ring. "Or did he have to gather all the courage he had in that very moment into a little ball, push it past the fear that settles in your stomach and throat, and spit it out of his mouth?" Clutching his side where the invisible ball of courage would be, James could be talking about Hasanatu, who has spent the past four years calling herself stupid before anyone else could, or Jovita, whose jaw quivered whenever Ann called on her in class.

"So many of you have had similar experiences. It may have been your first day of class after having arrived in this country only a few days before, or maybe it was that day when your only friend, the only person in the room who speaks your language, is absent," James says, and he might as well be talking about Chit Su. "And now, you're here. After the English Regents, or, for some of you, the math Regents, after college essays, SATs, and final presentations . . . you're here. But that's just the part of the story that happened in the building. Many of you have traveled by boat, or on foot across deserts and mountains, swum across rivers, sometimes with family, sometimes completely alone, some of you through war zones and refugee communities, all to get right here," James says, and he might as well be talking to Ngawang, or Mohamed Bah.

"Then, of course, there was the discrimination, the laughing, the ignorance, the nights of working seven or eight hours after a full school day to be followed by another full school day, the longing for absent parents, difficulties at home, even deaths. And still, after all that, you've arrived here. You should know that the adults in this school are amazed and inspired by you, that we are changed as a result of having just known you," James tells the Class of 2009.

Looking out at the silver and gold balloons eddying through the crowd, James tells the graduates that there are people in this room, their parents, teachers, and friends, who have witnessed the beauty and magic in each of them. He tells them that, with every passing year, there will be times when life will seem small—made to feel even smaller by the pressures of work, family, and unforeseen obstacles—but that really it is just the opposite.

"One of my favorite quotes is by a famous author, and it's a simple quote but very profound to me. She said, 'Life is big.' Life is big—so simple, but so powerful," James says, resting his eyes on the sixty familiar faces in the two front rows.

"What big lives you have lived. Big, big, huge amazing lives—and so young. I ask you, if it is possible to go from *pencil* to here, how much bigger can your journeys become?"

Shortly before graduation, James Rice's advisory met in Room 407 for the last time. For the occasion, he wanted to do a special final exercise, and when the class took their seats around the conference table, he put the question out there. "Today is June 11, 2009," he began. "In twenty years, the year 2029, what do you think these people are going to be doing? We're going to guess. Just go around."

Over the next hour, predictions were made and futures forecasted over juice and cookies. It was decided that Yangi Sherpa—the Nepali girl who had changed her name to "Angie" after Angelina Jolie—would be a housewife. In addition, there was a Haitian girl bound to be a famous singer, a Chinese boy who would live a regimented life as a lawyer with a house in the suburbs, a longhaired Mexican boy who was destined to star in Spanish telenovelas, and a Mexican girl, Berely Garcia, who everyone thought would be a botanist; in fact, she loved plants so much someone said that she would be a plant, and Berely herself chimed in that she would be a forget-me-not.

Then it was Yasmeen's turn. "You can't say that she's gonna be married," James joked, and everyone laughed. The Haitian girl, Rachelle, said that, twenty years from now, she imagined Yasmeen and her husband would be living in California, where they would raise their children.

"Her kids will probably want to be different from her, and she probably will be more open to them than her parents were to her," Rachelle added. "She won't be as strict."

"You think so?" James asked doubtfully.

"It depends on the father," someone else put in.

"Yasmeen," James said, "My question is, if your teenage daughter wants to go to prom with a boy, will you let her?"

Yasmeen considered her answer for a moment, and nodded. "I'll go with her," she said, unintentionally setting off a chorus of dissenting moans and groans.

Once the laughter died down and her cheeks drained back to their normal color, Yasmeen turned the original question back to James. "What do you view for me?" she asked, as if he held her future in his hands, like a Magic 8-Ball, and all he had to do was shake it.

"I think you're going to be a teacher," James said finally. "I think you're going to be working with small children, too—I can totally see that."

"And I want to be an activist for women's rights," Yasmeen said, before changing her mind and saying that she wanted to be a playwright.

For once, the future seemed full of possibilities that were not just meant for other people, and in her final minutes of high school, Yasmeen struggled to put into words exactly what it was that had gotten her through this year—and would get her through the next twenty.

"Just think about tomorrow, what are you going to do tomorrow? I mean, take me for example. How many times I called you and told you I'm not coming to school?" she asked James. "But then I think about who's going to be affected, and in that case I think about my siblings. Especially The Girl. The things that you care for, they drag you, they push you to move on. Inside of me, I felt like I am nothing, I felt dead—but I was breathing. You will get there, as long as you keep hope alive. Keep it breathing."

"That's a good one," James said, moments before class was dismissed forever. "Keep hope breathing."

Epilogue: It Goes On

It is impossible to predict where the graduates of the Class of 2009 will be in twenty years. Some will return to their home countries, some will continue to carve out lives for themselves in this country, and others will exist in some liminal space between. But wherever they end up, chances are good that they will have kept a copy of their burgundy-colored senior yearbook titled "Our Story" in a florid mustard-yellow font. When they turn the pages, they will recognize the smiling, semi-veiled face of a Muslim classmate whom they almost lost. And next to her picture, they will read the words of Robert Frost: "In three words, I can sum up everything I've learned about life: It goes on."

The same can be said about life at the International High School at Prospect Heights. In February 2010, Alexandra Anormaliza left her post as principal to work at the DOE's Office of Achievement Resources. As deputy executive director, she now supports the rollout of the Common Core State Standards, as per the Division of Performance and Accountability. In other words, "We want more schools to be organized around the needs of their students, and to have that as their first and foremost priority," Alexandra says. "I think we did that very well at the International High School at Prospect Heights." Former assistant principal Nedda de

Castro took over as principal as Alexandra settled into her new office at the DOE's downtown Manhattan headquarters, otherwise known as Tweed. At first, it felt strange. "Often, all I could think was, 'I want to go home,'" Alexandra says, "and home was the school."

International continues to be a second home to its new students. Only a few weeks after the Class of 2009 graduated, the Class of 2013 began showing up to enroll for the fall; with 112 freshmen, they would be the biggest class that the school had ever seen. Many of the freshmen came from countries that recently had been in the news. Like their predecessors, they arrived in dribs and drabs, looking lost and scared, some with parents or relatives and some alone, drifting through the halls. They wore nervous expressions and clothing that they probably shouldn't have; one Haitian boy turned up in high-waisted pants and a T-shirt that said "GAP," but on closer inspection actually stood for "God Answers Prayers." On the first day of school, he sat alone at lunch.

On the second day of school, a new boy appeared in the guidance office. The only word that he seemed to know was "Bamako," the capital city of Mali, where he was from. He had huge hands and huger feet and a heavy brow. He wore a pale yellow polo shirt, dark blue jeans, and bright white sneakers, and he spoke Bambara—the only student to speak his language in the whole school. As he waited for his class schedule, he sat at the conference table outside Miguel Antunes's office and worked on a word-search puzzle that one of the social workers had passed out to a couple of other boys who were also waiting for schedules.

"Imma done! Imma done!" a gangly Uzbek boy shouted when he had circled all of the found words in the puzzle, which had a sports theme. "Do you need help?"

A scowl slid over the face of the boy from Mali, and he scooted down the table, bending protectively over his paper as if using his body to shield it from glancing blows. In blue ink, he tentatively circled the letters ASKETBA, and abruptly stood up and threw the paper in the trash.

"What's the matter?" one of the social workers asked. "It's just a game. Don't worry."

Her gentle tone did nothing to soothe the boy's nerves, and for a moment another freshman boy from Senegal who had watched the whole exchange looked even more confused.

"He doesn't speak English," he said to Miguel. "How is he going to understand?"

It was a logical question, and there was only one answer. "Slowly but surely," Miguel said.

In fact, there was someone who spoke Bambara: Suzannah Taylor, Chit Su's freshman advisor, who had spent time abroad in Mali. Later in the period, the social worker sent for her, and she took over from there, explaining the class schedule to the boy from Mali, who learned at least one new English word that day, which he repeated over and over: Suzannah.

Suzannah had convinced Chit Su's family to let her stay at International until the end of the school year, and, in June, Chit Su left much the way she had arrived—with little fanfare, after an exit interview in Miguel's office. She did not end up moving to Texas, though she did visit her mother there once for a long weekend. In the end, the family relocated to Chicago, where her mother got a job making sushi at a Japanese restaurant that hired Chit Su part-time. For her first few months of living in Chicago, Chit Su wrote to Suzannah semiregularly via instant message chats.

Suzannah saved some of their Gmail chats, including one from October, almost a year and a month since Chit Su had walked into her classroom for the first time as a timid freshman.

> **10:45 PM Chit:** *hi ms i like chicago but i am no't happy like in my new york school . . . i miss you and all teacher,,, and all my friend . . . please say for me i miss all my teacher and my all friend*
> **10:52 PM Chit:** *i am not happy here in my school*
> **Suzannah:** *oh no! why not?*
> **Chit:** *i don't have friend.*
> **Suzannah:** *what! how can that be? is it true?*
> **10:53 PM Chit:** *no body not call me*
> *yes i really told you*
> *i am no't lie*
> **10:54** *now i always go to my jobs then i go to school*

A couple weeks later, Chit Su wrote again, at around two o'clock in the morning, but Suzannah was asleep. When she woke up and checked her computer, Suzannah found this message waiting for her:

1:52 AM Chit: *hi ms happy whith your family for halloween*
1:53 AM *your student*
chit su
bye
good night and good luck for ever. . . . . for you
bye
oh

Several weeks passed, and then Suzannah heard from Chit Su again, one last time, in January. From what Chit Su said in her message, her new high school in Chicago had placed her in the twelfth grade—two grades ahead of where she would have been at International—and she was having trouble keeping up, both academically and socially. It was hard for Suzannah to tell whether or not she was dropping out. The only thing that was clear was that Chit Su, even a year after leaving International, had not completely left in spirit. She still signed her name, "your student Chit Su."

Over the summer before his junior year, a judge at Family Court in Brooklyn heard Mohamed's testimony for the first time. After weeks of waiting and months of worrying about what he would say when he was called, he finally got to see the inside of a courtroom. It was a small space with wood-paneled walls, beige linoleum floors, and a seal that said In God We Trust in plain view. In many ways, the courtroom resembled the ones that Mohamed had seen on TV and in his imagination, only there was no jury, and there were no video cameras to record his every word. There was just his new lawyer, a young male attorney from The Door, and the intimidating judge, a black woman with close-cropped hair and glasses, who seemed to look right through Mohamed in a way that no one else ever had. After taking a seat by himself at a small table, with Cindy sitting nearby, he answered his lawyer's questions, and in short nervous bursts, Mohamed told the judge the same story that he had been telling for years.

As soon as Mohamed had finished, the judge's raised eyebrows said it all. "I find that portion of the story incredible—that a church would bring a child to New York City and just leave him there," she said, addressing Cindy and the lawyer. "I find that very incredible. You all need to get in touch with that church."

Before the hearing was adjourned, the judge advised Mohamed once again to get in touch with the people in Farmington; he needed the church to verify his testimony, at least the parts of it that they could. Mohamed's lawyer eventually contacted Pastor Ned Edwards, who agreed to write an official letter to the court that confirmed Mohamed's story about winning a scholarship and a trip to Connecticut, and left other questions unanswered, though not unturned.

Despite some dissenting voices in the congregation, the church as a whole agreed to take an official position to support Mohamed. At first, he was nervous about their sudden reappearance in his life. If the congregation had had the power to bring him here from Africa, surely they could send him back. Gradually, though, Mohamed is getting used to their marginal presence in his life—and all the complicated feelings that come with that. One day, on hearing about how Polly Hincks had fallen apart after he disappeared that afternoon at Macy's, he squirms in his seat, saying nothing for a few seconds. "I admit that I've wronged a lot of people, and I feel that's really evil of me," Mohamed finally croaks, sounding like a punished child. He knows that the congregation expects some sort of atonement, and he seems genuinely remorseful about causing the church so much worry, hurt, and embarrassment, if not 100 percent sorry for the way everything has worked out.

Since Ned Edwards sent his letter to the court, Mohamed has reopened relationships with some of the members. He sent letters to several people, including Polly. Though he did not go into detail about that day at Macy's, Mohamed began his letter with an apology. "I am so sorry to hear that you were worried and sick when I disappeared from the group. I apologize for not calling all this while," he said. "I am writing this letter just to say that I am doing great and no need to worry."

The congregants' reactions to Mohamed's sudden reappearance in *their* lives have ranged from shock to elation to patriotic pride to deep-rooted resentment. Mohamed still has not seen anyone in person, but several of the parishioners wrote letters to him, expressing how his disappearance almost three years before has affected their lives.

Polly told Mohamed more about what happened after he vanished. She recalled how the store alerted two hundred security officers, and how she, Pat Reville, and Mohamed's teacher Salamatu had driven home in a heavy downpour that matched their moods. "You may be turning what seemed to have been a tragedy—lost boy, illegal alien—into a possible victory—boy found, becoming an educated man and possibly an American Citizen and a credit to his place of birth," she wrote. "One result of hearing your wonderful story is that, if it's possible, I love my country even more than before. I am a passionate patriot and imagine you will become one, too."

Since Polly emailed her letter, she has rescinded some of her enthusiasm; she fluctuates between feeling proud of Mohamed for how far he has traveled, and angry with him on behalf of everyone whom she believes he has used and hurt along the way.

Pat Reville, who had opened her house and her family to Mohamed during his weeks in Farmington, also wrote. "Well, old man, good to hear from you again," she began her email. She went on to say how, after he disappeared, her children had felt betrayed, Henry in particular, and she regretted not having listened more closely when Mohamed said that he didn't want to go back to Sierra Leone. "I should have fought for you then," Pat continued. "Please, don't hold it against my kids for thinking you betrayed them. They cannot conceive of the challenges you face in Sierra Leone and so think it was an easy choice for you to stay here and not return. I am hoping you can come up and visit with us again soon. Then you and Henry can form a renewed friendship and laugh about the old times."

Not everyone is ready to forgive Mohamed, however, and in October, after getting a call from Mohamed's lawyer requesting the church's participation in his case, Pastor Ned Edwards delivered a sermon that finally captured in words the congregation's perennially fractured position on the subject of What To Do About Mohamed Bah. The sermon was titled, "From Past to Future," and it was inspired by the parable of The Prodigal Son in Luke 15:11–24. Almost three years to the day since Mohamed had walked into their lives, slept in their beds, and dined at their tables, Pastor Edwards told the parishioners the parable about an ungrateful son who squanders his share of his father's fortune, only to return begging for mercy. Instead of allowing his youngest son to repent, however, the father forgives him instantly and even fetes him with a fatted calf, much to the anger and disapproval of his oldest son. "We had to celebrate and be glad, because this brother of yours was dead and is alive again," the father says. "He was lost and is found."

As Pastor Edwards pointed out, among their own congregation, there were a lot of older brothers, parishioners who felt that Mohamed deserved to be punished, not rewarded and showered with kindness. "Now, this is a young man who has hurt and betrayed us deeply," Pastor Edwards said that Sunday in October, standing at the same lectern where he had introduced Mohamed to the church for the first time. "He has taken advantage of our hospitality and used us to get into this country. He has not called or written to let us know he was safe. And all of a sudden, a judge says, 'Make nice with the church in Farmington.' And he knows that if he wants to stay in this country, he had better do what the judge says."

"So on this World Communion Sunday, we have a living, breathing international parable before us. A parable about a son who has squandered his love and trust and wants to come home to our good graces. And the question is, how do we respond? Do we respond like the pharisees and the scribes who want to make sure the rules and structures are not violated, and that proper consequences are paid for violations so that the boundaries and expectations can remain clear? That is a worthy goal; we need to protect boundaries. We need the police and the courts.

"Or," Pastor Edwards continued, "do we risk the consequences of loving like God, so wastefully, so lavishly, so extravagantly, that we render all the rules inconsequential and celebrate that the lost has been found?

"The question really is bigger than how we respond to Mohamed,"

Pastor Edwards concluded his sermon that morning. "The question is how do we respond to the prodigals we encounter every day, in our families, in our neighborhoods, our church, in the news? The Juans and the Amahls, the Hyung-juns, the Aminas, the Sallys, and the Joes. Those who betray us, take advantage of us, slight us or hurt us."

Gazing out at the sea of white faces, he asked the congregation again: "How do we respond?"

In the end, the church responded the way they always have in regard to Mohamed: they let him be. Pat Reville still hopes that Mohamed will come back to Farmington for a visit, back to where it all began. "I think it's just natural that he would come back," she says one afternoon in her kitchen, where Mohamed had eaten grilled cheese for the first time. "It would be natural that we could help him make it through the next leg of his life." Whether he returns or not, now Pat doesn't need to imagine an ending to the story of "What Happened to Mohamed Bah." It is clear to everyone that his story is one of new beginnings. "Closure is one way to deal, but I think the other thing is continuum. This isn't something that suddenly died," she says. "It goes on."

Not long after he got his court letter that he had requested from the church, Mohamed was one of several students in New York City chosen to speak at the United Nations, in honor of the International Day of Peace. Mohamed also appeared in a short documentary on the subject, and popped up on the church's radar again after emailing them the video, which was posted online. Certain members of the congregation took issue with the fact that, in the film, Mohamed called himself a refugee—which he technically is not. Regardless of whether the fallacy was intentional or not, they fear that if he continues to misrepresent himself so boldly and publicly, the truth will catch up. The video created a stir the following Sunday at church, when Polly Hincks circulated word of Mohamed's rising fame. "Too much, too soon," she said. "Pride goeth before the fall."

The church continues to question Mohamed's sincerity. As for Cindy, she continues to defend his honor like a bear protecting her cub. When it comes to her attention that Mohamed incorrectly called himself a refugee, she points out that he probably misunderstood the term; after all, English is not his first language, and he has said that he lived at a refugee camp in Guinea for almost three years. "You go live in one of those camps and see what you call yourself," Cindy fumes. She has a similar reaction after hearing about the day Mohamed beat Pat Reville's son Henry at a game of checkers, and how Pat later wondered if Mohamed had just pretended not to know how to play at first. "Mohamed is a quick study, and if they thought that was a setup, and he's a shark—no," she says. "He picks up on things quickly, and he's gonna beat your *ass*, so get over it. Just because he's good at something doesn't mean he's a hustler."

Still, in quieter moments, Cindy says she understands where the congregation's suspicions are coming from, and one fall day in her dining room, when Mohamed is out of the house, she takes a few minutes to consider a question that the church has raised, again and again, behind closed doors. "Is he trustworthy? Yeah. But I think that he's always going to take the road that's going to lead him to where he wants to go. That's the way it is. He's ambitious," Cindy says. "It has occurred to me that maybe I am a step on the way to something else, as he moves through. Could be. I just have to wait and see."

There was a time in her life when Cindy thought she might never get the chance to leave a mark on someone, but the more time passes, the more she sees how different Mohamed's life has become with her in it. And in many ways, the inscription on that first Mother's Day card that he ever gave her has turned out to be true—SO MUCH OF THE PERSON I AM IS BECAUSE OF THE MOM YOU ARE. Because of Cindy, who was officially appointed by the court as Mohamed's legal guardian, he now has a chance at getting his papers and going to college. This is the year that Mohamed will visit campuses of schools like MIT, Yale, and Williams, along with his classmates. He and Cindy have begun looking into private scholarships, but in the event that he doesn't get one, she is prepared to help pay Mohamed's tuition at one of the colleges that make up the City University of New York. "A friend of mine said Mohamed has a charmed life. I think that's funny, with all he's been through, because everything he has is so tenuous," Cindy says. "I think he'll calm down once he gets into a school. That's what he's been aiming for all this time—that's been the prize."

Cindy no longer opens her house up to couch-surfers looking for a place to crash; she stopped around the time Mohamed moved in. She doesn't think about renting out the upstairs bedroom anymore, either. That is Mohamed's room now, and as long as she lives in the same house, he can call it home. The choice is up to him, whether he wants to keep coming back. "He is at a point where he could go in one of several directions. He could end up back in Sierra Leone willingly, or he could end up back there against his will. He could end up staying here, or he could end up in Europe. I don't know. It depends on what else comes along," Cindy says. "What he's feeling now may not be what he's feeling two years from now. With anybody, you don't know if you're going to be in the same place, with the same people. It's not something I have to build my life around and worry about—if he moves on."

Sitting at the long dining table where soon Mohamed will join her for dinner, Cindy grows silent. "Whether or not he moves on or not," she says at last, "he's not going to forget me."

For now, at least, Mohamed is rooted to the spot, just another high school junior being pummeled by homework assignments and getting ready to apply to colleges. Soon, the eleventh-grade teachers will begin talking about the importance of writing a great personal essay, an area in which Mohamed has excelled in the past but now seems to regard warily. As he gets older, he is finding that he can't talk about himself without the inevitable question being raised: *How did you get here?* From that point on, there is no exit—just an exhausted story about the day he got lost in New York City.

"I know people don't believe me," Mohamed says, "It's something that's really depressing to me. I don't want people to think of me as a rascal, because I'm not. I'm just trying to find a better life." Now when someone asks how he ended up living in the United States, he simply says, "I came here on a scholarship with some Christian missionaries," and stops there.

It's hard to know what is the truth, but Cindy prefers not to dwell on the past. "It's not that important because it's over, he's here, and we just need to deal with what's happening now. He made the decision he made, and it was to set his life in a different direction," she says, merely speculating. "Most people wouldn't have the *balls*. Or, they would have been too closely tied to their parents to make a break like that. But if you don't feel bound to your parents, your family . . ."

Cindy shakes her head. There's no point in trying to undo what has been done. They'll just have to brace themselves for whatever happens in court and hope that, maybe next time, the judge will see it their way.

"I was wondering: What would have happened if Mohamed had gone into court and said, 'I ran away. I come from a place where they don't even have toilets, and if you take me to Connecticut with some of the richest people in the country, I'm supposed to turn around and go back?'" Cindy asks. "What would you do?"

Despite moving forward with his life in America, Mohamed still lives in fear of being deported—some days. Other days, he seems to block out the possibility of being deported altogether, and it is hard to say which is worse: living with fear, or living without it, in a fantasy world where consequences don't seem to exist. Since Mohamed moved in with Cindy, he has had a couple of run-ins with the police. One time on his bike, he accidentally hit a pedestrian in Prospect Park, and a cop came over to investigate. Nothing came of it, other than a verbal lashing from Cindy, who has warned Mohamed countless times about his reckless riding. She is afraid that even the simplest mistake, like using his student MetroCard on the weekend, could get Mohamed into trouble with the law, and lead to his deportation. "You're right," he says, whenever she gets going about how he'll be on the next slow boat back to Africa, and promises it won't happen again. He chooses not to tell her about other run-ins that he has had, like the time he bumped into one of his Fula "uncles" from the apartment in Bed-Stuy. "At first I thought they were going to be really mad at me," Mohamed says. Instead, his old roommate asked him how he was doing at school and talked about how he and the other men had gone their separate ways after Mohamed moved out. "He told me if I hadn't left, none of them would have wanted to take care of me after all," Mohamed says. "Everything is cool now."

On Facebook, Mohamed no longer hides behind his American alias, Jadon—the two have become one. In so many ways, Mohamed has become a real American boy. This year he is in Ann Parry's eleventh-grade English class.

Ann spent the summer in Ghana, where her uncle lives. For nearly two months, she ate *fufu* and took bucket baths, and slowly acclimated to life in a foreign country. She feels that the experience helped her freshen her approach to teaching immigrant students after an emotionally draining year. "It's kind of like when doctors are talking about their patients' illnesses. Sometimes you're wondering how you could possibly ever treat this person. You almost get numb to it, to the point where you can joke around with your coworkers," she says, reflecting on the times that her students' problems simply seemed insurmountable. "When I went to Ghana, I reconnected with that very real side of their experience—they have done something amazing, and we're right here in the middle of it."

In September, when Ann returned to the sprawling brick school building on Classon Avenue on the first day of classes, so did the old delusion of everything seeming sparkly and new. In addition to a new pixie cut—she chopped off her hair after taking out the tight braids that she had worn all summer long in Ghana—Ann had a new silver bike, a new classroom, new kids, and in her English class alone, thirty-one new names to learn. Names like Shuarb, Guiseppe, Saphir, Fatoumata, and Xinnong. One of the first assignments she gave her students was to write three questions that they wanted to ask their classmates. "What's 'classmates'?" one Yemeni boy asked. "All of *you*," Ann replied, a little taken aback. They had a long way to go.

Now that most of Ann's advisees from last year have graduated, she accepts their friend requests on Facebook. A couple of years since she chose her American name out of a dictionary, Dinice Liu finally settled on calling herself "Denise," and enrolled at CUNY, where she is studying to be a pharmacist. Freeman, aka Pollo Frito, also seems to have found himself, at least for now. At the University of Vermont, he is known around campus as Burlington's one-and-only Togolese salsa and *bachata* dancer. "In Vermont, I am considered the best bachata dancer by ladies and gentlemen," he reports. "I got deeply involved in Latin dancing, and I'm looking for part-time jobs as a salsa/bachata instructor." These days Freeman goes by the self-appointed nickname El Mandingo, and sometimes Spicy Daddy Dingo. When he's not tearing up the dance floor, he balances the coursework for his major, film and television studies, and a minor in French. (It turned out that "acting and zoology" wasn't really a viable double major.) Once in a while Freeman runs into Mukta, a fellow Seinfeld scholar who got accepted into UVM's honors college and is studying to become a resident nurse.

Despite Ann and her colleagues' concern about Ngawang, he managed to pay the tuition at Syracuse with a combination of financial aid and federal loans. He is thinking of majoring in international relations and starring in student films on the side. Now and then, Ngawang stops to chat with Harold, who is considering transferring to Drexel University to study business and engineering—and to be closer to Jessica.

Of course, not everyone made it to college. After graduating from high school, Jovita is unemployed and looking for work. She still comes to see Ann once in a while. On her last visit, Jovita came to school bearing three days' worth of Mexican food, a gift that Ann appreciated now that she is pregnant with her first child with her long-term, live-in boyfriend. As her teacher and advisor, Ann always had high hopes for Jovita, but since high school has ended, her situation has proven more complicated. "Affording school with no government support is a bit unrealistic for Jovita. Her family is significantly less better off than most," Ann says. "I am actually going to try to hire her to take care of my little one if she is available and wants the opportunity."

As for Genesis, she already has her hands full. Over the summer, she gave birth to twin boys, whom she named Leandro and Leonardo. "She called me like two days later and said, 'I'm studying for the Regents. Tell Ms. Alexandra that I'm still going to take the Regents,'" Ann recalls. "Great, but it's kind of delusional that she thinks she's going to pass these tests after not studying."

In fact, Genesis did come back to school after giving birth, and she currently spends first periods with Ann, who reports: "She is still study-ing for her Regents exams. Now we are having conversations about motherhood. I am trying to convince her not to have Doritos and soda for breakfast." Back when the kids were freshmen, Ann made a pact with her advisees, saying that she would stay at the school as long as it took them to graduate. So far, she hasn't broken her word.

Neither has Yasmeen. Not long ago, when the men in her family were busy making plans on her behalf, Yasmeen made a promise to herself: she vowed to go to college, regardless of how difficult her responsibili-ties were at home, being a wife to Saif, and a mother to her two younger siblings. At the time, it was hard to imagine how she could pull it all off. But much like James predicted in their last advisory meeting, Yasmeen enrolled in classes to study early childhood education at the Borough of Manhattan Community College. In January of 2010, she also had a big white wedding at a banquet hall in Coney Island, and this time there were formal invitations, strewn with pearly doves and pink roses, to honor the presence of the parents she had lost. Saif moved in with Yasmeen and her siblings shortly thereafter.

Jessica was already in Philadelphia and unable to make it to Yasmeen's wedding. They haven't seen each other since. Although they exchanged a few emails, Yasmeen eventually stopped returning Jessica's messages and calling her on the phone, even though her number hasn't changed. At first, Jessica thought that Yasmeen was angry with her for not making it to the wedding. However, as time passes, she has begun to view the sudden dissipation of their friendship less as a result of hurt feelings and more as an eventuality beyond her control, now that Yasmeen lives under the same roof with her husband. "I wish I could have a conversation with her to know what she is thinking. Then, I would tell her what I think," Jessica says. "Right now, I can only tell by my imagination. I would say she might be a bit trapped."

James Rice has imagined a similar fate for Yasmeen. Before she gradu-ated, he worked on getting her to open a Facebook account, and for a while she actively checked in on her friends' and teachers' pages, using a fake name and a computer graphic of white butterflies as her profile picture. Throughout the summer and fall, Yasmeen posted playful status updates, birthday wishes, and even a postcard wishing her Muslim friends a blessed Ramadan. But gradually she started logging on less and less, and her voice disappeared in the News Feed. The next time she wrote, it was in Arabic.

Yasmeen seemed to be disappearing in person, too. The night before her wedding, for her henna ceremony, she wore a burgundy ball gown that gave her the appearance of a blossoming rose. But unlike at her engagement party, this time her face was covered by a veil of golden coins, the only skin visible the glittery folds of her eyes, which blinked rapidly as she waited for Saif. "Don't be nervous," a friend advised her, "because someday you're going to look into his eyes and think, 'I hate his guts.'"

James Rice might have laughed if he had been in the room, but he wasn't invited to the henna ceremony or to the wedding the next day, when several female teachers and staff were in attendance. He wasn't allowed to see Yasmeen in her wedding dress, and he wasn't interested in attending the all-male ceremony. After the wedding, James didn't hear from Yasmeen for a while. Days passed, then weeks, and about three months after her wedding, he grew concerned. Even though Yasmeen wasn't his student anymore, James called her at home and demanded that she come into school to see him, just as he had done almost a year before, the day before her engagement party.

"I thought, 'Oh my God, she's pregnant, and she's ashamed to tell me,'" James recalled in an email, one week after her visit. "Result: Not pregnant and still in school."

Jessica was the last of her friends to leave for college. Over the summer, she spent almost two months in Xiangtan, China, and when she got back to New York City, she was ten pounds heavier, thanks to her mother's cooking. Nearly two years had passed since Jessica and her mom had seen each other last, and it was hard to say good-bye again. Long ago, Mr. Tan made plans to bring his wife and daughter to America, where they would all live together in their new home. Reality intervened and plans changed, but the dream hasn't wavered. Jessica hopes to become an American citizen in the near future, and as soon as that happens, she will apply for her mother to come join her in the United States. Until then, they continue to talk on the phone almost every day. Sometimes Jessica tells her mom about Harold. Since graduating, they have broken up and gotten back together several times, but as usual Jessica isn't sure if Harold is the right boyfriend for her. "I don't want to lose him. I just want him to know who I really am," Jessica says. "I'm moving forward all the time, and for him to stay with me, he has to move at the same speed. If he slows down and needs me to wait for him, I will not do that." If anyone understands, it is Jessica's mother, who has spent a lifetime waiting. At the airport checkpoint before Jessica boarded her flight back to the United States, her mother told her, "Don't look back."

When she returned in September, Jessica moved back in with her granduncle and grandaunt, whose apartment she had stayed in after her stepmother kicked her out. But earlier in the summer, Mr. Tan's wife and sons were away in China, and Jessica and her father lived together for almost a month. The day she moved back in was not momentous. Leaving most of her belongings behind to pick up later, she packed everything she would need for the next four weeks at her father's apartment into a single carry-on suitcase. It wasn't much; just a clean towel, summer clothes, teddy-bear pajamas, underwear, and face wash. She packed as if she were going camping, not as if she were going home.

Mr. Tan picked Jessica up in the morning, after his family had left to go to Hong Kong. Almost as soon as she walked into the old building, Jessica was struck by a sense of déjà vu. The superintendent still sat behind a desk in the lobby, with its mirrored walls and linoleum floor, but this time Mr. Tan made an introduction. "This is Jessica," he said, and paused. "My daughter." Inside the copper elevator, Jessica punched in the floor number. "Three, right?" she asked, though she already knew the answer. When Mr. Tan unlocked the door to the apartment, Jessica instinctively held her nose. "Aaah!" she screamed. "It smells like babies!" "Well," her father said sheepishly, "we *have* babies."

Most of the evening went like that, with Jessica sniffing around and Mr. Tan tiptoeing around her. He apologized for the state of the living room, which was filled with his sons' toys and crayon scribbles, and occasionally he told her a little tidbit about one of her half brothers, such as: "My son, he loves the letter Q. He gets so excited when he sees the letter Q."

Jessica was only half-listening. When they walked in, she had offered to help her father with some computer maintenance, and within minutes of setting her bag down, she had picked up his laptop and begun running a disk cleanup program to make more space on the hard drive. As she defragmented his files, he cooked for her, just as he had always done. Only, he didn't lay a towel on the floor under the stove, because he was in his own kitchen. And instead of wearing his work clothes and changing into the slippers that he used to leave by her front door, Mr. Tan wore black socks, flip-flops, white boxers, and a T-shirt with a red dragon on it. They barely exchanged a word as he began to coat a frying pan with oil for the whole flounder that he had bought earlier in the day. He had given Jessica a bowl of watermelon to snack on before dinnertime, and while he put on the rice, she munched on the cool red flesh and began to organize the files on her father's second computer. He cooked; she defragmented. Bit by bit, the files began to fall into their right places.

Chop, drop, hiss. Mr. Tan started to hum. He slid the fish into the pan and let it sizzle until the scaly skin was as thin and crispy as parchment and the tail curled up like an ancient scroll. Next, he sliced the chicken to stir fry, before starting the squid with carrots and spicy green peppers and washing the head of Chinese lettuce that he planned to steam and wilt as a side. "Oh, my God, I'm so hungry!" Jessica said as the familiar vapors of garlic and ginger weighted the air. When the chicken was ready, Mr. Tan set the first plate down next to her, and Jessica pushed the computer aside. He scooped a fistful of white rice into a small bowl and brought that over, too.

Platter after platter and bowl after bowl, Mr. Tan delivered dinner to Jessica, each new dish bathing her face in steam. Then he took out two plates and four chopsticks, and for the first time in a very long time, Mr. Tan sat down with his daughter to eat.

Eventually, Jessica left for China, Mr. Tan's family returned, and life went back to normal. But almost two years since he watched his wife banish his daughter from their home, he is trying to be a father to her again. Jessica was scheduled to go to Drexel in mid-September, and on moving day Mr. Tan did what thousands of fathers across the country do every fall when their sons and daughters head off to college: He packed up the car and drove her to her dorm.

It was a cool, overcast morning in lower Manhattan, one of the first true autumn days, and as Jessica waited on the curb for her father to arrive in his silver Toyota SUV, she had goose bumps. She wore lavender jeans and her sequined, yellow T-shirt plastered with pictures of Garfield in various poses. Her hair was longer than it had ever been, and she held it back with a pink plastic headband decorated with small molded bunnies. In her earlobe, a single earring resembling a Sweet Tart swung slightly in the breeze. Her outfit did not exactly scream business school, but that was where she was headed: to the business and engineering program at Drexel University in Philadelphia, a couple of hours away.

Mr. Tan showed up a little after nine o'clock, just in time to drop his youngest son off at the day-care center across the street from Granduncle's apartment in the Hong Ning Housing for the Elderly. Outside, a few of the residents were doing their morning tai chi, stretching their arms toward the sky. "Say good-bye," Mr. Tan told his son, bundling the little boy in a khaki raincoat as Jessica kneeled down for a hug. "Bye," the boy said and wrapped his arms around his half sister's neck.

After walking his son across the street, Mr. Tan returned to the car and began making room for Jessica. He left the T-shirts wrapped around the front seats to protect the upholstery, but removed a car seat to the trunk and cleared out space in the back for Jessica's stuff—and there was a lot of stuff. A few days before, he had taken her to BJ's Wholesale Club and a Chinese supermarket in Flushing, Queens, to buy everything from school supplies to toiletries and packaged food. She had been assigned a single room, and in many ways, it wouldn't be so different from the room she had rented in Chinatown.

As the sky brightened and more residents ventured outside to sit on the green benches in front of the housing complex, Jessica and her dad took turns going up to Granduncle's apartment and carting down various bags and boxes. There were sixteen in all. One by one, they loaded her bubblegum-pink sack packed with clothes and tied with twine, her heavy black suitcase, her new portable canvas wardrobe, her laptop computer, a plastic container filled with books, and crates of water, tissues, and maxi pads, packaged in bulk. With each trip down, the boxes got lighter, and everyday needs were replaced by flimsy afterthoughts: flip-flops for the shower, a pack of orange-flavored gum, and a bottle of spicy Szechuan chili sauce, a special gift from her father to help get her through her first winter without home-cooked Chinese food.

Grandaunt, graying by the minute and shivering in a purple sweater vest, waited and watched from the sidewalk. The elderly tenants of Hong Ning had been up for hours already, and a few residents tended to a little patch of green behind the brick housing project, where bitter melons and amaranth still grow. A woman with wet eyes and skin like a moldy onion came and sat on a bench and gazed out at the street, where Mr. Tan did a final check before shutting the car door.

"It's time to go," he said.

Jessica climbed into the passenger seat beside her father, and he started the car. From Norfolk Street they turned left onto Delancey, and in Jessica's rearview mirror, the Williamsburg Bridge got smaller and smaller. The pigeons had begun pecking for crumbs near New Roma Pizza, where the pie-maker could be seen through a large window adjusting his red apron and kneading his first mound of dough. Outside Amigo Mini Mart and Smoke Shop, two men drank coffee in the weak morning light, not far from the orange-vested construction workers who were drilling into a nearby sewer line, vibrations running up and down their arms.

No one noticed the silver SUV or the girl inside of it, feeding her father a pastry from the palm of her hand as he gripped the wheel. Soon, they would be whirring through the Holland Tunnel and onto the New Jersey Turnpike, joining thousands of cars also heading south. Mr. Tan would take Exit 4 toward Philadelphia and the Betsy Ross Bridge.

At that point, the city that Jessica Tan had lived in, loved in, cried in, and survived, would be replaced by a new city, with its own mass transit system to learn and bargain stores to raid. And yet, the further they drove, the more the old one would begin to seem like home.

Acknowledgments

For the past few years, I have been carrying around a fortune-cookie message that I received during one of my first interviews with Ngawang Thokmey at a Chinese restaurant. The paper is now torn and crumpled, but the message is clear: "Determination will get you through this." At the time, I imagined that "this" meant writing my first book; and since then, determination certainly has helped. However, so have a lot of people—family, friends, and colleagues whom I am fortunate enough to have in my life.

On a personal note, I would like to start by thanking my parents, Terry and Michelle Hauser, who in addition to being my first readers are, respectively, the first great writer and the first inspiring teacher I ever met. Their support and belief in me has been and continues to be invaluable, as was the experience of growing up in Miami, another polyglot city of exiles and immigrants. Having listened to some of the stories within these pages, I could never take for granted the importance of home and family, and I am so grateful for mine.

Speaking of family, ours has a new addition, my amazing husband, Addison MacDonald. During the 2008–9 school year, I got used to the question constantly asked by several girls in the senior class who were married already, about to get married, or just plain nosy: "Miss Brooke, has he proposed yet?" In June after school let out, Addison finally proposed, and we started planning our own wedding as I began the laborious process of sifting through thousands of pages of notes and transcripts. Writing this book has been one of the most challenging endeavors I've ever taken on, but marrying Addison was easy. I can't imagine having a better partner in life. He has provided love, encouragement, and ballast as well as some much-needed levity and laughter along the way.

Before the book came the book proposal, and for the countless hours that went into shaping it, I want to thank my agent Larry Weissman and his wife and partner in all respects, Sascha Alper. They not only helped me craft my vision of what the book would be, they fed me while doing it—chicken salad and brussels sprouts in their living room. Larry and Sascha championed this project from the beginning and found the perfect home for it in the end. I feel so fortunate to be publishing this book with Free Press, and I want to express my heartfelt gratitude to publisher Martha Levin, editor-in-chief Dominick Anfuso, and my editor Leslie Meredith, who challenged and guided me, and made this book better in ways big and small. It has been a wonderful experience having an editor who is rooting for these students just as much as I am, and I'm indebted to her for helping me bring their stories into sharper focus. Thanks also to assistant editor Donna Loffredo for her skillful and friendly assistance, and to my publicist Meredith Wahl-Jones.

This book would not have been possible without Alexandra Anormaliza. She is, after all, the school's founding principal, and the halls of the International High still reflect her original vision, even though she has graduated to Tweed, where she recently got promoted again following the appointment of Cathleen P. Black as the New York City schools chancellor. (Alexandra is now the executive director of the Office of Achievement Resources in the Division of Academics, Performance, and Support.) Few people are able to combine professionalism and passion for what they do so smoothly and powerfully. I also want to thank Nedda de Castro, who became principal shortly after Alexandra left and continues to advocate for the kids who need her most; Miguel Antunes, who patiently explained how the intake process works; and the entire staff at International for letting me hang around and ask so many questions. There are too many teachers who lent their time and insights to thank personally here (Ann Parry, for one, was indispensable, and Cynthia Chatman opened her home and her heart), but as a group they inspired me deeply, to the point that, since leaving the school, I have been pursuing the idea of teaching part-time.

With every big assignment I've worked on, there is always that one person who emerges as a guide—someone who helps you see, hear, smell, and feel the larger truth of a place. From the start, my guide for this project has been Dariana Castro. I first met Dariana while reporting "This Strange Thing Called Prom," an article about the school's first-ever prom that I wrote for the City section of *The New York Times*. In this book, as in the article, Dariana is responsible for some of the best insights and observations that I coyly have passed off as my own. She is one of the most resourceful people I know, and also one of the most caring—qualities that gelled together in December of 2010 when, after applying for college early in his senior year, Mohamed Bah found out that he was accepted into a well-regarded liberal arts college on a four-year scholarship. The day he opened his acceptance letter, Dariana was there to videotape Mohamed and Cindy celebrating and dancing to the tune of James Brown's "Say It Loud—I'm Black and I'm Proud." The resulting music video, which Dariana edited and set to Janelle Monáe's "Tightrope," became a bit of a YouTube sensation, and rumor has it that it even reached the president of the college. The victory, however, was bittersweet. The same day that Cindy hosted a congratulatory dinner for Mohamed, the U.S. Senate blocked the Dream Act, the bill that would help grant legal status to hundreds of thousands of undocumented students, including many activists who christened themselves "Dreamers" and staged protests and phoned lawmakers in the months leading up to the vote. It was a disheartening blow, but the Dreamers are rallying for the 2012 election.

In addition to the names above, several people helped me from behind the scenes. I would like to thank my friend Ronnie Saha, who was the first person to make me aware of the Internationals Network for Public Schools, back when he was working at the International Rescue Committee. Claire Sylvan, the Network's founding executive director and a nationally recognized leader in improving education for immigrants who are also new English-language learners, helped me to see the bigger picture. Also at the Internationals Network, Daria Witt provided essential resources and introductions; and Sanda Balaban, a mover and shaker at the Department of Education, helped me to get this project off the ground. Finally, I want to thank an authority in the field of immigration law, Allan Wernick, who is the author of *U.S. Immigration and Citizenship: Your Complete Guide*, now in its fourth edition, as well as a widely read columnist and a professor at Baruch College, City University of New York (CUNY). When I needed answers, he generously lent his time and expertise.

As I got deeper and deeper into my research, friends and family saw less and less of me, and when we did get together, they asked a lot of questions about the school that reawakened my own curiosities. Thanks to all of my relatives with inquiring minds, including Greg MacDonald, Wendy Soliday, Luke MacDonald, Brooke MacDonald, and Andy Morse; as well as my close friends, Hannah Burroughs, Taryn Drongowski, Alicia Fessenden, and Kelly Borgeson.

On a daily basis, I received additional moral support from the Brooklyn Writers Space, and from a handful of colleagues who read my early drafts. Susan Kittenplan brought a magazine editor's keen eye to every line, and bolstered me with her enthusiasm; Kerrie Mitchell asked tough questions that led me to uncover important answers; and *New York Times* editor Francis Flaherty offered wisdom over coffee and between the covers of his book, *The Elements of Story: Field Notes on Nonfiction Writing*. At the *Times*, I also want to thank the inimitable Constance Rosenblum and the unstoppable Lynda Richardson, who edited "This Strange Thing Called Prom," among many other stories that I wrote for the City section, which closed in 2009. It was one of my favorite sections in any publication, and I am honored to have been a part of it.

Finally, I want to thank all of the students at the International High School at Prospect Heights. I think that James Rice put it best in his graduation speech for the Class of 2009 when he told them, "You should know that the adults in this school are amazed and inspired by you, that we are changed as a result of having just known you."

I am changed having known these students, too.

A Note on Sources

The first time I stepped foot into the International High School at Prospect Heights in the spring of 2008, I was overcome by the sense that I had everything to learn, and everyone to learn from. Since then, the students themselves have been my greatest sources, inviting me into their lives and living rooms. However, I also want to acknowledge the many journalists, authors, scholars, and historians whose work has influenced and guided me along the way.

I knew from the start that I wanted to write a book that, while set at a school, wasn't necessarily about school—but, rather, about people. Tracy Kidder's *Among Schoolchildren* and Samuel G. Freedman's *Small Victories: The Real World of a Teacher, Her Students, and Their High School* both transcend the genre of books about education and left me thinking about the stories of individual students and teachers long after I had finished reading about them.

Before I even met many of the students in the Class of 2009 at International, I had read their essays in a self-published anthology entitled *Narrating America: Immigrant Youth Tell Their Stories*, which they put together during their junior year. As seniors, many of the same kids shared their journals and college essays with me. (In these pages, some excerpts have been trimmed or condensed for space.) Overall, I took the students at their word and presented their stories as they had recounted them in written recollections, casual conversations, and more formal interviews. At the same time, I wanted to leave room for the idea that some of the stories might be missing important chapters. These are teenagers, after all, and many are recalling events that happened in their childhood in another country, while speaking in a relatively new language: English. It is possible that some details have been lost in translation, or altered in transit. I verified the students' stories with older relatives whenever I could, and when I couldn't, I tried to make that clear to the reader. I am thankful to the members of The First Church of Christ–Congregational in Farmington for sharing their side of the story about the events leading up to and following Mohamed's disappearance, as well as various documents, including email correspondences and Pastor Ned Edwards's Sunday sermon. An article about Mohamed's visit to Connecticut that appeared in the *New Haven Register*, "City Schools Welcome African Visitors" by Maria Garriga, provided additional background, as did an article in *The New York Times* about Farmington, " 'A Village of Pretty Houses,' Where Women's Lives Were Reshaped," written by Eve Glasberg.

For the most part, I relied on the students as "guides" to their own cultures—a few served as my translators in a pinch—but I also consulted a handful of sources whose insights have been illuminating. In particular, I would like to thank Loukia K. Sarroub, who is the author of *All American Yemeni Girls: Being Muslim in a Public School* and a professor of education at the University of Nebraska–Lincoln, as well as Peter C. Andersen, who is the editor of The Sierra Leone Web (www.sierra-leone .org), an online treasure trove of information about that country's history, culture, languages, and people. Additionally, I want to acknowledge Burmese translator and Karen activist Myra Dahgaypaw, who met with me and Chit Su in New York, and Sally Thompson, who is deputy executive director at the Thailand Burma Border Consortium and helped me to better understand life at the Nu Po refugee camp.

While I didn't want to write a book about issues per se, I did depend on the work of many colleagues to enlighten me about important developments in education and immigration, both on the local and national levels. The following articles shed beams of light: in *The Village Voice*, "The Maze of America: Finding a High School for an Immigrant Child is Tougher Than You Think" by Jessica Siegel; in the *Carnegie Reporter*, "Educating Immigrant Students" by Lucy Hood; and in *The New York Times*, "A Teacher Who Helps the Many Become One" by Sol Hurwitz; "Taught to be Principals, and Now Facing the Test" by Elissa Gootman; "Student's Prize Is a Trip Into Immigration Limbo" by Nina Bernstein; "In School for the First Time, Teenage Immigrants Struggle" by Jennifer Medina; "Where Education and Assimilation Collide" by Ginger Thompson; "With Diplomas in Hand, but Without Legal Status" by Fernanda Santos; and "Coming Out Illegal" by Maggie Jones.

At the International High School at Prospect Heights, the college counselor Joanna Yip provided me with important background about the college-application process as well as the number of undocumented students in the senior class, an estimate based on information that the students volunteered during their conversations with her. During the 2008–9 school year, in addition to distributing consent and release forms to all of the students, I handed out an informal survey to the seniors to learn more about their backgrounds at a glance. The surveys were optional and, again, the information was volunteered. In a few cases, I used pseudonyms to protect people's identities.

Outside of the school, several reports and studies provided me with important statistics as well as perspective. For a clearer understanding of the longitudinal effects of the Internationals model, I want to credit researchers at the Graduate Center of the City University of New York, Michelle Fine, Brett Stoudt, and Valerie Futch, who published the 2005 report, "The Internationals Network for Public Schools: A Quantitative and Qualitative Cohort Analysis of Graduation and Dropout Rates: Teaching and Learning in a Transcultural Academic Environment." I also benefited from reading "So Many Schools, So Few Options: How Mayor Bloomberg's Small High School Reforms Deny Full Access to English Language Learners," published in 2006 by The New York Immigration Coalition and Advocates for Children of New York; and "DREAM vs. Reality: An Analysis of Potential DREAM Act Beneficiaries," authored by Jeanne Batalova and Margie McHugh and published in 2010 by the

Migration Policy Institute. For a better grasp of the enormous health crises in Sierra Leone, I referred to the following two reports from the World Health Organization: "The World Health Report 2000: Health Systems: Improving Performance," and "Maternal Mortality in 2005."

I also spent many hours visiting the following websites: Internationals Network for Public Schools (www.internationalsnps.org), This Week In Education (www.thisweekineducation.com), and Insideschools.org (www.insideschools.org), which featured a review of the International High School at Prospect Heights by Pamela Wheaton originally published in April of 2005. Readers interested in learning more about this particular International High School may visit www.ihsph.org.

Finally, Facebook has been an invaluable resource. Many of the students have "friended" me over the past three years, and shared their online profiles, status updates, and posts. Whenever possible, I have tried to see the students through the lenses that they themselves have provided.